MW00445083

H2H Marketing

Philip Kotler • Waldemar Pfoertsch • Uwe Sponholz

H2H Marketing

The Genesis of Human-to-Human Marketing

Philip Kotler
Kellogg Graduate School of Management
Northwestern University
Evanston, IL, USA

Waldemar Pfoertsch
Pforzheim Business School
Pforzheim University of Applied Sciences
Pforzheim, Germany

Uwe Sponholz
Faculty of Business and Engineering
University of Applied Sciences
Würzburg-Schweinfurt
Schweinfurt, Germany

ISBN 978-3-030-59530-2   ISBN 978-3-030-59531-9   (eBook)
https://doi.org/10.1007/978-3-030-59531-9

© The Editor(s) (if applicable) and The Author(s), under exclusive license to Springer Nature Switzerland AG 2021
This work is subject to copyright. All rights are solely and exclusively licensed by the Publisher, whether the whole or part of the material is concerned, specifically the rights of translation, reprinting, reuse of illustrations, recitation, broadcasting, reproduction on microfilms or in any other physical way, and transmission or information storage and retrieval, electronic adaptation, computer software, or by similar or dissimilar methodology now known or hereafter developed.
The use of general descriptive names, registered names, trademarks, service marks, etc. in this publication does not imply, even in the absence of a specific statement, that such names are exempt from the relevant protective laws and regulations and therefore free for general use.
The publisher, the authors, and the editors are safe to assume that the advice and information in this book are believed to be true and accurate at the date of publication. Neither the publisher nor the authors or the editors give a warranty, expressed or implied, with respect to the material contained herein or for any errors or omissions that may have been made. The publisher remains neutral with regard to jurisdictional claims in published maps and institutional affiliations.

This Springer imprint is published by the registered company Springer Nature Switzerland AG.
The registered company address is: Gewerbestrasse 11, 6330 Cham, Switzerland

Foreword

The book introduces us to the theme of human integrity and honor in the context of the marketplace. The book emphasizes that human values of trust and service to others are the foundations of human economic activity rather than the sale of commodities and luxuries. The book has reframed marketing as a way of solving crucial human problems, by emphasizing that human beings should be given primacy over the products we engineer or the profits we make.

For scholars and practitioners of marketing and business, the book takes one through a refreshing journey of exploring what truly constitutes human integrity in marketing. It encourages us to question our approach to marketing—from a consumeristic frame to a service-dominant frame. It invites us to approach marketing as a tool for the holistic development of human societies and for meaningful viable business.

To achieve business goals, respecting the individual/human subject is fundamental rather than accelerating consumerism. The H2H marketing model evolved in this work is unique in several ways. Influenced by design thinking, service-dominant logic, and digitalization, it explains why marketing needs renovation. Further, it emphasizes how marketing needs to be practiced—as a mindset, operational process, and management task characterized by a human-to-human interaction. Finally, it espouses the importance of trust and empathy in stating what marketing should be used for. I believe that the publication *H2H Marketing* is more than a book; it is a way of life that forces traditionally understood notions of marketing to be dispelled and replaced by human-centric approaches with wider social implications.

Christ University   Fr Thomas C. Matthew
Bangalore, India

Preface

How does the future of marketing look like? Marketers around the world have been wondering. Many things have rattled the principles of marketing, and this is just the beginning of the re-orientation. The power of the customer has increased through the spread of the Internet, and tech companies are trying to utilize the scope of applications to change the habits of customers fundamentally. The 2020 Coronavirus Pandemic has added new uncertainties and brought new insights and geared the customer more to the real essentials of a human being. Around the globe, information creation and distribution have initiated new dynamics in markets, and customers have become more aware of options and possibilities available to them. In various degrees, digitalization has reached every corner of the world. Marketing automation and the use of artificial intelligence (AI) are making their way into everyday life. Marketing science now has the challenge to create new approaches to address the current situation.

Evolving and expanding from business-to-business (B2B) marketing, we have developed a new concept for human-to-human (H2H) marketing. With this publication, we wanted to bring together our cumulative experience and insights to help to form a better way of marketing. We are combining the latest marketing concepts, advances in design thinking, and newest service-dominant logic approaches, as well as the latest insights into digitalization.

During the last few years, we intensively researched in these areas, writing articles and books, designing and conducting courses, and working on many industrial and consumer strategy projects. It became clear to us that the way marketing was understood and how it was implemented was essentially responsible for its success. We concluded that the "mindset" in marketing was responsible for its outcome. To stay relevant and powerful, marketing thinking has to shift.

Over the years, marketing concepts have changed to create value and to stay relevant. Under the current circumstances, it is necessary to have a clear value orientation for any marketing activity. It has to be aligned with a focus on people-for-people benefits. The creation of human-to-human marketing establishes a new approach that puts human beings at the center of marketing. It taps into the conscious and subconscious priorities of humans as a means to successful marketing. Marketing should work for the people, not against them.

Many marketing concepts do not achieve the goals of this new human-to-human (H2H) mindset. Push marketing oriented on the 4P marketing mix no longer fits into the realities of the digital world. The Internet is bidirectional, if not multidirectional. Customer knowledge, customer pull, or even user-generated content is playing an increasingly important role. Logically, marketers must cleverly adapt to the influences of digitalization. Therefore, in this book, we introduce a new "H2H marketing model" to describe and clarify the approach needed to develop a new concept for H2H marketing.

A Few More Didactic Hints

This book is based on a German language publication called *Das neue Marketing Mindset* (Springer-Gabler 2019) from Waldemar Pfoertsch and Uwe Sponholz. It introduced the principle of storytelling, which we would like to use in this English publication too.

We do this because a story told can attract the readers' attention much more easily than a factual address. Over thousands of years, man has handed down knowledge through storytelling, and this method is being used increasingly in modern business today. Our storytelling approach is diagrammed in Fig. 1. All figures and Tables in this publication are compiled by the authors. Therefore, we do not mark them individually as "Authors' own figure" or "Table compiled by author".

We start with the "Call for Adventure" to introduce the current state of marketing and ask ourselves where marketing is heading. "Marketing-Quo Vadis?" is not a theoretical question. It leads to the fundamental understanding of our profession by addressing the need to change. We look at the evolution of the marketing mix and its consequences. In recent years, other concepts and ideas have emerged, which need to be considered. Raj Sisodia, Jag Sheth, and David Wolfe provided us with inspiration and encouragement with their study *Firms of Endearment*.

Marketing cannot neglect the sustainability challenge; it needs to find appropriate dimensions to judge its own principles. Built upon this, our own observations and reflections of applied marketing in the field as consulting

THE NEW MARKETING PARADIGM
H2H MARKETING

ELEMENTS OF
H2H MARKETING

GREAT JOURNEY

BRAVE ACTION

H2H
MARKETING

CALL FOR ADVENTURE

SOLUTION AND RETURN

THE CURRENT STATE
OF MARKETING

FINDING MEANING IN
A TROUBLED WORLD

Fig. 1   The genesis of H2H marketing as a story

companies enabled us to develop the H2H marketing model and the evolution to the H2H marketing concept. After the "call for adventure" and description of the current state of marketing, we continue the "great journey" with the development of the "new marketing paradigm" and the presentation of the H2H marketing model. In the initial version of this publication, H2H marketing model was called the "Bangalore model" because it was developed on the Christ University Campus in Bangalore. Synonym to the acronym H2H, we used the term "mensch marketing". The American language noun "mensch" originates from the Yiddish: מענטש mentsh, which emphasizes a human-orientated behavior. The website for this book is also called Mensch Marketing.

This new model adds design thinking (DT) as an innovation method for any marketing activity. As a first step, its human-centered mindset should lead to human-centered marketing. Secondly, its toolbox and process-oriented approach can bring marketing even further to meet current human needs. This is also true for service-dominant logic (S-DL) concept, which we want to see bundled with all marketing activity. S-DL is also human centered and delivers the theoretical basis for H2H marketing. As the third step of the H2H marketing model, we see current developments of digitalization as a great opportunity for redirecting the focus of marketing to a more stakeholder-oriented concept. This new way of marketing management in the form of H2H marketing needs some brave actions, which we introduce in the elements of H2H marketing. As in any good story, the hero needs the right attitude, which in our case is called H2H mindset.

The foundation for this mindset is trust, which we see this as the key currency for any business transaction in a hyper-connected world. In detail, we present profound insights into a map of the unknown terrain that will be explored in our journey. The "solution and return" of the story is then told through the introduction of the operative marketing, which focuses on the H2H process and the necessary steps in the new forming of the marketing mix. It is an iterative process, based on new technological capabilities through the digitalization and deep thinking in H2H marketing. This marketing approach challenges the core competencies needed to create and deliver meaningful value propositions to customers and other collaboration partners. At the end of the story, we offer new solutions to finding meaning in the troubled world we live in. This will provide a path for the future for many companies led by our hero—H2H marketing mindset. To illustrate feasibility, case studies are mentioned in this publication and are fully displayed in the upcoming *H2H Marketing Case Study Collection.*

This book addresses global decision makers, executives, professors, students, and the curious general audience. At the end of each chapter, we ask questions to reflect on, which depend on your personal situation and perspective, and which we, therefore, cannot give a blanket answer for in this book.

Please note, in our writing, we use the female form (she, her) for simplicity and uniformity, but it should be understood as gender-neutral! In admiration of excellent management thinkers like Vargo & Lusch, Michael Porter, and many more whom we have met and worked with, we are concerned with the sustainable improvement of the world and people-oriented marketing. Such thought leaders, together with ongoing technical developments, give us inspiration, which we would like to discuss and adapt to in the future through lively exchange.

Many thanks go to our collaborators and helpers from our all around the world. This publication was created in cooperation with Maximilian Haas. Special thanks go to Guido Morhardt and Yoshiyasu-Simon Kono for creating the design language of the figures.

For updates and further information, contact our website or the authors: https://mensch.marketing/

The website is built like a magazine and will feature special topics and provide updates and serves as our co-creation platform for researchers and practitioners. Various chapters of the book are offered for a limited period for free download. We are looking forward to be in touch with you.

Longboat Key, FL	Philip Kotler
Stuttgart, Germany	Waldemar Pfoertsch
Schweinfurt, Germany	Uwe Sponholz
August 2020	

Endorsements

"A compelling and comprehensive message about how marketing can serve society and not just the consumer. The human-centric perspective in *H2H Marketing* enlarges and enables the company to serve the customer more holistically as a human who is also an employee, a supplier, an investor, and a citizen."

—Jagdish N. Sheth is the Charles H. Kellstadt *Professor of Marketing at the Goizueta Business School, Emory University, Atlanta, GA, USA*

"Perhaps too often forgotten, people are always at the core of all aspects of marketing. *H2H Marketing* builds on that rich insight to offer a creative and long overdue reexamination of marketing.
Thought-provoking and inspiring, its focus on human-to-human interactions will change how marketers can and should approach their craft."

—Kevin Lane Keller, E.B. Osborn *Professor of Marketing, Tuck School of Business, Dartmouth College, Hanover, NH, USA*

"Sui generis, marketing has always been focusing on the customers. However, corporations often focus predominantly on their product portfolio and try to maximize sales instead of concentrating on customers' needs and wants and their problems by offering innovative and value-adding solutions. Today's customers' needs and wants—in particular when it comes to Gen Y and Z—often transcend traditional functional and emotional benefits as they call for more encompassing stakeholder value management-oriented companies which are acting responsible with respect to the environment and society as well as the world as a whole. In this innovative book, the authors demonstrate how enterprises can live up to this kind of human-to-human marketing approach."

—Marc Oliver Opresnik, *Professor of Marketing, Technische Hochschule Lübeck, Germany*

"There is nothing more exciting than the evolution and creation of our planet's biosphere. Humans are one result of this deep time process. And as it seems—we could be the big disrupter. Therefore, we all should welcome smart wake-up calls in our specific professional and personal lives. This book is a great offering to dedicated marketing experts and branding brains to understand the deeper meaning of purpose creation. It also offers you a bright spectrum of tools to do our transmission work in the human fabric."

—Achim Kuehn, *Head of Group Marketing and Corporate Communications, Herrenknecht AG, Schwanau, Germany*

"H2H Marketing is a paradigm change in marketing. The book helps to see marketing as what it essentially always has been: a human-to-human interaction. Incorporating the ground principles of value co-creating, this book provides the much-needed actionable marketing tools for a new customer-centric era."

—Patrick Planning, *Professor of Business Psychology, Stuttgart Technology University, Stuttgart, Germany*

"We live in a world where people are flooded with thousands of advertising messages every day. H2H Marketing thinks ahead and focuses on the valuable interaction between humans instead of unethical business approaches to message potential customers whatever the cost.

What I find most exciting about the book is how the authors break down the walls between the core elements and innovative approaches of marketing to create a holistic and balanced picture of the future of marketing without losing its roots.

The scientific foundation of the articles in conjunction with clearly stated instructions for a practical implementation of the contents makes this book a required reading for marketing professionals."

—Christian Koch, MS, *Marketing Manager, Müller—Die lila Logistik AG*

"In the end it comes back to where it all should start—finally a human-centric approach of marketing. This book reveals impressively how design thinking, the service dominant logic, and digitalization serve as building blocks of H2H Marketing. Rethinking existing marketing strategies with the eyes of this new paradigm will lead to striking insights. Everybody who was waiting for the next leap in marketing will be inspired by this book."

—Adam-Alexander Manowicz, *Professor Business and Mathematics, Bielefeld University for Applied Science, Bielefeld, Germany*

Herzlichen Glückwunsch, lieber Waldemar! Das sieht ja toll aus ☺

—Prof. Dr. Thomas Cleff, *HS PF Pforzheim University, Dean of the Business School, Pforzheim, Germany*

Contents

About the Authors

Philip Kotler is one of the leading authorities in marketing. He was the S. C. Johnson & Son Distinguished Professor of International Marketing at the Kellogg School of Management, Northwestern University, Evanston, Illinois. He received his Master's Degree at the University of Chicago and his PhD Degree at MIT, both in economics. He did postdoctoral work in mathematics at Harvard University and in behavioral science at the University of Chicago.

Professor Kotler is the author of *Marketing Management: Analysis, Planning, Implementation and Control*, the most widely used marketing book in graduate business schools worldwide; *Principles of Marketing*; *Marketing Models*; *Strategic Marketing for Nonprofit Organizations*; *The New Competition*; *High Visibility*; *Social Marketing*; *Marketing Places*; *Marketing for Congregations*; *Marketing for Hospitality and Tourism*; *The Marketing of Nations*; *Kotler on Marketing*; *Building Global Bio Brands*; *Attracting Investors*; *Ten Deadly*

Marketing Sins; Marketing Moves; Corporate Social Responsibility; Lateral Marketing; and Marketing Insights from A to Z. He has published over one hundred articles in leading journals, several of which have received best article awards.

Professor Kotler was the first recipient of the American Marketing Association's (AMA) "Distinguished Marketing Educator Award" (1985). The European Association of Marketing Consultants and Sales Trainers awarded Kotler their prize for "Marketing Excellence." He was chosen as the "Leader in Marketing Thought" by the Academic Members of the AMA in a 1975 survey. He also received the 1978 "Paul Converse Award" of the AMA, honoring his original contribution to marketing. In 1989, he received the Annual Charles Coolidge Parlin Marketing Research Award. In 1995, the Sales and Marketing Executives International (SMEI) named him "Marketer of the Year."

Professor Kotler has consulted for such companies as IBM, General Electric, AT&T, Honeywell, Bank of America, Merck, and others in the areas of marketing strategy and planning, marketing organization, and international marketing.

He has been Chairman of the College of Marketing of the Institute of Management Sciences, a Director of the American Marketing Association, a Trustee of the Marketing Science Institute, a Director of the MAC Group, a former member of the Yankelovich Advisory Board, and a member of the Copernicus Advisory Board. He has been a Trustee of the Board of Governors of the School of the Art Institute of Chicago and a Member of the Advisory Board of the Drucker Foundation. He has received honorary doctoral degrees from Stockholm University, the University of Zurich, the Athens University of Economics and Business, DePaul University, the Cracow School of Business and Economics, Groupe H.E.C. in Paris, the University of Economics and Business Administration in Vienna, the Budapest University of Economic Science and Public Administration, and the Catholic University of Santo Domingo.

He has traveled extensively throughout Europe, Asia, and South America, advising and lecturing to many companies about how to apply sound economic and marketing science principles to increase their competitiveness. He has also advised governments on how to develop stronger public agencies to further the development of the nation's economic well-being.

Waldemar A. Pfoertsch is professor emeritus of international business at the Pforzheim University, Germany, and lectures about B2B marketing and industrial brand management. He is lecturer at the Mannheim Business School, Tongji SEM, Shanghai, and TUM (Technical University Munich), Heilbronn. He also teaches at the Indian Institute of Management Calcutta (IIMC), ITM, Sweden, and Graduate Business School of ESAN, Lima Peru. From 2007 to 2010, he was professor of marketing at China Europe International Business School Shanghai (CEIBS). His other teaching positions have been at the Executive MBA Program at the University of Illinois, Chicago. He was visiting Associate Professor at Kellogg Graduate School of Management, Northwestern University, and Lecturer for Strategic Management at Lake Forest Graduate School of Management. He has taught online with the University of Maryland-Graduate School. At the start for his career, he was Research Assistant at the Technical University of Berlin.

Dr. Pfoertsch has extensive experience in management consulting in the USA, Europe, and China. In his years at UBM/Mercer Consulting Group, Arthur Andersen Operational Consulting, and LEK Consulting, he worked throughout Europe, Asia, and North America, assisting companies in developing international strategies. His earlier positions include sales and strategy positions at Siemens AG in Germany/the USA and being an Economic Advisor to the United Nations Industrial Development Organization (UNIDO) in Sierra Leone, West Africa.

His research interests have evolved around the globalization of high-tech companies and their marketing and branding efforts. His newest research is focusing on human-to-human marketing of industrial companies.

Uwe Sponholz is professor of service engineering, innovation management and design thinking, B2B marketing, and sales as well as strategic management at FHWS—University of Applied Sciences Würzburg-Schweinfurt. He also teaches at Christ University, Bangalore, India, and other foreign universities. As dean of the Faculty of Business and Engineering at FHWS, he was a strategic driver of the internationalization of the university and the introduction of innovative teaching methods. Today, in addition to his teaching duties, he is responsible for the degree program management of the MBA Business with Europe and the management of two laboratories (Creative Cube and VR Laboratory).

His professional career began at the Institute for Trade Research at the University of Cologne, initially as a researcher and later as head of department of the newly founded consulting division of the institute. He then moved to Alliances Management Consultants in Paris, a small consulting firm specializing in providing strategic advice to large service providers. From there he went to FAG in Schweinfurt, where he was significantly responsible for the development and implementation of a global service concept.

For years, he has supported companies with design thinking workshops and consulting projects. He is also shareholder and founding partner of in-cito management consulting and Bodystance GmbH. He uses the second company to test his conceptual ideas of H2H marketing.

Maximilian Haas worked as research assistant at Pforzheim Business School before starting work as a consultant. He graduated 2019 in International Business at Pforzheim University. His interests lie mainly in the area of branding and international business.

List of Abbreviations

4Cs	Consumer, Cost, Communication, Convenience
4P	Product, Price, Place, Promotion
5As	Aware, Appeal, Ask, Act, Advocate
5Cs	Communication, Channel, Cost, Customer Solution, Community
5Es	Evolve the Solution, Exchange the Knowledge, Expand the Value, Extent the Access, Engage the Brand
A2A	Actor-to-Actor
AI	Artificial Intelligence
AR	Augmented Reality
B2B	Business-to-Business
B2B2C	Business to Business to Consumer
B2C	Business-to-Consumer
BFD	Brand-formative Design
CB	Collaborative Branding
CBV	Customer-Based-View
CEO	Chief Executive Officer
CFO	Chief Financial Officer
CMO	Chief Marketing Officer
CPS	Cyber-Physical Systems
CRM	Customer Relationship Management
CSR	Corporate Social Responsibility
CVP	Cost Volume Profit
CX	Customer Experience
CXM	Customer Experience Management
DT	Design Thinking
e-commerce	Electronic Commerce
ERP	Enterprise Resource Planning
EY	Ernst & Young

f-factor	Factor for Friends, Family, Followers, Facebook, etc.
FMOT	First Moment of Truth
FoEs	Firms of Endearment
FP	Fundamental Premise
G-DL	Goods-Dominant Logic
H2H	Human-to-Human
HPI	Hasso Plattner Institut
IDEO	Innovation Design Engineering Organization
IoT	Internet of Things
IT	Information Technology
MBV	Market-Based-View
MVC	Minimum Viable Content
NGO	Non-Governmental Organization
P&L	Profit & Loss
POV	Point of View
RBV	Resource-Based View
ROI	Return on Investment
RRM	Review and Rating Management
SAVE	Solution, Access, Value, Education
S-DL	Service-Dominant Logic
SIVA	Solution, Information, Value, Access
SMART	Specific, Measurable, Achievable, Reasonable, Time-bound
SoLoMo	Social Local Mobile
STP	Segmenting Targeting Positioning
UBI	Universal Basic Income
UGC	User-generated Content
UX	User Experience
VBV	Value-Based-View
VR	Virtual Reality
VUCA	Volatility, Uncertainty, Complexity, Ambiguity
YMCA	Young Men's Christian Association
ZMOT	Zero Moment of Truth

List of Figures

List of Tables

1

The Current State of Marketing

We believe marketing can change the world for the better. During the last decades, marketing experienced many revolutionizing changes that added to the quality of life for many people. However, changes have not all been for the better. Due to some unethical practices of over-zealous profit-minded marketers, the current image of marketing, as perceived by employees and customers, has deteriorated to a point where "most people associate negative words, such as 'lies,' 'deception,' 'deceitful,' 'annoying,' and 'manipulating,' with marketing".[1] Public scandals, like falsified market research results, add further aggravation to this bad image.[2]

A general lack of trust prevails, which results in the exact opposite of what marketing is trying to achieve. Brands like Amazon, Airbnb, FlixBus, Mercedes-Benz, Salesforce, Tesla, Whole Foods Market, or Uber could not survive if customers would not place their trust in them. Amazon digitally displays more than 350 million different products and promises, to be delivered after a customer pushes the purchase button without ever having seen the product physically. Such an act of trust had to be earned with much effort on Amazon's part. Without trust, it becomes nearly impossible for a company to build a meaningful relationship with the customer on a human level. The belief by many today is that consumer marketing rarely keeps its promise about the customer and market orientation and, instead, practices a tendency

---

[1] Sheth, J. N., & Sisodia, R. S. (2005). Does marketing need reform? p. 10 in Marketing Renaissance: Opportunities and Imperatives for Improving Marketing Thought, Practice, and Infrastructure. *Journal of Marketing, 69*(4), pp. 1–25. https://doi.org/10.1509/jmkg.2005.69.4.1.

[2] See also Kotler, P. (2017). *Criticisms and Contributions of Marketing*. Retrieved from https://www.marketingjournal.org/criticisms-and-contributions-of-marketing-an-excerpt-from-philip-kotlers-autobiography-philip-kotler/.

© The Author(s), under exclusive license to Springer Nature Switzerland AG 2021
P. Kotler et al., *H2H Marketing*, https://doi.org/10.1007/978-3-030-59531-9_1

to outsmart and trick customers rather than convincing them in an honest way.[3]

Taking this into account, it does not come as a surprise that the diminishing importance and credibility of marketing departments have been proven empirically.[4] The founder of marketing in Germany as a scientific discipline, Professor Meffert,[5] points out that marketing is meant to be a "dual management concept" – on the one hand a corporate function and on the other hand a "corporate governance concept" that integrates the "market-oriented coordination of all operational functional areas." While this dual understanding is predominant in scientific discourse, marketing in professional practice is more and more limited to the corporate function, while a leading function is successively denied.[6]

This problem is not new: Marketing has been struggling with diminishing importance for some time now. Already in 2005, Sheth and Sisodia postulated that "marketing has come to view itself too narrowly and, in many cases, merely as sales support".[7] Meffert warned: "Restricting marketing to a sales-supporting instrument does not do justice to the dual leadership claim of marketing and carries the danger that marketing orientation is only anchored operationally, but not strategically, in the company and its corporate culture".[8]

Many researchers see shareholder value orientation[9] as the primary reason for this development. According to them, successful, market-oriented corporate management and the shareholder value approach are not mutually exclusive. Problematic developments arise when firms, in pursuit of short-term capital gains, try to save costs and reduce marketing budgets, which in the short term does not have a negative impact on customer loyalty. In the long

---

[3] Sheth & Sisodia (2005), *op. cit.*

[4] Homburg, C., Vomberg, A., Enke, M., & Grimm, P. H. (2015). The loss of the marketing department's influence: is it really happening? And why worry? *Journal of the Academy of Marketing Science, 43*(1), pp. 1–13. https://doi.org/10.1007/s11747-014-0416-3.

[5] Meffert, H., Burmann, C., Kirchgeorg, M., & Eisenbeiß, M. (2019). *Marketing: Grundlagen marktorientierter Unternehmensführung Konzepte – Instrumente – Praxisbeispiele* (13th. ed.), pp. 12–13 Wiesbaden, Germany: Springer Gabler.

[6] Benkenstein, M. (2018). Hat sich das Marketing als Leitkonzept der Unternehmensführung wirklich überlebt? – Eine kritische Stellungnahme. In M. Bruhn, & M. Kirchgeorg (Eds.), *Marketing Weiterdenken: Zukunftspfade für eine marktorientierte Unternehmensführung* (pp. 49–64). Wiesbaden, Germany: Springer Gabler.

[7] Sheth & Sisodia (2005), *op. cit.*, p. 11.

[8] Meffert et al. (2019), *op. cit.*, p. 14.

[9] Benkenstein (2018), *op. cit.* and Rebecca Henderson (2020). Reimagining Capitalism in a World on Fire, New York, USA: PublicAffairs. "WHEN THE FACTS CHANGE, I CHANGE MY MIND. WHAT DO YOU DO, SIR?" Shareholder Value as Yesterday's Idea.

run, however, the image, brand positioning, and customer loyalty suffer considerably.

1.1 Marketing: Quo Vadis?

The corporate management of a market-oriented firm is often subject to criticism because it only reacts to market developments instead of proactively shaping market developments in a resource-oriented manner. For marketing to yield effective results, firms ought to aim for a healthy mix between market orientation (market pull) and resource orientation (technology push) instead of clinging to only one perspective. Marketing needs to be both market-oriented and resource-oriented. Both aspects form part of a marketing mindset that should infuse the entire company, not only the marketing department.

A few companies like Whole Foods Market and Patagonia have this mindset. In all its offerings, a positive customer experience is the overriding goal. Seamless access to products, services, software, content, and solutions is the core of all their offerings. Similar approaches can be found in B2B companies such as SKF (Svenska Kullagerfabriken) Gothenburg, Sweden, and Schaeffler Technologies, Herzogenaurach, Germany, also known as Schaeffler Group. Another positive example has developed in recent years: Microsoft. Under the leadership of Satya Nadella, the company changed from a "blue screen" company to becoming very customer-oriented. In this context, we would like to mention Salesforce and its founder and Co-CEO Marc Benioff. He's an angel investor in dozens of tech start-ups and a prolific philanthropist and delivers a vision for the need for a new kind of marketing, one where businesses and executives value purpose alongside profit and that changing the world is everybody's business.

In addition to the aforementioned lack of market orientation, marketing in its corporate function is being questioned increasingly.[10] Partly, this is due to the behavior and the capabilities of the marketing experts themselves. While consuming big budgets, marketers are often struggling with low efficiency and effectiveness. In addition, as the results of measures are hard to quantify, the lack of professional accounting for the often badly spent financial resources create the impression of marketing being lavish and ineffective.[11] Strategic tasks of high importance, e.g., parts of the business development process, are

---

[10] Sheth and Sisodia (2005), *op. cit.*

[11] Sheth, J. N., & Sisodia, R. S. (2002). Marketing productivity: Issues and analysis. *Journal of Business Research, 55*(5), pp. 349–362. https://doi.org/10.1016/S0148-2963(00)00164-8.

no longer assigned to marketing departments,[12] instead, marketing gets reduced to the conception and execution of sales policy instruments, mostly in the area of communication.

It must be understood that these changes are not due to the diminishing significance of marketing but are associated with a misinterpretation of the role of marketing by both practitioners and academics. At a symposium on the question: *Does Marketing Need Reform?* Rajiv Grover, the holder of the Sales and Marketing Chair of Excellence at the University of Memphis, concluded:

> If marketing is defined as satisfying the expressed and latent needs of customers, it is well accepted out there, so marketing is not really being marginalized. But marketers are being marginalized, in the sense that many strategically important aspects of marketing e.g., pricing, ad budgeting, new product decisions are being taken away by other functions in the organization.[13]

Marketing must return to the core of value creation tackling long-term problems that profoundly affect people's lives. Even though being equipped with good intentions, marketers often fall into the trap of several malpractices. They find that "the bulk of 'marketing in practice' differs greatly from the normative construct"[14] and that marketers are following practices that only reap positive results for one party at the expense of the other – *unethical marketing* at the expense of the customer or *inane marketing*, what they describe as "marketing actions [...] so poorly thought out that they leave the company vulnerable to exploitation by increasingly deal-savvy consumers"[15] at the expense of the marketer – or, even worse, marketing measures that are just wasteful and of no benefit at all. When the customers are losing out and the organizations wins, most of the time the gains are short-lived. The company can achieve short-term profits, until other competitors arrive or government regulations are becoming necessary. This is clearly not an ethical way to conduct marketing activities.

The most ruthless example is the price increase of more than 5000% of the AIDS treatment Daraprim. In 2015, Turing Pharmaceuticals jacked up the price for this life-saving medication from $13.50 to $750 per dose and clearly

---

[12]Voeth, M. (2018). Marketing und/oder marktorientierte Unternehmensführung? In M. Bruhn, & M. Kirchgeorg (Eds.), *Marketing Weiterdenken: Zukunftspfade für eine marktorientierte Unternehmensführung* (pp. 67–78). Wiesbaden, Germany: Springer Gabler.

[13]Sheth and Sisodia (2005), op. cit., p. 11.

[14]Sheth, J. N., & Sisodia, R. S. (2007). Raising Marketing's Aspirations, *p. 141. Journal of Public Policy & Marketing, 26*(1), pp. 141–143. https://doi.org/10.1509/jppm.26.1.141.

[15]Sheth and Sisodia (2007), *op. cit.*, p. 141.

downed the not so ethical orientation of Martin Shkreli, the company's CEO. If the customers are short-term winner, this is clearly not so smart for the product or service providers; it becomes inane on a long-term basis. When both sides are losing, then we talk about wasteful marketing. We are gearing for long-term gain for the customer and the company, and when it is oriented to the people, we talk about H2H Marketing (see Fig. 1.1[16]).

To our understanding, it is the task of any Chief Marketing Officer (CMO) to create the highest benefits for their customer and the company. This could be achieved if they work for a higher purpose by creating Human-to-Human Marketing. Sonya Oblisk, CMO of Whole Foods Market said, "We're always striving to better understand our customers' passions when it comes to food."[17] She belongs to the group of CMOs who drive for customer orientation and growth. She sets new standards for how marketing should be, moving away from product-led to experience-led business. Linda Boff of General Electric (GE) is steering the 130-year-old industrial conglomerate to a true customer-centric way of doing business. With no doubt, GE and other similarly large established enterprises like Unilever and Caterpillar are struggling with their marketing strategy.

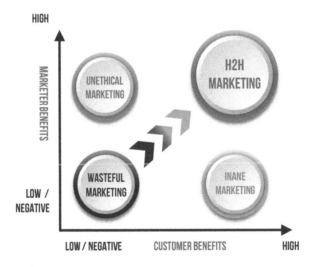

Fig. 1.1 H2H marketing orientation

[16] Adapted from Sheth and Sisodia (2007), *op. cit.*, p. 142.

[17] Wholefoodsmarket (2020). *Quality and Transparent Sourcing Drive Millennial Food Choices, According to New Whole Foods Market Survey.* Retrieved from https://media.wholefoodsmarket.com/news/quality-and-transparent-sourcing-drive-millennial-food-choices-according-to.

Under the category of marketing malpractices also falls what Seth Godin criticized as *Interruption Marketing*, to which he proposes *Permission Marketing* as an antidote to unwanted spam emails, phone calls, and banner ads flooding people's daily lives and constantly interrupting their attention flow. With Permission Marketing, he makes a compelling case for a collaborative, non-intrusive approach to marketing that asks people for permission to educate them on products and services instead of overpowering them and brute-forcing a way into their minds, for which especially the digital space provides plenty of opportunities. This enables companies to provide information that has relevance to the customers, information that is welcomed not ignored. Such an approach would be much more valuable for building trust with the customer and could help to improve the bad image of marketing and its practitioners.[18]

The authors of *Inbound Marketing* argue that the interruptive *outbound marketing* measures pushed onto customers are not only costly and yield almost no positive results, but also they put them under unwanted distress, which further adds to the bad reputation of the field.[19] Instead of only trying to get across a message, firms should "attract visitors by providing them with relevant information, publishing useful content and generally trying to be as helpful as possible".[20]

Internet search provided the basis for inbound marketing, and many traditional companies are experimenting with the same. Giants like IBM, SAP, Apple, and many small companies have made the shift. Tesla completely relies on inbound marketing – they have no sales force. CEO and Chairman, Elon Musk, represent the brand; the rest is done online, including all ordering or pre-ordering. The same is true for Airbnb and Uber. Even Mercedes-Benz is creating a pull-effect from young customers who are inspired by social media activities of the brand.

H2H Marketing has the ambition to leave malpractices behind, offering an *ethical and collaborative way of engaging with customers*, by co-creating value together as a team rather than at the expense of each other. Marketing needs higher aspirations and competitive goals to finally be taken seriously again. H2H Marketing makes a contribution to that! Some companies and brands are already applying this principle on their own or using some elements. Whole Foods Market approach of providing sustainably grown produce is

---

[18] Godin, S. (2007). *Permission Marketing*. London, United Kingdom: Simon & Schuste, UK.

[19] Halligan, B., & Shah, D. (2018). *Inbound-Marketing: Wie Sie Kunden online anziehen, abholen und begeistern* (D. Runne, Trans.). Weinheim, Germany: Wiley-VCH.

[20] Halligan and Shah (2018), *op. cit.*, p. 19.

encouraging a healthy lifestyle and great shopping experience with a clean conscience of doing well for the planet. Their employees and suppliers are also included in the picture as the company continues to come up with offerings to benefit them. Airbus also provides excellent customer experience and continuous product innovation by applying some of the H2H Marketing principles.

These companies aim for higher goals by combining resource orientation with market orientation and communication with action (as shown in Fig. 1.1). The aim does choose to concentrate on either market orientation or resource orientation, because they are not considered to be contrary but complementary concepts. Firms need to develop core competencies out utilizing their key resources with their key activities, but the resulting service offerings must also be in line with the market.

Firms practicing H2H Marketing are focused on co-creating value together with their customers and communicating their value offerings properly. Amazon has done it with customer-created product reviews and Spotify with their private user named listings. DeWalt Power Tools has established an insight community so that customers can contribute new product ideas. Ikea introduced "Co-Create Ikea" in the form of a digital platform where customers and fans could make proposals for new product developments. Such companies do not communicate empty promises on which they do not deliver, and they do not fail to communicate their success stories when they do well.

1.2   Firms of Endearment: Pioneers of the H2H Philosophy

H2H firms have a strong ethical commitment to all their stakeholder groups, from their customers, suppliers, and employees to society as a whole. They share a character trait, what Sisodia, Sheth, and Wolfe call *Firms of Endearment* (FoE), where "[n]o stakeholder group benefits at the expense of any other stakeholder groups and each prospers as the others do".[21] In their book of the same name, the authors summarize positive results from companies like 3M, Adobe Systems, and Autodesk that human marketing based on collaboration, empathy, and respect can have:

---

[21] Sisodia, R. S., Sheth, J. N., & Wolfe, D. (2014). *Firms of Endearment: How World-Class Companies Profit from Passion and Purpose* (2nd ed.), p. 7. Upper Saddle River, NJ: Pearson Education.

Earn a place in the customer's heart and she will gladly offer you a bigger share of her wallet. Do the same for an employee and the employee will give back with a quantum leap in productivity and work quality. *Emotionally* bond with your suppliers and reap the benefits of superior offerings and responsiveness. Give communities in which you operate reasons to feel pride in your presence, and enjoy a fertile source of customers and employees.[22]

For the authors, endearing behavior towards interest groups of a company is not just another Corporate Social Responsibility charade, but rather the very essence of their approach to doing business. Firms of Endearment overcomes the "me first, others second" thinking and adopts a stakeholder approach where the interests of all parties are respected and taken into account. Typical character traits of Firms of Endearment are[23]:

- They pay higher wages than their competitors and invest more time and money into the education of their employees.
- Suppliers are treated as collaborative partners, not as inferior vassal. They get support to boost their business and grow together.
- FoEs create an emotional bond with customers, employees, and the communities they are operating in.
- Lower employee turnover is characteristic.
- FoEs are driven by long-term goals and do not fall victim to short-term, rash actions.

These FoEs like CarMax, Chipotle, Cognizant, and Costco have a win/win situation. By contributing to the outcome of improving the lives of others, they in turn receive strong financial rewards. Sisodia et al.[24] note:

All this may seem counterintuitive, but in case after case, FoEs with higher labor costs actually have lower labor costs per dollar of income as well as lower marketing costs.

The emotional connection between FoEs and their customer fosters loyalty and willingness to advocate for a brand. This shows that being a FoE/H2H Marketer is not about being an idealistic new trendsetter; it is a clear competitive advantage that makes it possible to be competitive *and* help others without trade-offs between parties.

---

[22] Sisodia, Sheth, & Wolfe (2014), *op. cit.*, p. 7.

[23] Sisodia, Sheth, & Wolfe (2014), *op. cit.*

[24] Sisodia, Sheth, & Wolfe (2014), *op. cit.*, p. 96.

H2H firms today are needed more than ever, not only for the social transformation of capitalism but also to ensure sustainable business practices. Apte and Sheth[25] in their book *The Sustainability Edge: How to Drive Top-line Growth with Triple-bottom-line Thinking* describe sustainability as one of the most essential and urgent goals of today's and future leaders. With increasing pressure coming especially from the younger generation, who voice their fears about an uncertain future and demand a radical change in the path of business, firms are expected to take things into their hands and reshape their businesses to make sure they leave behind an intact planet to future generations.

The authors add a long list of companies including Harley-Davidson, IBM, Marriott Hotels, MasterCard Worldwide, and many more. All of these companies address some of the elements of FoE, but not all the requirements of this concept. Southwest Airlines, Starbucks, and United Parcel Service care about their customers and employee needs; some of them may use ethically sourced products, and some have numerous innovations. All of them do have in common that they thrive for a common good. In the words of Bill Marriott, "Take good care of the employees and they will in turn take good care of the customers who will return again and again."

1.3   Sustainable Management Challenge

Sustainability is in the forefront in current issues of society, politics, and the economy. Advocates have created a sense of urgency and managed to demand immediate attention. Other than steps that individuals can take, people are increasingly looking towards companies to tackle bigger problems, because trust in government has diminished on the whole. In regard to sustainability, Apte and Sheth add an important dimension to the spectrum of brand activism and H2H Marketing. They describe that while some companies are catching up to the sustainability movement, others resist because they view "sustainable growth" as a concept that is contradictory in itself. For brands like Patagonia, Timberland, and Jack Wolfskin, their "green" approach is widely recognized. This is not so much the case for Walmart or Procter & Gamble. They offer some sustainable products, but for most of their product offerings and practices, they are heavily criticized.

At first glance, growth and sustainability seem to be two mutually exclusive goals. The two authors on the other hand make a case for sustainable growth

---

[25] Apte, S. & Sheth, J. (2016) *The Sustainability Edge: How to Drive Top-line Growth with Triple-bottom-line Thinking*, Rotman-UTP Publishing.

with the conviction that achieving revenue growth while remaining true to sustainability principles are very much in the realm of what's feasible. They argue that the business world needs positive examples, something they call *sustainability champions*, which proves this feasibility. In their work, they outline three different strategies to create sustainable growth:

- 1st strategy: "[D]ecouple revenue growth from depletion of virgin natural resources."[26]

By establishing a *circular economy*, where firms care about products after they have been used, the use of resources can be lowered. For new products, firms can use renewable resources (Ikea) or material that has been recycled (Nike).

- 2nd strategy: "[B]usinesses can produce fewer and better products."[27]

In times of the shared economy, firms can adjust their business models and incentivize customers to share (Airbnb, Uber, Grab, DriveNow), rent, or lease products. This can create new revenue streams while also making the business more sustainable (GE, Siemens Gamesa).

- 3rdstrategy: "[R]edefine growth."[28]

Is financial growth in the traditional sense all there is? Growth has many facets, like societal growth or the growth of well-being on a personal level. Firms should set growth goals considering other perspective than just financial ones.

Similar to the authors of Firms of Endearment, Apte and Sheth view the collaborative engagement of all stakeholder groups as the only sustainable source of competitive advantage. For them, sustainability is not an add-on but a necessity expressed in their assessment of the current situation:

The scope and magnitude of challenges that business faces, currently and in the future, are enormous. The world's physical resources are limited and becoming ever costlier, the advantage of scale and automation are declining, new innovations are copied at a faster pace, and societal problems are growing at alarming rates. Incremental change won't address these challenges. What is required is a

---

[26] Apte & Sheth (2016), *op. cit.*, Foreword section, Para. 7.
[27] Apte & Sheth (2016), *op. cit.*, Foreword section, Para. 9.
[28] Apte & Sheth (2016), *op. cit.*, Foreword section, Para. 10.

transformational change in business strategies, practices, and tactics with triple-bottom-line thinking.[29]

To successfully implement triple bottom line thinking, taking into account social, economic, and ecologic issues, they introduce an amplified stakeholder model that can serve as extension to the **SPICE** stakeholder model: **S**ociety, **P**artners, **I**nvestors, **C**ustomers, **E**mployees. This will be introduced in detail in Chap. 3.

Developments and findings of recent years show without a doubt that customer priorities are shifting. Especially, the younger generations in the USA request sustainable product and service offerings. This will have a strong impact in the coming years because the millennials are demanding sustainability prioritizing the improvement of the environment. In Fig. 1.2, it shows millenials, it is important for them that companies implement programs to improve the environment (83%) and 75% will change their purchasing behavior.[30]

Moreover, these sustainability-conscious customers are willing to pay a premium for sustainable products:[31]

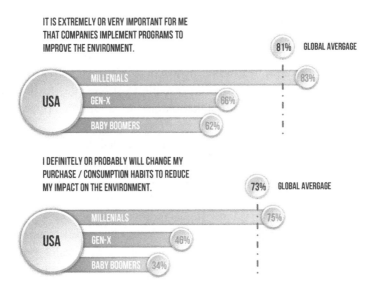

Fig. 1.2   Demand for sustainability among different age groups in the USA

---

[29] Apte & Sheth (2016), *op. cit.*, Preface section, Para. 3.

[30] Adapted from Nielsen (2018). *Sustainable Shoppers buy the change they wish to see in the world* [Report]. Retrieved from https://www.nielsen.com/wp-content/uploads/sites/3/2019/04/global-sustainable-shoppers-report-2018.pdf.

[31] Apte & Sheth (2016), *op. cit.*

- Many markets (e.g., Europe, USA) have reached high maturity levels making sustainable growth inside traditional, narrow paradigms almost impossible.
- As the emerging economies are catching up to higher living standards, the amount of required resources to satisfy their ever-growing demand is rising and poses an imperative for sustainable business practices, because the planet's resources are limited.

However, what can companies actually do? Companies can change the direction of their business concept: from shareholder orientation to stakeholder focus. Companies have a direct impact on their consumers and customers. Their employees are the ones who deliver the solutions and services. With these groups, the company is in constant direct interactions. The government has indirect impact on various administrative layers local, regional, or national. Companies are paying taxes and follow regulations. Nevertheless, media and other intermediaries are impacted indirectly. In addition, there are non-government organizations (NGOs), which get affected by a company's operations. Enablers are communities. They provide infrastructure, basic services, etc. Investors provide a financial basis, and the suppliers deliver the necessary components and any more. The sole focus on the investors is to narrow. Companies need a broader scope and have engage with each of the nine stakeholder groups. With this approach, a 360-degree stakeholder model could be created (see Fig. 1.3). The principle to success lies in the intention "maximizing benefits for all stakeholders as a source of competitive advantage".[32]

In line with these authors, we believe that sustainability will enable companies to reach a competitive advantage if they apply sustainability thinking in the right way – systematic and holistic – and if they adopt it as a crucial part of their organization and provide the basis for a more human-oriented marketing approach, the H2H Marketing.

Companies can directly affect their business clients, end customers, and employees. They can make conscious choices about their value propositions, processes, and relationships. Indirectly, they can influence media, governments, NGOs, etc. through lobbying, financial, and moral contributions. Additionally, they also can have an enabler impact to their suppliers, investors, and communities. We agree with the authors that businesses that embrace sustainability will contribute positively to their stakeholders, and we would like to incorporate this thinking in our approach.

---

[32] Apte & Sheth (2016), *op. cit.*

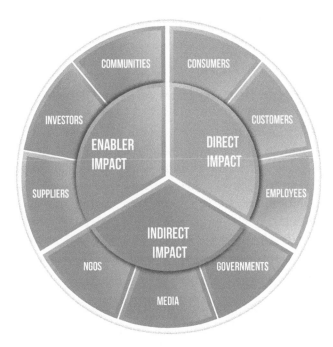

Fig. 1.3 The 360-degree stakeholder model

We see that many companies are struggling with the demand to embrace sustainability. For example, Nestlé Global gets heavily criticized for its water extraction practice at many locations, and Procter & Gamble and Walmart are in similar trouble. Industrial component and systems suppliers like GE, Siemens, and Johnson Controls are trying to improve their carbon footprint by manufacturing equipment which is more effective and energy efficient. One specific example is the Herrenknecht AG, which engineers, produces, and operates equipment for building underground passageways. With their tunneling equipment, they mechanized tunnel boring and increased efficiency and safety. As effect for the consumer, these tunnels save drivers millions of kilometers by shortening the route. Unfortunately, the construction consumes a huge amount of energy to drill this tunnel. With these energy-intensive investments, great savings could be achieved. Chemical companies find similar conditions. They are creating materials, which are longer lasting and more durable. An extreme example is the company Lamoral Coatings. They offer a fluoride polymer, which could extend the lifetime of metal, wood, or cloth surface areas more than tenfold, but their production process must be controlled very diligently to avoid environmental damages. These examples illustrate the options for incorporating human orientation and sustainability into the marketing activities.

1.4   The Evolution to H2H Marketing

To put H2H Marketing into context, a look at the evolutionary timeline of marketing is helpful. Marketing thinking had a constant development over the past 200 years. Before the shaping of the marketing orientation, there have been several periods of different views and concepts. Since the first industrial revolution, national economics were the origin of modern marketing science with its orientation to production. After 1900, followed a product-oriented approach, which led to trade and export science on one side and market theory and market policy on the other side. The failures of the production orientation during the Great Depression paved the way for change. The reshaped orientation was sales-focused that holds good to a certain extent even today, but it paved the way for the general marketing theory. The classical sales theory was at first an institution-oriented approach and then moved to goods-oriented and function-oriented. In the 1960, the different approaches of modern marketing theory appeared. There were various approaches: behavioral, decision-oriented, system-oriented, and situational.

Then from 1980, the "newer" paradigms in marketing theory appeared with emphasis on information economics, resource/competence orientation, relationship-orientation, process-orientation, and the digital marketing. Heribert Meffert provides a detailed overview of the evolution of marketing theory since its creation and the corresponding contextual topics (see Fig. 1.4[33]).

Still, marketing is a relatively young and dynamic discipline. In the 1930s, Procter & Gamble introduced brand management for their consumer offerings. GE's long time CEO Jack Welch brought it to new heights for industrial companies. Companies like Yahoo, AOL, and Google built the foundations for digital marketing, which gained phenomenal speed and continues to do so. Especially two aspects underwent constant changes over the decades: innovations in marketing and its importance in corporate management. Marketing had to continually adapt to structural changes in the market and build new success factors to stay relevant. These new success factors and their deriving tasks, in general, did not replace the former ones, but rather, they

---

[33] Adapted from Meffert et al. (2019), *op. cit.*, p. 31.

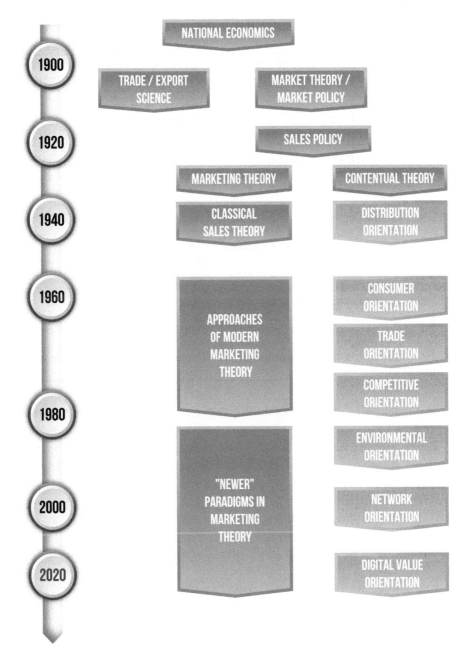

Fig. 1.4   The evolution of marketing theory

Table 1.1   Key themes and behaviors during different phases of marketing

Phases	Key themes	Behavior of market participants
1950s	Activation/shaping of the existing brands and distribution	Reactive behavior of customers and retailers and high receptiveness (*seller's market*)
1960s	Development and modification of sales channels	Consumer pent-up demand, development of different trade types, entry of new competitors
1970s	Differentiated market cultivation through market segmentation	Differentiated customer behavior, stronger trade (*buyer's market*)
1980s	Development and securing of strategic competitive advantages	Increasing customer awareness, intensified retail competition, intense competitive behavior
1990s	Fast reaction to environmental changes	Differentiation in customer behavior, strong retail concentration
2000s	Management of long-term customer relationships	Lifestyle buying behavior, high intensity of competition, emergence of e-commerce
2010s	Reaction and use of technological dynamics and digitalization	Digital interactions during purchase, new business models for suppliers and retailers
2020s	Shaping co-creation networks and eco-systems, firms taking stands on political, social, and economic issues	Digital interactions through the whole life cycle, high influence of the community and the personal environment

accumulated to an ever more complex task structure and an elevated competence level of marketing.[34] Sephora and Amazon are good retail examples.

Bruhn summarizes how the tasks of marketing and customer behavior changed during the observed decades (see Table 1.1). By analyzing the developments, he points out three crucial milestones[35]:

1. "Thinking in the 4Ps (*The Instrumental Paradigm*)"
2. "Thinking in Competitive Advantages (*The Competition Paradigm*)"
3. "Thinking in Relationship Marketing (*The Relationship Paradigm*)"

Comparing the milestones to the development processes shown in Fig. 1.4 and Table 1.1,[36] the absence of a paradigm for the current phase (*phase of*

---

[34] Bruhn, M. (2018). Marketing Weiterdenken in der marktorientierten Unternehmensführung – Entwicklungen und Zukunftsthemen der Marketingdisziplin. In M. Bruhn, & M. Kirchgeorg (Eds.), *Marketing Weiterdenken: Zukunftspfade für eine markt orientierte Unternehmensführung* (pp. 25–48). Wiesbaden, Germany: Springer Gabler.

[35] Bruhn (2018), *op. cit.*, p. 31.

[36] 1950 to 2010 is adapted from Bruhn (2018), *op. cit.*, p. 29. The phase from 2020s is based on current developments in the Service-Dominant Logic and digitalization.

digital connectivity,[37] *phase of digital value creation*[38]) stands out. H2H Marketing considers *Thinking in Co-Creative Service Exchange* as a new milestone with the Service-Dominant Logic, introduced by Vargo and Lusch[39] as a new paradigm and applied in companies like IBM, Goldman Sachs, McKinsey, KPMG, Deutsche Bank, and their peers.

Today, marketing faces strong challenges by several disruptive developments, the dominating one being digitalization and increasing ecological awareness. This is evidenced by the ever-present sustainability discussions in the news, supported by the first tangible effects of global warming and smog situation of cities around the globe. Energy providers are particularly affected by this new development, and as answers, Siemens, ABB, and GE are providing smart grid technology, wind turbines, solar applications, etc. Even oil companies are ready for change. British Petroleum (BP) changed its business focus and renamed its company to Beyond Petroleum.

On the buyers' side, the buying process has changed and is now based on a variety of communication and sales channels between which the customers constantly switch. This poses a challenge for firms to adequately manage and integrate them. Information transparency provided by the Internet produces well-informed customers who compare offerings online and have higher price sensitivity. Furthermore, the influence of the social context, subsumed under the term *f-factor* (family, friends, fans, followers) on the individual's purchasing decision, has also increased significantly, which reduces firms' direct influence on the customers. This makes change in thinking in marketing necessary and "[c]onnectivity changes the key foundation of marketing: the market itself".[40]

The study "Marketing Organization of the Future"[41] verifies that digitalization is the principal driver for the main challenges in marketing. In the study of participants with a marketing background, the study found that three out of the top four challenges for marketers are created by digitalization changes. These involve the explosion of sales and communication channels, with the consequence that marketers have to deal with extensive data and increased general velocity. Overall, most of the participants (60%) foresee growth in the

---

[37] Bruhn (2018), *op. cit.*

[38] Meffert et al. (2019), *op. cit.*

[39] Vargo, S. L., & Lusch, R. F. (2004). Evolving to a New Dominant Logic for Marketing. *Journal of Marketing, 68*(1), pp. 1–17. https://doi.org/10.1509/jmkg.68.1.1.24036.

[40] Kotler, P., Kartajaya, H., & Setiawan, I. (2017). *Marketing 4.0: Moving from Traditional to Digital*, p. 22. Hoboken, NJ: Wiley.

[41] Bathen, D., & Jelden, J. (2014). *Marketingorganisation der Zukunft* [Report]. Retrieved from https://www.marketingverband.de/marketingkompetenz/studien/marketingorganisation-der-zukunft/.

relevance of marketing departments for the future. Although optimistic in the outlook for future relevance, a high level of uncertainty about the future organization of marketing was expressed. 29% of respondents consider it necessary to completely restructure marketing departments, while 48% of the asked marketers call for at least small changes in order to live up to the claim of high relevance.[42]

The study further foresees that marketing experts are not keeping up with technological changes. Even their last remaining function – marketing communication – is challenged. It could possibly be taken away from them, as the necessary expertise lies more and more in the IT departments. Marketers will have to broaden their competences and skills, especially in technology to be able to leverage the potential that lies in digitalization developments and to avoid leaving the field to other departments.

We invite the reader to challenge marketing and marketers by defining the core competencies of marketing as a corporate function. What is the measurable contribution of marketing to innovations today? Why are sales processes defined well and are transparent in their effects on the company's targets while marketing procedures and effects are opaque?

Digging deeper into the current phase of marketing, connectivity challenges traditional views on access and ownership.[43] Paraphrasing Chen[44] and Marx,[45] Bardhi and Eckhardt state: "Instead of buying and owning things, consumers want access to goods and prefer to pay for the experience of temporarily accessing them. Ownership is no longer the ultimate expression of consumer desire".[46] The trend towards the *Sharing Economy* changes customer behavior and preferences, while co-creation of service gains more importance. The prime example of the Sharing Economy, car sharing (Uber, Lyft, DiDi, Grab, Share Now, Ola, etc.), only works with strong customer collaboration, and a smaller share of the task done by firms, as picking up, returning, as well as cleaning and refueling, is all done by the customer.[47] "The dematerialization of consumption, loss of importance of ownership, and new forms of

[42] Bathen & Jelden (2014), *op. cit.*, p. 8f.

[43] Bardhi, F., & Eckhardt, G. M. (2012). Access-Based Consumption: The Case of Car Sharing. *Journal of Consumer Research, 39*(4), pp. 881–898. https://doi.org/10.1086/666376.

[44] Chen, Y. (2009). Possession and Access: Consumer Desires and Value Perceptions Regarding Contemporary Art Collection and Exhibit Visits. *Journal of Consumer Research, 35*(6), pp. 925–940. https://doi.org/10.1086/593699.

[45] Marx, P. (2011, January 23). The Borrowers: Why buy when you can rent? *The New Yorker*. Retrieved from https://www.newyorker.com/magazine/2011/01/31/the-borrowers.

[46] Bardhi & Eckhardt (2012), *op. cit.*, p. 881.

[47] Bardhi & Eckhardt (2012), *op. cit.*

use"[48] as a consequence of connectivity are becoming more important. Furthermore, we see a rise of new customer needs, especially a rising interest in information and knowledge:

> Through industrialization and mass consumption, consumption of products slowly became a common habit. Thanks to advertising and decay, demand here is not saturated, but comparatively stagnant. This creates space for new needs and desires, including more knowledge and information and more service.[49]

These developments form part of a comprehensive "social transformation of capitalism".[50] They call the transitional phase in which we find ourselves the *Age of Transcendence*, in which the needs, desires, and dreams of customers are fundamentally changing, more focused on purpose, passion, and experience beyond materialistic needs. A major driver of this development is the demographic change taking place worldwide. With an aging society, passionate and purpose-driven issues are gaining much more momentum, and issues that dominate social discourse and thought are shifting. And when people live longer, their values, mentalities, and spiritual ideals are passed on to the next generation and anchored in it.[51]

With the shift from product-centricity to service-centeredness,[52] *experiential* co-creation of value becomes a new reality. That value creation is dependent on individual experiences, and the context in which they take place is also recognized by Prahalad and Ramaswamy, who state that "value creation is defined by the experience of a specific consumer, at a specific point in time and location, in the context of a specific event".[53]

In their paper *The New Frontier of Experience Innovation*, they introduce the idea that sustainable growth in the digitalized world requires an approach to innovation that is cut loose from the traditional fixation on the products and services of a company. Microsoft has successfully transitioned to this new

---

[48] Wallaschkowski, S., & Niehuis, E. (2017). Digitaler Konsum, p. 129. In O. Stengel, A. van Looy, & S. Wallaschkowski (Eds.), *Digitalzeitalter – Digitalgesellschaft: Das Ende des Industriezeitalters und der Beginn einer neuen Epoche* (pp. 109–141). Wiesbaden, Germany: Springer VS.

[49] Wallaschkowski & Niehuis (2017), *op. cit.*, p. 129.

[50] Sisodia, Sheth, & Wolfe (2014), *op. cit.*, p. XXII.

[51] Sisodia, Sheth, & Wolfe (2014), *op. cit.*

[52] It is important to note that for Vargo & Lusch *service* is different from *services* in their traditional sense. For them service constitutes "[...] the application of specialized competences (knowledge and skills) through deeds, processes, and performances for the benefit of another entity or the entity itself" (see Vargo & Lusch, 2004, p. 2).

[53] Prahalad, C. K., & Ramaswamy, V. (2003). The New Frontier of Experience Innovation, p. 14. *MIT Sloan Management Review, 44*(4), pp. 12–18. Retrieved from https://sloanreview.mit.edu/article/the-new-frontier-of-experience-innovation/.

Table 1.2   Comparison of traditional innovation and experience innovation

	Traditional innovation	Experience innovation
Focus of innovation	Products and processes	Experience environments
Basis of value	Products and services	Co-creation experiences
View of value creation	• Firm creates value • Supply-chain-centric fulfilment of products and services • Supply push and pull demand pull for the firm's offerings	• Value is co-created • Experience environments for individuals to co-construct experiences on contextual demand • Individual-centric co-creation of value
View of technology	• Facilitator of features and functions • Technology and systems integration	• Facilitator of experiences • Experience integration
Focus of supply chains	• Supports fulfilment of products and services	• Experience network supports co-construction of personalized experiences

frontier, and IBM, with the Red Hat acquisition, is determined to reinvent itself. Goldman Sachs, Deutsche Bank, and Bank of America are also moving to experience innovation. Besides these large conglomerates, there is room for small companies with focus on specific applications and market niches:

> The intent of experience innovation is not to improve a product or service, per se, but to enable the co-creation of an environment populated by companies and consumers and their networks — in which personalized, evolvable experiences are the goal, and products and services evolve as a *means* to that end.[54]

We identify strong implications that the shift towards experience will produce. This is presented in Table 1.2.[55] Underlying the concept of experience innovation is a fundamentally different understanding of how value is created and which role firms take in this process. While before, customers had a passive role in business, today's connected and empowered customer acts as active co-creator in collaboration with companies, providing companies with their competence, "a function of the knowledge and skills they possess, their willingness to learn and experiment, and their ability to engage in an active dialogue".[56]

---

[54] Prahalad & Ramaswamy (2003), *op. cit.*, p. 18.

[55] Adapted from Prahalad & Ramaswamy (2003), *op. cit.*, p. 17.

[56] Prahalad, C. K., & Ramaswamy, V. (2000). Co-opting Customer Competence, p. 80. *Harvard Business Review, 78*(1), pp. 79–87. Retrieved from https://hbr.org/2000/01/coopting-customer-competence.

This results in a fundamental change in perspective for the firms as they are no longer seen as "value producers" but as collaborative actors in a co-creation process. The S-DL postulates that firms cannot unilaterally produce value embedded into products and services but can rather provide value propositions out of which customers derive value. In line with what the S-DL firms[57] can only provide experience opportunities, the experience itself, from which the customer individually derives value, cannot be "produced" by companies but is brought to life by the customer.

The example almost everybody can relate to is the Swedish company Ikea. Their offerings are unassembled pieces of furniture, which need to be assembled by the customers' own hands. The stylish and reasonable priced offerings are co-created with their customers. Ikea continues to open stores worldwide and expand their e-commerce offerings. They have been growing more than double the market growth and want to reach half of the world market by 2025. Similar developments could be witnessed with many industrial service providers, started out as product companies and became solution providers, many: 3M, Alfa Laval, Alcatel, Atlas Copco, Bosch Rexroth, DATAIKU, Fujitsu Global, KUKA, MCK AUTOMAÇÃO, Omron, Sinomation, Sumitomo, Thales, and Tetra Pak.

Marketers need to understand the new reality of co-creation, which forms an integral part of H2H Marketing. Because of its essential significance for success in today's marketplace, service orientation in the sense of the S-DL further is a key character trait of the H2H Mindset (see Chap. 3).

All too often, marketing is only involved in the innovation process at the "back end of innovation." It is called to action shortly before market launch, but it should take more responsibility in innovation, especially at the "fuzzy front end of innovation".[58]

- The new H2H Marketing approach relies on *Design Thinking* as a means of participating in all (especially the early) stages of innovation, as well as the *digitalization* and *S-DL* (the three factors of the H2H Marketing Model will be explained in detail in Chap. 2), that provide a fertile environment for both incremental (*exploitation*) and ground-breaking (*exploration*) innovations. Marketing itself can learn a lot from Design Thinking as mindset and innovation method, not only because of early intervention

---

[57] Prahalad & Ramaswamy (2000), *op. cit.*

[58] Gassmann, O., & Schweitzer, F. (2014). Managing the Unmanageable: The Fuzzy Front End of Innovation. In O. Gassmann, & F. Schweitzer (Eds.), *Management of the Fuzzy Front End of Innovation* (pp. 3–14). Cham, Switzerland: Springer International Publishing.

into innovation but also because of its customer or, better put, human focus, which it takes, unlike in the case of marketing, very seriously.

- Marketing departments have lost part of their importance, which has been documented empirically.[59]
- Marketing has built up a poor image and reputation due to untrustworthy behavior of marketers and the respective departments. "[M]arketing is being driven by corporate goals that are increasingly divergent with customer and societal goals".[60]
- Marketing is under pressure to provide financial accountability and measurable success of its activities, with pressure coming both from the shareholders and CFOs, as Kumar underlines: "This request [for more transparent measurement of success] from all quarters of the organization is due in part to previous marketing practices that focused on acquisition rather than retention, price rather than added value, and short-term transactions rather than the development of lasting, profitable relationships".[61]
- Marketing has gotten increasingly reduced to only the communication function. Connectivity in this context poses a challenge for marketers, as they run into the danger of seeing the last function left to them – communication.[62] The digital transformation of the economy can be seen as a driver for the increasing insignificance of marketing departments. Everybody communicates with everybody; the customers are better informed than ever before and do not depend on information from the firms anymore, when they are in doubt about a product or service. People's information and decision-making behavior are fundamentally changing; the customer at all times decides freely when and where he wants to access exactly which information, lowering effectively the influence of communication measures taken by marketing departments.
- Marketing suffers a lack of trust, which is fatal, as trust is the lead currency for a sustainable business practice.
- The business world as a whole is experiencing a shift from product centricity towards service centricity. Marketing needs to adapt to these changes.

So, marketing has a big task in the transition from intrusive outbound marketing to permission-based human marketing, from "shareholder myopia"[63] to

---

[59] Homburg et al. (2015), *op. cit.*

[60] Sheth & Sisodia (2007), *op. cit.*, p. 142.

[61] Kumar, V. (2015). Evolution of Marketing as a Discipline: What Has Happened and What to Look Out For. *Journal of Marketing, 79*(1), p. 5. https://doi.org/10.1509/jm.79.1.1.

[62] Homburg et al. (2015), *op. cit.*

[63] Sheth & Sisodia (2007), *op. cit.*, p. 141.

real human affection for every stakeholder, and from dominating passive consumers to co-creatively collaborating with customers, together making a conscious effort to contribute to the good of society. Consulting companies and agencies like HubSpot, Accenture, and WPP Group are helping to make the shift, but companies have to make this conscious decision to become a H2H company. Whole Foods Market, Salesforce, FlixBus, and Tesla are frontrunners, and the rewards are outstanding. Amazon paid $13.7 billion for 400 Whole Foods Market stores and its stock price continuous to outpace all other retail companies in the USA.

Many more decision-makers of American, European, and Chinese companies have started to implement this concept or elements of it. Farm and construction equipment maker John Deere offers farming and road construction solutions. The Swiss pharmaceutical company Roche applies co-creation, and the Chinese Changzhou Smart Automation integrates intelligent IoT solutions for energy efficiency.

The "Fridays for Future" movement places sustainability as a serious and urgent problem of humanity at the center of the media and thus at the center of political and social discussions. The youth criticizes that current representatives of the older generation in politics and economy talk far too long about problems such as growing poverty, climate change, and a dramatic decline in biodiversity but do not really act. Young people thus address one of the core problems: Although there are enough figures, data, and facts to prove the last two of the abovementioned problems, there is no change in people's behavior. This may be due to the world's dominant industrial worldview, which believes in limitless economic growth and postulates a positive relationship between rising incomes, rising consumption, and happiness.[64] This can be supported by data.[65] The relationship between higher income and satisfaction was confirmed in a study from the USA.[66] The two Nobel Prize winners found that Americans become increasingly happier as their annual income increases, with the caveat that after reaching $75,000 a year, additional income does not necessarily make people happier. Despite the study, the stance that growing middle income has no limits is clearly expressed in the following statement.

---

[64] Heath, T, & McKechnie, S. (2019). *Sustainability in Marketing. Incorporating Sustainability in Management Education: An Interdisciplinary Approach*, edited by Amaeshi, K., Muthuri, J.N., & Ogbechie, C., pp. 105–31. Cham: Springer International Publishing. https://doi.org/10.1007/978-3-319-98125-3_6.

[65] Rosling, H, Rönnlund, A, & Rosling, O. (2018). *Factfulness: Ten Reasons We're Wrong About the World--and Why Things Are Better Than You Think*. Flatiron Books.

[66] Kahneman, D., & Deaton, A. (2010). High Income Improves Evaluation of Life but Not Emotional Well-Being. *Proceedings of the National Academy of Sciences 107* (38): 16489–93. https://doi.org/10.1073/pnas.1011492107.

"There are 5 billion potential consumers out there, improving their lives in the middle, and wanting to consume shampoo, motorcycles, menstrual pads, and smartphones."[67]

With the invention of the "ecological footprint," a measure is now available to determine resource consumption at the individual, corporate, and national levels.[68] However, such measurements have not led to any noticeable change in behavior among the people themselves, companies, or nations. While most people are aware of the negative effect of increased consumption, this does not seem to be enough to change one's own behavior. It is often "the others," not "we" or "me," who are responsible for climate change. In times of smartphones as an access instrument to the mobile service cloud, people have reached an unprecedented level of egocentrism, which makes actions that pursue the common good a low priority. Everybody wants to get everything immediately, at any time and as comfortably as possible. But sustainability requires less egoism and transition from an anthropocentric to a bio-centric paradigm.[69] Although efforts can be made to buy "more sustainable products," these products also require their own resources in production and distribution and cannot compensate for the negative ecological balance of higher consumption levels.

It could be that the people believe that technology will somehow solve whatever human and social problems that arise in the future. Marketing plays a contributing role, since it fuels hyper-consumption, taking advantage of the "head in the sand" tactic used by people. In this context, marketing is more of a causal factor than a solution. Lately, more voices are calling for marketing to play a vital role within the framework of sustainability, but marketing research itself is hardly involved in such a discussion.[70, 71, 72] If marketing has been successful in influencing human behavior to hyper consume, it can also be instrumental in encouraging more sustainable behavior. Changing the currently dominating egocentric and consumption-oriented mindset is a challenge that marketing can take on as a higher goal.

---

[67] Rosling et al. (2018), *op. cit.*, p. 32.

[68] Wackernagel, M., & Rees, W. E. (1996). Our Ecological Footprint. *The New Catalyst Bioregional Series*; 9.

[69] Kemper, J., Hall, C., & Ballantine, P. (2019). Marketing and Sustainability: Business as Usual or Changing Worldviews? *Sustainability 11* (3): 780. https://doi.org/10.3390/su11030780.

[70] Kemper et al. (2019), *op. cit.*

[71] McDonagh, P., & Prothero, A. (2014). Sustainability Marketing Research: Past, Present and Future. *Journal of Marketing Management, 30* (11–12): 1186–1219. https://doi.org/10.108 0/0267257X.2014.943263.

[72] Jones, P., Clarke-Hill, C., Comfort, D. & Hillier, D. (2008). Marketing and Sustainability. *Marketing Intelligence & Planning, 26* (2): 123–30. https://doi.org/10.1108/02634500810860584.

H2H Marketing puts the human being and the solution of relevant human problems (*H2H problems*) at the center of its attention in order to tackle what is lacking presently: credibility, honesty, integrity, empathy for each other, vulnerability, and constructive dialogue as well as sustainability and other problems.[73, 74]

> Let us revitalize the human side of marketing and reap the fruits of purpose- and passion-driven business making the world a better place!

Storyline

Before we will move to the "Great Journey of H2H Marketing" of our story (see Fig. 1 in preface), we summarize what happened so far. We criticized the current state of marketing and used the poor image and reputation of marketing departments in companies worldwide as a "call for adventure" or let us say as a call for change. We learned that traditional marketing can embrace practices that can be referred to wasteful, inane, or unethical marketing. You have been introduced to firms of endearment, which already are on the way to change their marketing practices and goals. We identified the increasing importance of other stakeholders than shareholders of companies – such as communities, the society in general, and our planet. Sustainability and the traditional industrial paradigm clash together, and it is one of the major tasks of H2H Marketing to solve this contradiction. We have shown the development of marketing theory ending up with H2H Marketing using the S-DL as the essential paradigm for a needed shift in marketing. H2H Marketing responds to major trends in society and business such as digitalization, increasing connectivity of humans embedded in ecosystems that co-create experiences. Three actors mainly affect this response of H2H Marketing itself: Design Thinking, S-DL, and digitalization. We will tell their story in our next chapter in more detail.

Questions

1. Why do we take trust as the key currency of successful marketing?
2. Try to find your own examples of corporations, which have started applying H2H Marketing partially and send them to us so that we can grow our database. Why do you think that we ask for a partial and not complete implementation of H2H Marketing?

---

[73] Rittel, H.W., & Webber, M.M. (1973), Dilemmas in a general theory of planning. *Policy Sciences, 4* (2), pp. 155–169.
[74] Buchanan, R. (1992), Wicked Problems in Design Thinking. *Design Issues, 8*(2), pp. 96–100.

3. H2H Marketing considers a certain paradigm as the next significant step in the development of marketing theory. Which is it? Why do you think that this paradigm might be the next essential paradigm for marketing (or why not)?
4. What are the consequences of an increasing connectivity on customer behavior and what are the consequences on existing business models mainly based on the sales of products and services?
5. What is the vital role of traditional marketing in the existing industrial paradigm and how does it clash with the efforts to contribute to sustainability? How might marketing contribute to a mindset shift of suppliers and customers?

References

Apte, S., & Sheth, J. (2016). *The sustainability edge: How to drive top-line growth with triple-bottom-line thinking.* Rotman-UTP Publishing.

Bardhi, F., & Eckhardt, G. M. (2012). Access-based consumption: The case of car sharing. *Journal of Consumer Research, 39*(4), 881–898. https://doi.org/10.1086/666376.

Bathen, D., & Jelden, J. (2014). *Marketingorganisation der Zukunft* [Report]. Retrieved from https://www.marketingverband.de/marketingkompetenz/studien/marketingorganisation-der-zukunft/

Benkenstein, M. (2018). Hat sich das Marketing als Leitkonzept der Unternehmensführung wirklich überlebt? – Eine kritische Stellungnahme. In M. Bruhn & M. Kirchgeorg (Eds.), *Marketing Weiterdenken: Zukunftspfade für eine marktorientierte Unternehmensführung* (pp. 49–64). Wiesbaden: Springer Gabler.

Bruhn, M. (2018). Marketing Weiterdenken in der marktorientierten Unternehmensführung – Entwicklungen und Zukunftsthemen der Marketingdisziplin. In M. Bruhn & M. Kirchgeorg (Eds.), *Marketing Weiterdenken: Zukunftspfade für eine marktorientierte Unternehmensführung* (pp. 25–48). Wiesbaden: Springer Gabler.

Buchanan, R. (1992). Wicked problems in design thinking. *Design Issues, 8*(2), 96–100.

Chen, Y. (2009). Possession and access: Consumer desires and value perceptions regarding contemporary art collection and exhibit visits. *Journal of Consumer Research, 35*(6), 925–940. https://doi.org/10.1086/593699.

Gassmann, O., & Schweitzer, F. (2014). Managing the unmanageable: The fuzzy front end of innovation. In O. Gassmann & F. Schweitzer (Eds.), *Management of the fuzzy front end of innovation* (pp. 3–14). Cham: Springer.

Godin, S. (2007). *Permission marketing.* London: Simon & Schuster.

Halligan, B., & Shah, D. (2018). *Inbound-Marketing: Wie Sie Kunden online anziehen, abholen und begeistern* (D. Runne, Trans.). Weinheim: Wiley-VCH.

Heath, T., & McKechnie, S. (2019). Sustainability in marketing. In K. Amaeshi, J. N. Muthuri, & C. Ogbechie (Eds.), *Incorporating sustainability in management education: An interdisciplinary approach* (pp. 105–131). Cham: Springer. https://doi.org/10.1007/978-3-319-98125-3_6.

Henderson, R. (2020). *Reimagining capitalism in a world on fire*. New York: PublicAffairs.

Homburg, C., Vomberg, A., Enke, M., & Grimm, P. H. (2015). The loss of the marketing department's influence: Is it really happening? And why worry? *Journal of the Academy of Marketing Science, 43*(1), 1–13. https://doi.org/10.1007/s11747-014-0416-3.

Jones, P., Clarke-Hill, C., Comfort, D., & Hillier, D. (2008). Marketing and sustainability. *Marketing Intelligence & Planning, 26*(2), 123–130. https://doi.org/10.1108/02634500810860584.

Kahneman, D., & Deaton, A. (2010). High income improves evaluation of life but not emotional well-being. *Proceedings of the National Academy of Sciences, 107*(38), 16489–16493. https://doi.org/10.1073/pnas.1011492107.

Kemper, J., Hall, C., & Ballantine, P. (2019). Marketing and sustainability: Business as usual or changing worldviews? *Sustainability, 11*(3), 780. https://doi.org/10.3390/su11030780.

Kotler, P. (2017). Criticisms and contributions of marketing. Retrieved from https://www.marketingjournal.org/criticisms-and-contributions-of-marketing-an-excerpt-from-philip-kotlers-autobiography-philip-kotler/

Kotler, P., Kartajaya, H., & Setiawan, I. (2017). *Marketing 4.0: Moving from traditional to digital*. Hoboken, NJ: Wiley.

Kumar, V. (2015). Evolution of marketing as a discipline: What has happened and what to look out for. *Journal of Marketing, 79*(1), 1–9. https://doi.org/10.1509/jm.79.1.1.

Marx, P. (2011, January 23). The Borrowers: Why buy when you can rent? *The New Yorker*. Retrieved from https://www.newyorker.com/magazine/2011/01/31/the-borrowers

McDonagh, P., & Prothero, A. (2014). Sustainability marketing research: Past, present and future. *Journal of Marketing Management, 30*(11–12), 1186–1219. https://doi.org/10.1080/0267257X.2014.943263.

Meffert, H., Burmann, C., Kirchgeorg, M., & Eisenbeiß, M. (2019). *Marketing: Grundlagen marktorientierter Unternehmensführung Konzepte – Instrumente – Praxisbeispiele* (13th ed.). Wiesbaden: Springer Gabler.

Nielsen. (2018). *Sustainable Shoppers buy the change they wish to see in the world* [Report]. Retrieved from https://www.nielsen.com/wp-content/uploads/sites/3/2019/04/global-sustainable-shoppers-report-2018.pdf

Prahalad, C. K., & Ramaswamy, V. (2000). Co-opting customer competence. *Harvard Business Review, 78*(1), 79–87. Retrieved from https://hbr.org/2000/01/co-opting-customer-competence

Prahalad, C. K., & Ramaswamy, V. (2003). The new frontier of experience innovation. *MIT Sloan Management Review, 44*(4), 12–18. Retrieved from https://sloan-review.mit.edu/article/the-new-frontier-of-experience-innovation/

Rittel, H. W. J., & Webber, M. M. (1973). Dilemmas in a general theory of planning. *Policy Sciences, 4*(2), 155–165. https://doi.org/10.1007/BF01405730.

Rosling, H, Rönnlund, A, & Rosling, O. (2018). *Factfulness: Ten reasons we're wrong about the world – and why things are better than you think.* Flatiron Books.

Sheth, J. N., & Sisodia, R. S. (2002). Marketing productivity: Issues and analysis. *Journal of Business Research, 55*(5), 349–362. https://doi.org/10.1016/S0148-2963(00)00164-8.

Sheth, J. N., & Sisodia, R. S. (2005). Does marketing need reform? In marketing renaissance: Opportunities and imperatives for improving marketing thought, practice, and infrastructure. *Journal of Marketing, 69*(4), 1–25. https://doi.org/10.1509/jmkg.2005.69.4.1.

Sheth, J. N., & Sisodia, R. S. (2007). Raising marketing's aspirations. *Journal of Public Policy & Marketing, 26*(1), 141–143. https://doi.org/10.1509/jppm.26.1.141.

Sisodia, R. S., Sheth, J. N., & Wolfe, D. (2014). *Firms of endearment: How world-class companies profit from passion and purpose* (2nd ed.). Upper Saddle River, NJ: Pearson Education.

Vargo, S. L., & Lusch, R. F. (2004). Evolving to a new dominant logic for marketing. *Journal of Marketing, 68*(1), 1–17. https://doi.org/10.1509/jmkg.68.1.1.24036.

Voeth, M. (2018). Marketing und/oder marktorientierte Unternehmensführung? In M. Bruhn & M. Kirchgeorg (Eds.), *Marketing Weiterdenken: Zukunftspfade für eine marktorientierte Unternehmensführung* (pp. 67–78). Wiesbaden: Springer Gabler.

Wackernagel, M., & Rees, W. E. (1996). Our ecological footprint. *The New Catalyst Bioregional Series, 9.*

Wallaschkowski, S., & Niehuis, E. (2017). Digitaler Konsum. In O. Stengel, A. van Looy, & S. Wallaschkowski (Eds.), *Digitalzeitalter – Digitalgesellschaft: Das Ende des Industriezeitalters und der Beginn einer neuen Epoche* (pp. 109–141). Wiesbaden: Springer.

2

The New Paradigm: H2H Marketing

In 2017, Psychology Today featured an article from Marty Nemko titled, "Marketing is Evil." The author claimed, "Marketers use many psychological plays to make you buy what you shouldn't."[1] He exemplified the crisis of marketing with overpriced products and services like Cartier watches, Liberty Mutual insurance, and T. Rowe Price investments, among other luxury products. Additional examples of overpricing would be pharmaceutical companies who take advantage of patients in need of their medication. Lannett, Purdue Pharma, and Valeant have unreasonable raised prices.

This kind of opinions is quite common. Credibility has seriously eroded as consumers wise up to the empty promises and aggressive tactics practiced by marketers. Their relevance in companies has also declined as their one last remaining function of communication is not being performed up to standards required by digitalization of the consumer market. Given this, the question arises as to whether marketing in its current form can continue to exist or whether it needs to change its paradigm.

To survive, marketing has to return to the core of creation of meaningful value propositions. Marketing must play a key role in innovation in the enterprise in finding and understanding customers' attitudes and behavior. In order for this to happen, marketers must have direct customer contact again by merging with the people involved: employees, customers, and partners. It would have to play an important role in transforming industrial companies

---

[1] Nemko, M. (2017). *Marketing is Evil: Marketers use many psychological ploys to make you buy what you shouldn't* [Blog post]. Retrieved from https://www.psychologytoday.com/us/blog/how-do-life/201701/marketing-is-evil

© The Author(s), under exclusive license to Springer Nature Switzerland AG 2021
P. Kotler et al., *H2H Marketing*, https://doi.org/10.1007/978-3-030-59531-9_2

into providers of product service systems based on customer-oriented competencies.

We even go one step further and suggest extending customer centeredness to human-centeredness and focusing on solving existential human problems. With this in mind, we have designed a new thinking model, which we call the "H2H Marketing Model" formerly called "Bangalore Model," as it has been developed on the campus of Christ University in Bangalore, India. This model incorporates current developments and trends simultaneously. It integrates current concepts in the form of a new human-oriented mindset, improved marketing process, and advanced management approaches and provides a paradigm shift for all marketing thoughts.

The H2H Marketing Model is a theoretical framework, which integrates the influencing factors of Design Thinking (DT), Service-Dominant Logic (S-DL), and digitalization (D) into a new marketing thinking approach. Design Thinking has essentially led to understanding human centricity and thinking based on deep customer insights as a mindset and marketing as an iterative innovation process. The Service-Dominant Logic provides the theoretical foundation for human marketing by integrating many fragments and emphasizes the importance of co-creation of value in collaborative ecosystems. Digitalization has given the customer and the marketer new options and gives all participants of the marketing interaction and transaction new possibilities. Insofar digitalization serves within the H2H Marketing Model as enabler, not only as trend. The H2H Marketing Model integrates all three elements into presenting an option for a new mindset and marketing action (see Fig. 2.1).

Fig. 2.1 The influencing factors in the H2H Marketing Model

Until now, all three concepts were treated separately. After trying to understand the inner logic of these concepts and their implications when applied, we concluded that amalgamating them would create something new– H2H Marketing. Today, there are a few companies applying this type of concept intuitively. The most prominent application we found was Whole Foods Market and Patagonia. Both are purpose-driven companies who put customer orientation in the center of their strategy. Whole Foods Market, for example, followed a Service-Dominant Logic from the beginning by introducing continuously healthy food solutions and established quality standards beyond existing government requirements. They apply Design Thinking to develop and improve their offerings and procedures. Online distribution and digital communication are used strategically to synchronize physical and digital message of purpose.

Another company with inclination to H2H Marketing Model is Airbnb. The company created a business model that is beyond transactional by establishing a deep emotional layer between the entrepreneurial host and the adventurous guest. The business model is completely digitalized, and with Design Thinking projects, they are continuously improving their services to strengthen the emotional bond between the host and guest. Other companies are the mobility company FlixBus, the German drug store chain "dm-drogerie markt," and Sephora, the French multinational chain of personal care and beauty stores. They have applied certain aspects of the H2H Marketing Model. The same could be said for Amazon, Salesforce, and Spotify, which are digital-born companies applying humanized approaches as their concepts. Traditional analogue companies have also applied elements of the new model as well. Deutsche Bank, Stanley Black & Decker, SAP, Siemens, and GE have heavily used Design Thinking to modify their offerings and become more human-oriented. The application of Service-Dominant Logic can be seen at Delta Airlines, SFR, the French telecommunication company, and Siemens Healthineers. Digitalization initiatives can also be found at GE Factory Automation and Bosch Industry, SKF, Schaeffler, and many other industrial machine builders.

Even in the automotive industry, there are great examples for digitalization. Tesla is the frontrunner in electrification and digitalization. They dismantled the physical sales channels by offering all sales and services online. Smart, the mini car from Daimler and Geely is going the same route, and others are sure to follow. The announcement of Sony to enter the automotive market with an own car is a clear hint that the automotive industry will transform from a dominating Goods-Dominant Logic (G-DL) to as S-DL. Also in banking, insurance, and heavy construction equipment, digitalization enables great improvement for their direct customers- the construction companies of buildings and infrastructures.

H2H Marketing is the new, overarching framework proposed to confront current developments and present challenges. Most recent literature and some advanced companies have identified it and have started to apply this concept already.

The H2H Marketing model consists of two fundamental layers. The first layer provides the conceptual framework (the H2H Marketing Model) with the three impact concepts Design Thinking (DT), Service-Dominant Logic (S-DL), and digitalization (D). The second layer represents the implementation of conceptual thinking in marketing. This layer itself covers three parts. First, the H2H Mindset as prerequisite for successful implementation of H2H Marketing; second, H2H Management providing strategic planning, alignment, and control of H2H Marketing; and, finally, the execution of the H2H Process to put H2H Marketing into practice (see Fig. 2.2).

The *H2H Marketing Model* on the first layer constitutes the theoretical framework. It is built upon three determining factors: Service-Dominant Logic, Design Thinking, and the Digitalization. It analyses the new dynamics that digitalization has brought to marketing. Customer behavior has changed, value propositions need rethinking, and firms experience a transformed relationship with their customers into valuable assets. With the S-DL, it also includes the theoretical foundation of H2H Marketing, revolutionizing the understanding of value creation, the role of the firm, and the necessity to manage and operate collaborative networks. With S-DL comes the recognition that value is always co-created and that firms can only provide value propositions, not "built-in" value in their products or services. These

Fig. 2.2 The complete H2H Marketing Model

paradigms shift in the understanding of markets and economic actors, and the role of the firm in co-creating value is one of the fundamental pillars of H2H Marketing.

Design Thinking as the second influencing factor of the framework provides the basis for a human-centered, experiential mindset and methodology for confronting marketing's claimed importance to meaningful innovations and real contribution in practice. While the H2H Marketing Model stands for the influence and repercussions of Design Thinking, Service-Dominant Logic, and digitalization on marketing, the next layer provides a model for a human response to it: H2H Marketing. It consists of three components that are strongly interconnected and represent different management layers (see Fig. 2.3) to form the basis of H2H Marketing.

The *H2H Mindset* (normative) is the central prerequisite for the implementation of strategic and operative management. It appears on both, on the individual level as a personality trait and on the organizational level as corporate culture. It is the firm's organizational guideline for personal thinking and acting for all people in the company and unites typical character traits of a design thinker (experimental, empathic, human-centered) with the service understanding of the S-DL (value is co-created in collaboration with the customer) and the connectivity thinking and "human touch" in a digitized world. This mindset sets up for a successful application of H2H Marketing: the strategic directions (H2H Management) and the operative execution (H2H Process).

H2H Management does not forget about the strategic importance of the classical Segmenting-Targeting-Positioning (STP) approach. It emphasizes the orchestrated handling of brand, experience of humans involved, and reputation of the brand or firm in the relevant communities. It links the STP

Fig. 2.3 The H2H marketing components corresponding different management layers

approach with branding by using the company's service to solve a human problem in order to answer the meaningful question "why" and not the simpler questions "what" and "how" according to the "golden circle" of Simon Sinek.[2] In a time of democratized brands, where companies are losing influence over their own brand, H2H Management embraces this development by laying emphasis on co-creating the brand together with the customers. The management of trust calls for a renewing impulse as well. Customer Experience Management (CXM) strikes out in a new direction, as it becomes increasingly important to deliver a seamless experience across all customer touchpoints, whether digital or physical.

Finally, the reputation management chapter provides tools to foster and protect reputation, a strategically important task in a highly transparent, low-trust world. Corporate Social Responsibility (CSR) needs rethinking, because in today's world, the traditional self-adulation– publicly proclaiming and showcasing a broad range of superficial assistance, short-term engagements, and philanthropic endeavors – is not enough anymore: action is needed! Walk the Talk!

The *H2H Process* complements the H2H Mindset and the strategic H2H Management tools with a highly flexible, experiential, and iterative approach that can be used variably to implement human-centered marketing operationally. Its specialty in comparison to the 4P marketing mix is its *iterative character* and that the starting point is always a human problem that needs to be solved. In addition, it explicitly integrates the marketing process with H2H Management and connects marketing with engineering and business development.

With the new marketing paradigm, the journey through H2H Marketing does not end with the improved implementation of advanced marketing thinking. It actually offers an outlook into the future of marketing where sustainable business is prime focus, and it helps by suggesting how companies can partake in the social transformation of capitalism.

After switching to H2H Marketing and committing themselves to its philosophy, companies can make a positive contribution to solving human problems by becoming proactive change agents. They benefit from stronger trust relationships, which brings themselves great benefits but also entails great responsibility. As society increasingly turns to companies to help with existential problems, the practice of H2H Marketing and brand activism becomes an indispensable imperative. In particular, the near future has a great deal of

---

[2] Sinek, S. (2009). Start with why: How great leaders inspire everyone to take action. New York: Penguin

conflict potential, which poses difficult questions for companies and societies. H2H Marketing can offer some guidance in these troubled times.

Leading companies in this sense are Patagonia, HiPP Organic baby and toddler food, and the Body Shop. These companies are doing good in all parts of their value chain. Patagonia's design is oriented towards body-friendly and mind-pleasing models. The production is environment friendly and marketing is trustworthy with all players taking care of the customer. The Body Shop adopted their "world awareness" campaign early when it was still a novel idea. Both companies are progressively active and promote the common good.

2.1   The H2H Marketing Model: The Three Influencing Factors

The value logics of *Design Thinking*, *Service-Dominant Logic*, and *digitalization* are the starting point for the creation of H2H Marketing. They widen the view on value creation in service innovation and implementation for companies oriented to human. Since some of the key principles underlying Service-Dominant Logic and Design Thinking are very similar and digitalization has opened up instant and multidirectional communication, a new way of thinking is possible.[3] All of these concepts came from different backgrounds and places, but they are all deeply concerned with the creation of value and the importance of understanding the humans involved. A few companies have already applied some of these concepts, such as Apple, Microsoft, IBM, Infosys, and Whole Foods.

The **H2H Marketing Model**, by integrating **Design Thinking, Service-Dominant Logic, and Digitalization**, creates the opportunity for Human-to-Human (H2H) Marketing. DT, S-DL, and D are the very essence of the first layer of the **H2H Marketing Model**, which acts as a theoretical framework for H2H Marketing. Companies and organizations taking up this new concept can make a difference to our planet earth and its inhabitants. They can be the leading pack of the future, contributing as well as benefiting. This is true for Business-to-Business (B2B) companies and Business-to-Consumer (B2C) companies, whether they offer products, services, or software.

Satya Nadella of Microsoft states, "We are the company that enables people to do more, play more, have more fun, create more. So, in some sense, we

---

[3] See Edman, K. W. (2009). Exploring Overlaps and Differences in Service Dominant Logic and Design Thinking. In her contribution to the First Nordic Conference on Service Design and Service Innovation she compared DT and S-DL and demonstrated the overlap. Available under http://www.ep.liu.se/ecp/059/016/ecp09059016.pdf

refer to ourselves as the 'do more company'."[4] Google considers itself as a "Don't be evil" company, and Elon Musk of Tesla says, "You want to have a future where you're expecting things to be better."

In the future, B2B and B2C companies' communication and transaction will become increasingly automated, but when problems arise, human intervention will be necessary. It should still be remembered that the final target customer for all business is humans and not machines. So, keeping in mind meaning and purpose is key for the success of sustainable relationships. Those companies understanding these new dimensions will adopt a Human-to-Human approach, inwards and outwards. Human-to-Human (H2H) Marketing has three components of *Mindset*, *Process*, and *Management*. They are strongly interconnected and interdependent.

Further, all three are grounded in the H2H Marketing Model, meaning that they are directly affected by the influencing factors. Simply put Digitalization, Design Thinking, and the Service-Dominant Logic have clear

Fig. 2.4   Three influencing factors inside the H2H Marketing Model

[4] McKinsey & Company (2018). *Microsoft's next act* [Podcast]. Retrieved from https://www.mckinsey.com/industries/technology-media-and-telecommunications/our-insights/microsofts-next-act

consequences for H2H Marketing as a whole, as well as each facet of H2H Marketing (see Fig. 2.4).

From the beginning, *Design Thinking* provided a useful tool for highly innovative companies, which were open for the new mindset of the concept. After all, the context is *deeply rooted in solving human problems* as well as the connection between the organizational cultures.

Service-Dominant Logic is considered as the "grand theory" for marketing, even though reception in Europe has been lagging. We are integrating its fundamental premises and axioms here and applying its central concepts. The stated change of the mindset of S-DL has become of great importance for H2H Marketing, so we will examine this in detail.

For a better understanding of *digitalization*, we will particularly focus on the opportunities to change the behavior of market participants. To not be negatively affected by digitalization, marketing needs to undergo its own digital transformation. The transformations should not be seen as a threat but as an opportunity: digitalization gives marketing the opportunity to gain in-depth knowledge of the *Homo Digitalis* and his changed buying behavior. It offers a powerful opportunity to design and enable seamless customer experiences along the whole customer journey. If marketing uses these findings creatively and interdisciplinary based on competences in data management and analysis for its own company's value proposition, then the importance of marketing can increase again.

Not only are companies from industrialized world engaged in H2H Marketing; we are seeing impressive developments in developing countries. For example, Grab Holdings Inc. is a ride-hailing company based in Singapore. Besides transportation, the company offers food delivery and digital payment services via mobile apps and many other services. Their solutions make life simpler. Beginning of 2020, they were active in nine Southeast Asian countries and covered 240 cities. They have now more than a billion happy users. Other examples are MercadoLibre online retail from Latin America, KakaoTalk from Korea, Zalo from Vietnam, and MyPursar a digital money transfer solution from Central Africa.

2.2 Design Thinking

In recent years, Design Thinking has gained considerable importance and has gotten adopted by many firms. IBM applies it and has trained more than 10,000 employees. Many firms like Procter & Gamble, IBM, and Deutsche Bank use it to confront rapidly changing business environments, where agile behavior and adaptation to new technologies are necessary for survival. Implementing crucial changes in the solving process of human-centered problems, as is offered by Design Thinking, appears to many as an option worth considering in order to remain relevant and on top of the competition. Corporate innovators like Airbnb continually look for a way of establishing a steady and reliable stream of new ideas. With the help of Big Data, for example, they now have access to more information about their customers but struggle to derive good use from it because that requires real human insights. Data can show patterns, but the interpretation of the findings and deriving inspiration for a new innovative service or product need human understanding, combining analysis with intuitive and creative thinking. Design Thinking by many is seen as this bridge between the analytical and creative, intuitive realm.[5]

The revival of the fashion brand Burberry would be a good example. The company realigned its business towards a brand-led and customer-centric model. Burberry restored its corporate heritage and core brand values. The changes in Burberry's business model triggered the need to renew and realign its supply chain strategy through consolidating and rebuilding manufacturing activities back in the UK, in order to support its brand repositioning as quintessentially British with the company's refocus on heritage products.[6, 7, 8]

Design Thinking usually aims at improving the approach to innovations, resulting in human-centered solutions with an enhanced customer experience, such as new products, services, or business models.[9] Many companies and organizations have used it successfully. Design Thinking was a part of Airbnb's success; in particular, they built a culture of experimentation: "It was only when they gave themselves permission to experiment with non-scalable changes to the business that they climbed out of what they called the 'trough of sorrow.'"[10] IBM created good results with it. Bank of America, Stanley

[5] Gobble, M. M. (2014). Design Thinking. Research Technology Management, 57(3), pp. 59-61. https://doi.org/10.5437/08956308X5703005

[6] Robinson, P.K., Hsieh, L. (2016). Reshoring: a strategic renewal of luxury clothing supply chains. Operations Management Research, 9, pages 89–101. https://doi.org/10.1007/s12063-016-0116-x

[7] see also Mower, S. (2017). How Christopher Bailey Transformed Burberry and Redefined Brand Revivals in the 21st Century. Vogue. Retrieved from https://www.vogue.com/article/burberry-christopher-bailey-legacy

[8] Ahrendts, A. (2013). Burberry's CEO on Turning an Aging British Icon into a Global Luxury Brand. Harvard Business Review. Retrieved from https://hbr.org/2013/01/burberrys-ceo-on-turning-an-aging-british-icon-into-a-global-luxury-brand

[9] Grots, A., & Pratschke, M. (2009). Design Thinking – Kreativität als Methode. Marketing Review St. Gallen, 26(2), pp. 18–23. https://doi.org/10.1007/s11621-009-0027-4

[10] First Round Review (2019) "How Design Thinking Transformed Airbnb from a Failing Startup to a Billion Dollar Business" outlines how the start-up AirBnB went from $200 a week profit to the "unicorn"

Black & Decker, and many more followed. Liedtka describes interesting examples in her Harvard Business Review article "Why Design Thinking works."[11] The following case study can shed some more light on the topic[12]:

German Carglass® company used Design Thinking to improve the customer experience. Carglass® has a dominant position in the German car window repair market and usually is the first choice in case of damaged car windshields. Although impressed by the technical ability of the Carglass® experts, some clients chose not to do business with them because they were somehow not adequately persuaded during their decision-making process. So, in 2015, the firm confronted this issue by starting a Design Thinking initiative called *"1fach!Erfolgreich!" (Simply Successful)* to make the employees not only repair experts but also customer experts. Optimization processes were implemented in over 300 service centers to create a more pleasurable customer experience. An interdisciplinary team including high-ranking executives and employees from sales, marketing, operations, human resources, and the service centers, together with an external consulting firm, was created. Taking the perspective of the customer, the whole customer journey with all possible contact points was analyzed and optimized using the typical Design Thinking process. The results spoke for themselves: the assisting external consulting firm presented higher profits, an improved Net Promoter Score, and a nationwide standardized service as a positive outcome of the Design Thinking project.[13]

To approach DT correctly, a look at a definition may prove helpful, because, sometimes, the terminology and different dimensions can get mixed up. In the course of this chapter, we will have a closer look at two dimensions of the issue: *Design Thinking as mindset or culture* and the more practical facet *Design Thinking as a useful toolbox, as methodology*. First, clarification on the term itself is necessary.

The ambiguity of DT and the incoherence between the theoretical and the practical side of it have been addressed by various authors.[14]

it is today. https://firstround.com/review/How-design-thinking-transformed-Airbnb-from-failing-startup-to-billion-dollar-business/

[11] Liedtka, J. (2018). Why Design Thinking works. Harvard Business Review, 96(5), pp. 72–79. Retrieved from https://hbr.org/2018/09/why-design-thinking-works

[12] Blatt, M., & Sauvonnet, E. (Eds.). (2017). Wo ist das Problem?: Mit Design Thinking Innovationen entwickeln und umsetzen (2nd ed.). München, Germany: Franz Vahlen.

[13] Reutemann, B. (2017). Service Design: Der Turbo für Ihr Business [Presentation]. Retrieved from https://bernd-reutemann.de/wp-content/uploads/2017/02/Servicedesign.pdf

[14] Carlgren, L., Rauth, I., & Elmquist, M. (2016). Framing Design Thinking: The Concept in Idea and Enactment. Creativity and Innovation Management, 25(1), pp. 38–57. https://doi.org/10.1111/caim.12153

Johansson-Sköldberg, Woodilla, and Çetinkaya[15] point out that there are currently two relevant discourses drifting away from each other without considerable thematic overlaps. The authors differentiate between the academic discourse, which they refer to as *Designerly Thinking*, backed up by extensive scientific research, and *Design Thinking* in a practical, managerial context, backed in its majority by positive experience reports about the effects of the practical implementation, not scientifically corroborated findings. H2H Marketing focuses on *Design Thinking* as one of the three influencing factors in the H2H Marketing Model, a thinking mode where "design practice and competence are used beyond the design context (including art and architecture), for and with people without a scholarly background in design, particularly in management."[16] The Hasso-Plattner-Institut (HPI) Academy, a spin-off of the HPI, specializing in DT and innovation, understands DT as follows:

> Design Thinking is a systematic, human-centered approach to solving complex problems within all aspects of life. The approach goes far beyond traditional concerns such as shape and layout. And unlike traditional scientific and engineering approaches, which address a task from the view of technical solvability, user needs and requirements as well as user-oriented invention are central to the process. [17]

Important is to note that DT is addressing human-centeredness, the focus on user needs, and focus on innovation, distinct from the classic approach to design. Such a definition shows explicitly the relation to marketing as a mindset (customer centricity). Similarly, Tim Brown, CEO of design and innovation consulting firm IDEO, in his article *Design Thinking* published in the Harvard Business Review, defines it as:

> [A] methodology that imbues the full spectrum of innovation activities with a human-centered design ethos. By this I mean that innovation is powered by a thorough understanding, through direct observation, of what people want and

---

[15] Johansson-Sköldberg, U., Woodilla, J., & Çetinkaya, M. (2013). Design Thinking: Past, Present and Possible Futures. Creativity and Innovation Management, 22(2), pp. 121–146. https://doi.org/10.1111/caim.12023

[16] Johansson-Sköldberg, U., Woodilla, J., & Çetinkaya, M. (2013). *op. cit.*

[17] Hasso Plattner Institute of Design. (2019). An Introduction to Design Thinking: Process Guide, para. 1. Retrieved from https://dschool-old.stanford.edu/sandbox/groups/designresources/wiki/36873/attachments/74b3d/ModeGuideBOOTCAMP2010L.pdf

need in their lives and what they like or dislike about the way particular products are made, packaged, marketed, sold, and supported. [18]

He clearly points towards the significance of putting human problems and needs at the center of all attention. He stresses that point especially when he goes on to state:

> Put simply, it is a discipline that uses the designer's sensibility and methods to match people's needs with what is technologically feasible and what a viable business strategy can convert into customer value and market opportunity. [19]

When speaking about technological feasibility and the viability of a business strategy, Tim Brown is referring to the so-called trifecta of innovation proposed by IDEO.[20, 21]

The concept states that a new idea is considered a valuable innovation if there is a congruence of three factors: human perspective, technology point of view, as well as the business side.[22] A positive overlap of these three criteria is seen as crucial, as laid out in the following:

- Every innovation process should have a real human problem as a foundation. That problem is the starting point for all further considerations.[23]
- With the human problem in mind, the proposed solution to it is then tested to match the first of the three factors for a valuable innovation: *desirability*.
- Is the solution a desirable one for the customers? Does it include a legitimate value proposition for them? An empathic change of perspective is required here to get to the center of what the customer really needs.[24]

---

[18] Brown, T. (2008). Design Thinking. Harvard Business Review, 86(6), p. 86. Retrieved from https://hbr.org/2008/06/design-thinking

[19] Brown, T. (2008). *op. cit.*

[20] Orton, K. (2017, March 28). Desirability, Feasibility, Viability: The Sweet Spot for Innovation [Blog post]. Retrieved from https://medium.com/innovation-sweet-spot/desirability-feasibility-viability-the-sweet-spot-for-innovation-d7946de2183c

[21] See also Grots, A., & Pratschke, M. (2009). *op. cit.*, pp. 18–23.

[22] Hasso Plattner Institute of Design. (2019), *op. cit.*

[23] IDEO, (2019). How to Prototype a New Business [Blog post]. Retrieved from https://www.ideou.com/blogs/inspiration/how-to-prototype-a-new-business

[24] IDEO, (2019). *op. cit.*

- The next condition that must be fulfilled is the one of *feasibility*: Does the solution work? Does the firm have adequate operational capabilities to offer it? [25]
- If so, then, it is also necessary to check whether or not the solution is *viable* in terms of being profitable and sustainable from a business perspective. What are the costs involved, and what are the economic benefits? [26]

These three factors should not be perceived as a chronological list of tick boxes but more as orientation when evaluating the innovative potential of an idea. If one of the factors is not met, possible associated risks and cost of the implementation may rise.[27] The only advice on can give is to start with the check of the desirability of an idea first. Ignoring this can waste a lot of resources.

Design Thinking is also used for social innovations. YMCA used DT to adopt their offerings to inner city situations. In Vietnam and Cambodia, new public toilets and washing facilities have been developed and broadly implemented. DT can be small but with big impacts for the users. There are inspiring examples of simple Design Thinking from Japan such as queueing markers for first and second trains, automatic taxi doors for passenger side rear doors, and transparent umbrellas that make it easier to navigate the crowds.

All three definitions presented above refer to Design Thinking as a mindset and a method or approach. Both will be discussed in more detail in Sects. 2.2.1 and 2.2.2. In addition, the organizational prerequisites for Design Thinking (Sect. 2.2.3) and the impact on H2H Marketing (Sect. 2.2.4) will be presented in this chapter.

2.2.1   Design Thinking as a Mindset

Looking at DT in its managerial, practical sense, two manifestations can be distinguished: Design Thinking as a mindset, philosophy or culture, and DT as methodology and toolbox. DT as a mindset aims at several core elements that define it. Primarily, this refers to a corporate culture in which innovations are made by people *for* people in a human-centered fashion.[28]

---

[25] Orton, K. (2017, March 28). Desirability, Feasibility, Viability: The Sweet Spot for Innovation [Blog post]. Retrieved from https://medium.com/innovation-sweet-spot/desirability-feasibility-viability-the-sweet-spot-for-innovation-d7946de2183c

[26] IDEO, (2019). How to Prototype a New Business [Blog post]. Retrieved from https://www.ideou.com/blogs/inspiration/how-to-prototype-a-new-business

[27] Orton, K. (2017, March 28). *op. cit.*

[28] Carlgren, L., Rauth, I., & Elmquist, M. (2016). *op. cit.*

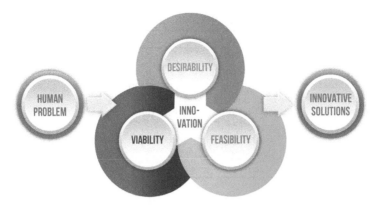

Fig. 2.5 The Trifecta of innovation

In H2H Marketing, the mindset also plays an indispensable role (in detail explained in Chap. 3). The mindset that should form the basis of a design thinker will be used therefore as a foundation: the H2H Mindset is a lineal descendant of it. It is one of the essential principles of Design Thinking to begin with the desirability for the human being, in most cases the user of a solution, before the profitability and the technical, as well as organizational feasibility for the provider, is discussed (as shown in Fig. 2.5[29]).

One of the principles to integrate is *fail early and often*. Errors or failure should not be avoided but should take place as early as possible in the innovation process. The earlier it is discovered that the development team is on the wrong track, the cheaper it will be to fix it. This requires companies to have high fault tolerance and the willingness to allow many repetitive loops in the development process, a kind of thinking that is not prevalent in all companies.

A design thinker personally should have certain character traits or thinking patterns[30]:

- *Empathy*: He should be able to see the problem through the lens of other stakeholders.
- *Integrative thinking*: Being able to go beyond the ordinary and analytical and take all aspects and perspectives of a problem into account.
- *Optimism*: The conviction that there's almost always a better solution to a problem than currently offered.
- *Experimentalism*: Abandoning the known routes of change and exploring the problem in novel directions (*thinking out of the box*).

[29] Adapted from Grots & Pratschke (2009) and IDEO (2019).
[30] For the following see Brown, T. (2008). *op. cit.*

Table 2.1 Framing model of design thinking

Characteristic themes	Alternative labels
User focus	User orientation, human-centeredness
Problem framing	Problem exploration, question the problem
Visualization	Making tangible, prototyping
Experimentation	Iteration and testing, action orientation
Diversity	Collaboration, systemic perspective

- *Collaboration*: Evermore complex problems, products, and services require the need for an interdisciplinary collaborative alliance.

Carlgren, with the help of empirical interview study, proposed a theoretical framework for DT,[31] in order to make it researchable and comparable, as definitions and literature approaches vary substantially. It adds a functional perspective to the personal perspective of the different character traits of a design thinker. The study included six major companies experienced in the use of the methodology and focused on the interviewees' perception and use of it. Based on the answers, they built a framing model with five characteristic themes and its corresponding alternative labels, as presented in Table 2.1.[32]

There are visible thematic overlaps between the personal and functional perspective. According to the interviewees, Design Thinking as methodology embraces user focus, and the question and solution approach are both human-centered. Problem framing refers to the diligent exploration of the problem, an analysis from all possible angles. Making ideas tangible by drawing, role-playing, or prototyping is an inherent part of Design Thinking, as is constant experimentation and diverse and collaborating in a team.[33]

2.2.2 Design Thinking as a Method and Toolbox

When it finally comes to the practical application, three factors are considered crucial to success: interdisciplinary project teams, the iterative execution of the Design Thinking process, and working space, giving room for

---

[31] Carlgren, L., Rauth, I., & Elmquist, M. (2016), *op. cit.*

[32] Adapted from Carlgren et al. (2016), *op. cit.*, p. 43.

[33] Carlgren, L., Rauth, I., & Elmquist, M. (2016), *op. cit.*

experimentation and creativity.[34] A team that consists of different disciplines, departments, and hierarchical levels, and may also include external members, forms the indispensable basis for every Design Thinking process. The mixing of disciplines is the strength of such teams, not only in the duplication of the respective thematic and methodological special qualities but also in the different points of view and experiences that every member brings to the table.[35]

When it comes to the structure of the Design Thinking process, literature gives various approaches that do not differ substantially when examined precisely. The difference mostly lies in the terminology as well as the number and segregation of the steps, while the fundamental content is similar. The process embodies the functional and personal perspective as described before. The process, as expressed in *fail early and often*, has an overlapping nature; often the steps are not finished completely before starting a new iteration. Different process designs have been proposed by authors, and the process adopted for this purpose is based on the process design of the HPI[36] shown in Fig. 2.6.

Understand

At the beginning of the entire innovation process stands the understanding and exploration of the problem and its associated problem space, which includes all aspects and influencing factors. In many cases, the result of the search phase lies in the fact that the initial problem itself must be modified and a deeper-lying question addressed. In this phase, the team members, with all their different skills and knowledge from the various disciplines, have to become "immediate experts" who examine the problem from all possible angles. As after each phase, the team visualizes and synthesizes the results of the problem exploration and decides provisionally in favor of one or more problem facet(s).

Observe

The essential part of the search for insights is done by qualitative research, like accompanying users, observing their behavior, and widening the perspective,

[34] Hasso Plattner Institute of Design. (2019). An Introduction to Design Thinking: Process Guide. Retrieved from https://dschool-old.stanford.edu/sandbox/groups/designresources/wiki/36873/attachments/74b3d/ModeGuideBOOTCAMP2010L.pdf

[35] Grots, A., & Pratschke, M. (2009). Design Thinking – Kreativität als Methode. Marketing Review St. Gallen, 26(2), pp. 18–23. https://doi.org/10.1007/s11621-009-0027-4

[36] Hasso Plattner Institute of Design. (2019), *op. cit.*

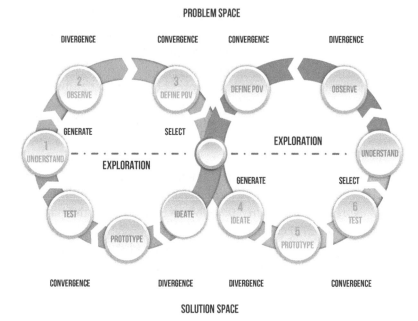

Fig. 2.6 The design thinking process and the double diamond model

not only focusing on the core problem, but also all surrounding aspects, which could provide inspiration for improvements. While observing, the design thinkers should watch the product or service in a user case scenario in a real-life context and ask questions, more in style of a conversation than an interview. The analyzed persons do not necessarily need to be actual customers. Often, other interest groups, such as extreme users, persons who deliberately refuse the product, or use it beyond its original purpose, are the most valuable information sources.

The collected findings are documented and then presented to each other. Here, as in almost every phase, the technique of storytelling is used. The aim is to analyze the possible user groups in such a way that as many valuable insights as possible can be determined by the team. On this basis, the team defines a precise problem for a concrete user group in the *define* phase.

Define Point of View

In order to be on the same page, the team specifies an exact, provisional, user group and creates a persona for it. A point of view (POV) statement is then formulated for this persona. In addition to that, also other tools, such as the empathy map (see Chap. 5), can be introduced to condense and visualize valuable findings of the team. The *define* phase is a synthesis process to filter the results with a special focus on visualization, as in the other steps as well. At the end of the search, it displays the result in a visually concise form, which prepares and communicates all previously generated data for the following steps.

Ideate

In the transition phase from the identification of a problem to the development of a solution, ideas for approaching it are generated. The goal is not to get one "perfect" idea but, instead, create the broadest range of possible solution opportunities. Generating ideas is done with the help of active, well-prepared brainstorming, based on the right questions, *How might we?* Generated ideas should be presented visually, using storytelling, drawings, and other tools for visualization. After structuring the ideas, the most promising ones are examined under the aspects of desirability, feasibility, and viability, with particular emphasis on the desirability factor to account for the human-centered nature of Design Thinking.[37]

Prototype

After the ideas have been condensed and prioritized by the team, an idea is selected and converted into a simple prototype for testing critical functions. In the case of prototyping a service, a show performance can serve as an experimental prototype. The *prototype* phase "is the iterative generation of artifacts intended to answer questions that get you closer to your final solution."[38] It serves the purpose of further developing the generated ideas, by building the prototype, often questions and critical details arise, that before were not considered.

Test

In the concluding phase, the prototype should be presented to the users in exchange for new insights and feedback. The team should not be emotionally

---

[37] Grots, A., & Pratschke, M. (2009), *op. cit.*
[38] Hasso Plattner Institute of Design. (2019), *op. cit.*, p. 7.

attached to the presented prototype for guaranteeing the objective treatment of the delivered feedback. Depending on the feedback, the team reacts by regressing to an earlier stage. This can even mean having to start from the initial phase again if modification of the initial human problem is necessary and repeats the process until reaching a satisfying result.[39]

An additional dimension can be used for providing more detailed information on the process, as was shown in Fig. 2.6. This additional dimension divides the process into two areas: *problem space* and *solution space*. The exploration of both areas first consists of divergent thinking patterns, followed by converging movement.[40] The first diverging thinking pattern starts with the initial problem: One problem is examined from all possible angles; all facets of it are analyzed to get a holistic understanding of the starting point. Diverging phases require the team members to be open-minded and ready to experiment. Analyzing the collected data starts a converging phase, where the insights and theories about the problem get synthesized and a selection takes place.

Then again, another divergence takes place, starting from this point of condensed information– exact user group, persona, and POV statements, followed by the generation of multiple ideas. The prototype phase then concludes the process with by selecting one idea out of the various created ideas for prototyping. In practice, design thinkers, especially those in charge of coordinating Design Thinking projects should always have in mind this interplay between explorative, diverging processes and condensing moments of selection and synthesizing.[41] The red process shown in Fig. 2.6 represents a first iteration and the blue one a second iteration. This should remind us that the innovation process in a Design Thinking project is highly dynamic and iterative.

2.2.3   Establishing the Organizational Prerequisites

The authors Elsbach and Stigliani have identified a clear link between a company's organizational culture and the use of Design Thinking tools. They note:

---

[39] See also Liedtka, J. (2018), *op. cit.*

[40] Lindberg, T., Meinel, C., & Wagner, R. (2011). Design Thinking: A Fruitful Concept for IT Development? In H. Plattner, C. Meinel, & L. Leifer (Eds.), Design Thinking: Understand – Improve – Apply (pp. 3–18). Berlin, Germany: Springer.

[41] Brown, T. (2008), *op. cit.*

First, we found that the effective use of design thinking tools in organizations had a profound effect on organizational cultures [...]. Second, and in a reciprocal manner, we found that organizational cultures influenced (both positively and negatively) the use of design thinking tools.[42]

In their work, they further identified various influencing factors, how the use of certain Design Thinking tools shapes the organizational culture, and, vice versa, how organizational cultures strongly affect the success or failure of practical Design Thinking:

• *Need-finding tools contribute to user-centric cultures*

These tools usually comprise user-oriented research activities like ethnography and netnography (more on that in Chap. 5) or analysis of the customer journey, during which the design thinkers immerse themselves in the environment of the user, his problems, and possible design solutions. Empathic engagement with the user is crucial, which over time affects the way an organization approaches its users, making it more user-centric.

• *Idea-testing tools contribute to cultures of openness to experimentation, openness to failure, and design-oriented strategic thinking*

Similar to need-finding and idea-testing tools, testing of a solution idea with a limited set of users can help to develop a culture that is open to the *fail early and often* concept and support employees that do not shy away from thinking out of the box. On the influence of the culture on the success of Design Thinking tools, Elsbach and Stigliani conclude:

Our [...] review provides evidence that organizational cultures defined by values, norms, and assumptions related to collaboration and experimentation (what we call "design thinking cultures") supported the use of design thinking tools, while cultures defined by values and assumptions related to productivity, performance, and siloed specialization, what might be thought of as more traditional corporate cultures, impeded the use of these tools.[43]

---

[42] Elsbach, K. D., & Stigliani, I. (2018). Design Thinking and Organizational Culture: A Review and Framework for Future Research. Journal of Management, 44(6), pp. 2274–2306. https://doi.org/10.1177/0149206317744252

[43] Elsbach, K. D., & Stigliani, I. (2018), op. cit., p. 12.

These findings corroborate the importance of the mindset of a design thinker that should infuse and cultivate into corporations Design Thinking activities, as well as the other way around. Besides tools, the design and supply of collaborative spaces facilitate the implementation of Design Thinking. Such spaces enable open communication, experimentation, and allow both intensive thinking and relaxation phases. The "New Work" initiatives of many firms today reveal that they understood the importance of collaborative spaces in order to manifest an agile working culture or mindset. However, such initiatives are useless when the corporate mindset applied and demonstrated by the C-level management does not fit into the proclaimed culture.

2.2.4 Design Thinking for the New Marketing

Deutsche Telekom and its mobile phone carrier T-Mobile have applied Design Thinking for the last 12 years and have changed the companies' DNA to a more user-friendly market approach. Through many projects organized by a competence center (creative center), the organization and its marketing went through many changes. The Switzerland telecom provider Swisscom went even one step further and created a human-centered division for mass market and business markets. They applied Design Thinking for many tasks. Small- and medium-sized companies are applying this concept as well.

The human-centered approach to innovation in Design Thinking is the reason it forms part of the H2H Marketing theoretical framework and is also the foundational basis developed into the H2H Mindset (as shown in Chap. 3). Design thinking breaks with the myth of unreachable design creativity popping out as perfectly developed ideas from the heads of ingenious masterminds. Instead, results can be achieved with "hard work augmented by a creative human-centered discovery process and followed by iterative cycles of prototyping, testing, and refinement."[44]

Successful use of Design Thinking, furthermore, involves two facets of integration: it can be introduced as *methodology*, but for that application to bear fruit, it also needs to be implemented as a *mindset*.[45]

In the past, design, similar to marketing, has been involved only at late stages of the development process, at a moment where the substantial innovation work is already done, and their job was to put a nice wrapper around the idea. However, with Design Thinking, the role of the designer is changing.

---

[44] Brown, T. (2008). *op. cit.*, p. 88. g

[45] For more detailed recommendations on implementation of Design Thinking in practical terms, the reader may be referred to the book *Design Thinking: Understand – Improve – Apply* by Hasso Plattner et al. (see reference list). Page XV for example provides basic rules for design thinkers.

The "new" designer is not limited by the boundaries of the traditional term, since the team combines knowledge of experts from various departments. While design was merely tactical, increasing the attractiveness of an already elaborated idea for customers, it now is becoming strategic– designers are requested to actively form ideas to better satisfy the customer's needs.[46] Design Thinking also ties in with the shift towards service-centricity and the Service-Dominant Logic as it offers more room for innovation:

> [...] innovation's terrain is expanding. Its objectives are no longer just physical products; they are new sorts of processes, services, IT-powered interactions, entertainments, and ways of communicating and collaborating—exactly the kinds of human-centered activities in which design thinking can make a decisive difference.[47]

Marketing should pick up this momentum to reclaim the position at the "fuzzy front end of innovation"[48] and to have an effective operational answer to face the shift from product-centricity towards a service focus and a shift from a focus of incremental innovation to a balance of incremental and radical innovations. Together with engineering and design, marketing can collaborate by using their specific knowledge and capabilities to innovate radically (see Fig. 2.7[49]).

Because of hyper-competition, companies today are searching for radical innovations, which might ensure their survival. Most of the established diverse industries are managing incremental innovations and in exploiting their existing products and services profitably. The focus is on engineering which is responsible for the technical performance of a product, not so much for services. We are convinced that the real power of marketing and design lies in service. While design is responsible to give a product/service the right form, marketing should delve below the consciousness level and meet latent needs and unfulfilled wants of users. To question the "why" is the key in this process, and marketing should not be satisfied until this is answered. This exploration needs expertise in psychology, sociology, and neurosciences. Together with the use of digital methods like (big) data analytics, this should be the core competency of marketing. With Design Thinking, H2H Marketing has a powerful

---

[46] Brown, T. (2008). *op. cit.*

[47] Brown, T. (2008). *op. cit.*, p. 86.

[48] Gassmann, O., & Schweitzer, F. (2014). Managing the Unmanageable: The Fuzzy Front End of Innovation. In O. Gassmann, & F. Schweizer (Eds.), Management of the Fuzzy Front End of Innovation (pp. 3–14). Cham, Switzerland: Springer International Publishing.

[49] Adapted from Verganti (2009), *Design-driven Innovation: Changing the Rules of Competition by Radically Innovating what Things Mean*, p. 32.

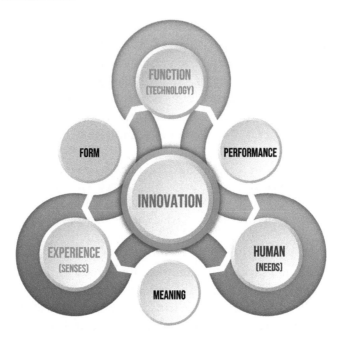

Fig. 2.7 The role of marketing to meaningful innovations

method and mindset that brings human-centered thinking into action and can infuse the whole company with its spirit. Over the last years, DT has gained a solid position in product development. In the other company processes, it is now achieving momentum. In sales teams there is a particularly high need. Salesforce has applied DT for itself, and it is promoting to change traditional sales methodologies with Design Thinking.

It is imperative to combining qualitative, mainly ethnographic research methods used in Design Thinking with the quantitative market research methods used in marketing. Together with the new possibilities enabled by the recent developments in data analytics and the use of artificial intelligence, marketing can regain reputation as the integral role in innovation processes.

2.3   The Service-Dominant Logic

Vargo and Lusch[50] offer a radical paradigm shift, rethinking the process of marketing; already in 1999, it was understood: "The very nature of network organization, the kinds of theories useful to its understanding, and the

---

[50]Vargo, S. L., & Lusch, R. F. (2004). *op. cit.*

potential impact on the organization of consumption all suggest that a para-digm shift for marketing may not be far over the horizon."[51] Moreover, Sheth and Parvatiyar point into the direction of relationship focus when stating that "an alternative paradigm of marketing is needed, a paradigm that can account for the continuous nature of relationships among marketing actors." [52]

In 2004, Vargo and Lusch introduced their new dominant logic for mar-keting, called the *Service-Dominant Logic* (S-DL), presenting a paradigm shift towards a logic that is inherently relational, embraces value co-creation, and proposes thinking in a network, and later an ecosystem perspective.[53] H2H Marketing agrees with the two authors and adopts it as a conceptual foundation.

S-DL stands in contrast to the Goods-Dominant Logic (GDL), from which, the S-DL evolved, shifting from a goods-centered model of exchange towards a service-centered model of exchange. Its authors advocate a reconsid-eration of the way goods and services are viewed and argue that a distinction is obsolete once realized that goods only offer another kind of service, some-thing Vargo and Lusch [54] find reflected in the following statement:

> Customers do not buy goods or services: they buy offerings which render ser-vices which create value […]. The traditional division between goods and ser-vices is long outdated. It is not a matter of redefining services and seeing them from a customer perspective; activities render services, things render services. The shift in focus to services is a shift from the means and the producer perspec-tive to the utilization and the customer perspective.[55]

The big differences between G-DL and S-DL are displayed in Fig. 2.8.[56]

In the following, the fundamental premises (FPs) will be discussed to understand the dominant logic shifting the focus from a manufacturing a tangible, standardized goods towards a service-centered view with a new understanding of value creation and the customer's role in the process.

---

[51] Achrol, R. S., & Kotler, P. (1999). Marketing in the Network Economy, p. 162. Journal of Marketing, 63, p163. https://doi.org/10.2307/1252108

[52] Sheth, J.N., & Parvatiyar, A. (2000). The Evolution of Relationship Marketing, p. 140. In J.N. Sheth, & A. Parvatiyar (Eds.), Handbook of Relationship Marketing (pp. 119–148). Thousand Oaks, CA: Sage.

[53] Vargo, S. L., & Lusch, R. F. (2016). Institutions and axioms: an extension and update of service-dominant logic. Journal of the Academy of Marketing Science, 44(1), pp. 5–23. https://doi.org/10.1007/s11747-015-0456-3

[54] Vargo, S. L., & Lusch, R. F. (2004). *op. cit.*

[55] Gummesson, E. (1995). Relationship marketing: Its role in the service economy, p. 250f. In W. J. Glynn & J. G. Barnes (Eds.), Understanding Services Management (pp. 244–268). New York, NY: Wiley.

[56] Adapted from Vargo & Lusch (2004, 2008, 2016) and Haeckel (1999).

Fig. 2.8 The shift from goods-dominant logic to service-dominant logic

This paradigm shift has happened in the real business world. Many new successful companies are pure service-oriented companies in the sense of Vargo and Lusch. Look at Google—all they offer is service. They may have some hardware offerings, like Google Home or Nest, but they are all driven by their service offerings. Google Chrome has some physical presence in the computing device, but the search, navigation, and communication capabilities determine the usefulness of Google's offerings. Facebook, WhatsApp, and Zoom service their customers in a similar fashion.

Brick and mortar companies have also made the shift to S-DL. The business transformation is in full swing in many industries from machine building to electrical equipment and heavy construction equipment. Service models offer significant benefits, for example, to the electric power companies. With advanced digital technologies and improved abilities, they guarantee better outcome. General Electric expands its offering from equipment (generators, switches, cables, controls, etc.) to also installing, maintaining, and operating the facilities. They even go one step further and offer to service even the equipment of competitors or companies that have left the market. From the $95 billion revenues in 2019, more than 45% was generated from services.

At IBM, the shift to service orientation has paid off. The transition happened after 2004, when IBM sold its PC division to Lenovo. Servers, storage facilities, and many more hardware components followed. IBM moved to customized software solution provider and offered "on-demand" service. For this period of time, their annual revenue level stood at $100 billion, but profitability increased dramatically. IBM is now handling mission critical and sensitive data of large corporations and government, from banking to health systems. Most of these businesses apply business models which are based on "as a service" and create recurring revenues, and most are highly scalable, like the cloud services. Companies will continue to invest in this direction, and the latest acquisition of Red Hat through IBM, the open platform Linux system, indicates the direction of the future.

2.3.1 Fundamental Premises of the S-DL

The S-DL is based on eleven fundamental premises (FP): in the original introduction, Vargo and Lusch proposed eight FPs,[57] to which modifications and two new FPs were added in 2008[58] and one new FP, as well as specifications, by giving axiom status to five of the FPs, was added in 2016.[59] Table 2.2[60] gives an overview of the current FPs and their evolutionary predecessors. The S-DL uses a definition of *service* differing from the traditional understanding of *service*s: Service in the S-DL means "[…] the application of specialized competences in knowledge and skills through deeds, processes, and performances for the benefit of another entity or the entity itself."[61]

Building on the definition of Constantin and Lusch,[62] Vargo and Lusch distinguish *operand resources*, "resources on which an operation or act is performed to produce an effect"[63] and *operant resources*, "[resources] employed to act on operand (and other operant resources)."[64] They see it as a characteristic of the shift from the G-DL, primarily focusing on operand resources– goods as basic unit of exchange and customers as operand resource on which the marketers perform acts, segmenting them, penetrating, etc., towards the S-DL, where exchange has the purpose of benefiting from the knowledge and skills of the counterparty and the customer is mainly an operant resource engaged as "co-producer of service."[65]

---

[57] Vargo, S. L., & Lusch, R. F. (2004). *op. cit.*

[58] Vargo, S. L., & Lusch, R. F. (2008). Service-dominant logic: continuing the evolution. Journal of the Academy of Marketing Science, 36(1), pp. 1–10. https://doi.org/10.1007/s11747-007-0069-6

[59] Vargo, S. L., & Lusch, R. F. (2016). *op. cit.*

[60] Adapted from Vargo & Lusch (2016), *op. cit.,* p. 8.

[61] Vargo, S. L., & Lusch, R. F. (2004). *op. cit.,* p. 2.

[62] Constantin, J. A., & Lusch, R. F. (1994). Understanding Resource Management. Oxford, Ohio: Planning Forum.

[63] Vargo, S. L., & Lusch, R. F. (2004). *op. cit.,* p. 2.

[64] Vargo, S. L., & Lusch, R. F. (2004). *op. cit.*

[65] Vargo, S. L., & Lusch, R. F. (2004). *op. cit.,* p. 7.

Table 2.2 The foundational premises of the service-dominant logic

FPs	2004	2008	2016
1	The application of specialized skills and knowledge is the fundamental unit of exchange	Service is the fundamental basis of exchange	No change **AXIOM STATUS**
2	Indirect exchange masks the fundamental unit of exchange	Indirect exchange masks the fundamental basis of exchange	No change
3	Goods are distribution mechanisms for service provision	No change	No change
4	Knowledge is the fundamental source of competitive advantage	Operant resources are the fundamental source of competitive advantage	Operant resources are the fundamental source of strategic benefit
5	All economies are service economies	No change	No change
6	The customer is always the co-producer	The customer is always a co-creator of value	Value is co-created by multiple actors, always including the beneficiary **AXIOM STATUS**
7	The enterprise can only make value propositions	The enterprise cannot deliver value but only offer value propositions	Actors cannot deliver value but can participate in the creation and offering of value propositions
8	Service-centered view is customer-oriented and relational	A service-centered view is inherently customer-oriented and relational	A service-centered view is inherently beneficiary oriented and relational
9		All social and economic actors are resource integrators	No change **AXIOM STATUS**
10		Value is always uniquely and phenomenologically determined by the beneficiary	No change **AXIOM STATUS**
11			Value co-creation is coordinated through actor-generated institutions and institutional arrangements **AXIOM STATUS**

With this perspective, the view on goods also changes. Before, goods (oper- and resources) were considered only as end products, while in the S-DL, goods are the carriers of operant resources, which are skills and knowledge incorporated in the goods, thus functioning as a vehicle, that fulfill an inter- mediary function. They connect two operant resources, the embedded knowl- edge in the goods and the customers. We can now move on to a detailed examination of the FPs.

FP1: Service is the Fundamental Basis of Exchange
In line with the abovementioned definition, Vargo and Lusch declare service the fundamental basis of exchange in the economic sense. In 2008, the word- ing was changed from "unit" to "basis" to leave aside G-DL terminology. This premise assigns the highest importance in exchange to operant resources, con- sidering that two or more actors exchange service.[66]

FP2: Indirect Exchange Masks the Fundamental Basis of Exchange
The S-DL argues that due to increasing division of labor (*Taylorism*) caused by the industrialization, it was no longer possible to exchange service for service because the actors involved were often no longer in direct contact with each other. Also, a monetization of exchange processes took place, replacing recip- rocal service with money, acts as storage for service, and is used as a medium of exchange.[67]

Because of increasing specialization that created micro-specialists with "the performance of increasingly narrow-skilled proficiencies,"[68] employees lost direct contact with the customer, as they were only passing the product to the next micro-specialized processing step, not to the customer. More impor- tantly, they also lost the sense for what they were doing and for whom they were doing it. From the viewpoint of the S-DL, the indirect exchange mecha- nisms provided by money, vertical marketing systems, and big organizations have an underlying fundamental basis of exchange, which is *skills-for-skills*, *services-for-services*.[69]

---

[66] Vargo, S. L., & Lusch, R. F. (2008). *op. cit.*
[67] Vargo, S. L., & Lusch, R. F. (2004). *op. cit.*
[68] Vargo, S. L., & Lusch, R. F. (2004). *op. cit.*, p. 8.
[69] Vargo, S. L., & Lusch, R. F. (2004). *op. cit.*

FP3: Goods are Distribution Mechanisms for Service Provision

In the traditional G-DL, the assumption is that products are a representation of the value "produced" by the firms. The firms produce the product with inherent value and sell it to the customer who then consumes the value. The customer, therefore, gets reduced to the role of a destroyer of value. In the S-D, goods are viewed as a distribution mechanism for the operant resources of the service providers, and the products are "encapsulated knowledge,"[70] service in disguise.

FP4: Operant Resources are the Fundamental Source of Strategic Benefit

Firms and other organizations today cannot rely anymore on operand resources (machines, production plants, etc.) to obtain a strategic benefit. Instead, resources like skills and knowledge are the deciding factors. The premise was modified over the years, changing "competitive advantage" to "strategic benefit" to shift attention from the mere competition orientation towards creating excellent value propositions for the customer. Only then should the firm take the competitive perspective into account because without the first step of value proposition, an exchange will not take place. The authors add the following: "Incidentally, 'strategic benefit' highlights an important implication of the service-for-service conceptualization of S-D logic, namely, that the service provider also has the role of 'beneficiary', given reciprocal service exchange."[71]

FP5: All Economies are Service Economies

The realization that service is the fundamental basis of exchange between economic actors (FP1) means that national economies are now considered *service economies*. This could be interpreted as the manifestation of the first FP on a global scale. A common misconception about the S-DL seems to be that national economies are becoming service economies. The reasoning in this argument is flawed in the sense that it still portrays the world inside the parameters of the G-DL (using G-DL's definition of services and service economies), while from the S-DL perspective, all of the exchange has its basis in service. Service economies are not a new phenomenon that only recently arose. Breaking it down to a smaller scale, Vargo and Lusch argue that not

---

[70] Vargo, S. L., & Lusch, R. F. (2004). *op. cit.*, p. 9.
[71] Vargo, S. L., & Lusch, R. F. (2016). *op. cit.*

only "all economies are service economies" but that also "all businesses are service business."[72]

FP6: Value is Co-created by Multiple Actors, Always Including the Beneficiary

The S-DL puts emphasis on value creation (*co-creation of value*) as a result of the collaboration of the producer and the customer.[73] FP6 should not be understood as *normative* statement of "firms should engage in co-creation of value and actively involve the customer" but as a *positive* one, a description of the actual value creation process of "value is always co-created," making it something binding, non-optional. [74, 75] Briefly put, this means "[…] the customer becomes primarily an operant resource (co-producer) rather than an operand resource ('target') and can be involved in the entire value and service chain in acting on operand resources."[76]

FP7: Actors Cannot Deliver Value but Can Participate in the Creation and Offering of Value Propositions

Initially, this meant that firms can only make a value offer, and not produce value. This results in a fundamental change in perspective for the firms, as they are no longer seen as "value producers" but as collaborative actors in a co-creation process. In 2008, the misconception that firms are finished with their side of value creation after making a value proposition needed clarification. "Rather, it [the FP7] was intended to convey that the enterprise cannot unilaterally create and/or deliver value."[77] This idea was then drafted into the 2008 version of the premise: "The enterprise cannot deliver value, but only offer value propositions."[78] In the current version (2016), "enterprise" got replaced by the term "actor" to open the S-DL up to the comprehension and analysis of value creation networks and service ecosystems.

---

[72] Vargo, S. L., & Lusch, R. F. (2008). *op. cit.*, p. 4.

[73] Vargo, S. L., & Lusch, R. F. (2008). *op. cit.*

[74] Vargo, S. L., & Lusch, R. F. (2008). *op. cit.*

[75] Vargo, S. L., & Lusch, R. F. (2016). *op. cit.*

[76] Vargo, S. L., & Lusch, R. F. (2004). *op. cit.*, p. 11.

[77] Vargo, S. L., & Lusch, R. F. (2008). *op. cit.*, p. 8.

[78] Vargo, S. L., & Lusch, R. F. (2016). *op. cit.*, p. 8.

FP8: A Service-centered View is Inherently Beneficiary Oriented and Relational

In the initial premise, it stated that a service-centered view is customer-oriented and relational. The service-centered view is considered "a model of inseparability of the one who offers and the consumer,"[79] In 2008, it was added that the customer orientation and relational character are *inherent* to the service-centered view,[80] in order to express that firms that think and act in a service-oriented way *always* end up being customer- and relationship-oriented. In the G-DL, firms had to put in active effort to get in touch with the customer; in the S-DL, this is integrated by default.

In the current version, the "customer" got replaced by "beneficiary" because it is not only customer relationships that can be viewed with the S-DL. "[…] 'beneficiary' centers the discussion on the current recipient of service and the referent of value co-creation."[81]

FP9: All Social and Economic Actors are Resource Integrators

This premise was not part of the original set of premises but was added later in 2006.[82] Here, the "actor" got introduced to demonstrate that there is more than only the dyadic relationship between customer and provider. The network character expressed in FP9 caused "a move from a single-minded concern with restricted, pre-designated roles of 'producers'/ 'consumers,' 'firms'/ 'customers,' etc. to more generic actors—that is, to an *actor-to-actor* (A2A) orientation."[83]

The A2A orientation has much in common with the B2B orientation, not with the B2C orientation of the marketing mainstream. Vargo and Lusch argue: "[…] as in B2B, there are no strictly producers or consumers but, rather, all actors are enterprises (of varying sizes, from individuals to large firms), engaged in the process of benefiting their own existence through benefiting the existence of other enterprises […]."[84]

This viewpoint is also central to H2H Marketing, which is expressed in the H2H orientation, adding human emphasis to the A2A approach of the S-DL. "Resource integration" is intended to emphasize that the business

---

[79] Vargo, S. L., & Lusch, R. F. (2004). *op. cit.*, p. 11.
[80] Vargo, S. L., & Lusch, R. F. (2008). *op. cit.*
[81] Vargo, S. L., & Lusch, R. F. (2016). *op. cit.*, p. 10.
[82] Vargo, S. L., & Lusch, R. F. (2008). *op. cit.*
[83] Vargo, S. L., & Lusch, R. F. (2016). *op. cit.*, p. 6.
[84] Vargo, S. L., & Lusch, R. F. (2016). *op. cit.*, p. 7.

model of the actors involved in the exchange is to integrate (mainly operant) resources and transform them into service. The actors, "generic resource integrators,"[85] are subject to high specialization causing them to exchange and integrate their operant resources to create value.[86]

FP10: Value is Always Uniquely and Phenomenologically Determined by the Beneficiary

FP10 suggests the nature of value and its creation: *only* the beneficiary of exchange determines the value; the firms cannot define the value of their propositions for a unique customer; therefore, used by different customers, the same product or service that the firm offers can lead to different results in value creation.[87]

FP11: Value Co-creation is Coordinated Through Actor-generated Institutions and Institutional Arrangements

Since the view of the S-DL has been extended from the consideration of the dyadic relationship of customer-firm to service ecosystems, Vargo and Lusch see the necessity for the service exchange processes in such systems to be regulated by service-oriented institutions. This further integrates S-DL on the way towards a "grand theory" of the market.[88]

2.3.2 Value Creation in the Service-Dominant Logic

Having seen that value is co-created in a collaborative process and is solely determined by the beneficiary, let us now lay out the chronological sequence of value creation (as shown in Fig. 2.9[89]).

S-DL distinguishes between two kinds of involvement of the beneficiary, temporally separated by the moment in which the exchange takes place as "transaction." The first kind of involvement is classified as *co-production*: it is

---

[85] Vargo, S. L., & Lusch, R. F. (2008). *op. cit.*, p. 9.

[86] Vargo, S. L., & Lusch, R. F. (2016). *op. cit.*

[87] Vargo, S. L., & Lusch, R. F. (2004). *op. cit.*

[88] Pfoertsch, W. A., & Sponholz, U. (2019). Das neue Marketing-Mindset: Management, Methoden und Prozesse für ein Marketing von Mensch zu Mensch. Wiesbaden, Germany: Springer Gabler.

[89] Adapted from Wilken & Jacob (2015), p. 152. Vom Produkt- zum Lösungsanbieter. In K. Backhaus, & M. Voeth (Eds.), Handbuch Business-to-Business-Marketing: Grundlagen, Geschäftsmodelle, Instrumente des Indu-striegütermarketing (2nd ed., pp. 147–164). Wiesbaden, Germany: Springer Gabler.

Fig. 2.9 The chronological sequence of value creation in the S-DL

the first, but optional, involvement of the customer in the creation and design of a value proposition. In this case, the customer takes an active role in the development of the properties of the value proposition, subsumed under *open innovation*, or does parts of the working process herself with *self-service*. While this kind of involvement is optional, the latter part of co-creation of value is not.[90]

The value itself is defined by the beneficiary "making use" of the value proposition— "value-in-use" instead of "value-in-exchange" is the consequence.[91] This takes place in the phase of co-creation of value, while co-production is considered a "strategic option for the preparation of value-in-use."[92]

The developments of the S-DL go hand in hand with a changing understanding of the customer role in the value creation process and power balance between the customer and the firm (see Fig. 2.10[93]). This transformation of the customer understanding was recognized already by Prahalad and Ramaswamy[94] before the introduction of S-DL in 2004 and was a precursor to subsequent developments. Additionally, value creation is also described as highly unique, depending on the individual actor and context. This understanding of value-in-context pointing out the supplier's need for information about the context of the user in order to estimate the individual value of a value proposition for the user. It is seen as one of the major benefits that in the

---

[90] Wilken, R., & Jacob, F. (2015). *op. cit.*

[91] Vargo, S. L., & Lusch, R. F. (2004). *op. cit.*

[92] See Wilken, R., & Jacob, F. (2015). Vom Produkt- zum Lösungsanbieter, p. 152. In K. Backhaus, & M. Voeth (Eds.), Handbuch Business-to-Business-Marketing: Grundlagen, Geschäftsmodelle, Instrumente des Industriegütermarketing (2nd ed., pp. 147–164). Wiesbaden, Germany: Springer Gabler. Translated from German to English.

[93] Table adapted from Prahalad & Ramaswamy (2000). For Age of Transcendence see Sisodia et al. (2014). Goods-Dominant Era adapted from Vargo & Lusch (2016).

[94] Prahalad, C. K., & Ramaswamy, V. (2000). *op. cit.*

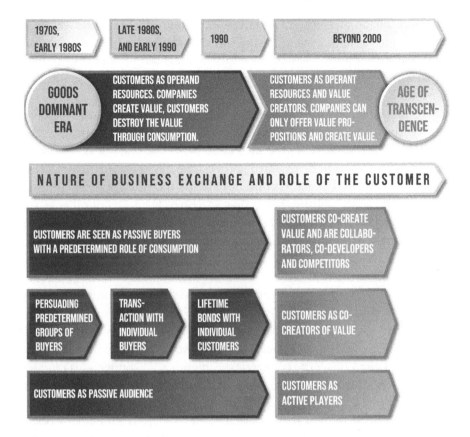

Fig. 2.10 The customer's changing role in value creation

S-DL co-creation of value is central to all considerations, taken seriously and not reduced to interaction in the sense of co-production, something the authors call "[…] a precursor to making better strategic decisions."[95]

2.3.3 Service Ecosystems

With the increased transparency and speed of the Internet, workers, vendors, customers, and other stakeholders are increasingly connected in real time, and economies and society are increasingly characterized by network structures. The significance and effects of networks and relationship systems cannot be explained by the sequential and separating G-DL, while in contrast, the S-DL

---

[95] Vargo, S. L., & Lusch, R. F. (2016). *op. cit.*, p. 19.

advocates collaborative system and network thinking.[96] The S-DL specifically tends towards a *service ecosystem* perspective, defined as "a relatively self-contained, self-adjusting system of resource-integrating actors connected by shared institutional arrangements and mutual value creation through service exchange."[97]

Like ecosystems in the biological world, service ecosystems emerge as a result of the interaction of actors engaging in service exchange to solve their (local) problems. Over time, the successful, beneficial share of the exchanges has a high likelihood to be repeated and become a system structure. The ecosystem contains itself as actors constantly adapt and react, and self-adjusting processes constantly reshape them. They also often form part of other ecosystems or are related to them. An example of this is the family: in itself, it forms its own service ecosystem with resource-integrating actors, but at the same time, it is embedded in other ecosystems of which it forms a part, e.g., the neighborhood or the country.[98]

This idea of service and value realization inside of network structures is not new[99] and is already being discussed in marketing and supply chain management, where exchange processes and actors are closely tied and chained together. The S-DL adds new facets to the network conceptualization, one of the more apparent being the connecting element: "[…] connections represent *service-for-service exchange*, rather than just connections of resources, people, or product flows […]."[100] Although being more difficult to grasp due to higher complexity, the ecosystem perspective provides a more accurate depiction of reality. It is not only the links and ties that matter; it is the "flows and exchanges between actors"[101] for which the ecosystem view gives a more adequate representation.

Institutions and institutional arrangements are the keys to understanding the service ecosystem perspective. "Service ecosystems need shared institutions (rules) to coordinate activities among actors and to function effectively."[102] Building on the definition of Scott, [103] institutions in the S-DL are not organizations as in the common use of the word but rather "the humanly devised

---

[96] Vargo, S. L., & Lusch, R. F. (2016). *op. cit.*

[97] Lusch, R. F., & Vargo, S. L. (2014). Service-dominant logic: premises, perspectives, possibilities, p. 24. Cambridge, United Kingdom: Cambridge University Press.

[98] Lusch, R. F., & Vargo, S. L. (2014). *op. cit.*

[99] See e.g. Achrol, R. S., & Kotler, P. (1999). *op. cit.*

[100] Vargo, S. L., & Lusch, R. F. (2017). *op. cit.*, p. 45.

[101] Lusch, R. F., & Vargo, S. L. (2014). *op. cit.*

[102] Lusch, R. F., & Vargo, S. L. (2014) *op. cit.*

[103] Scott, W. R. (2008). Institutions and organizations: Ideas and interests. Los Angeles, CA: Sage.

rules, norms, and beliefs that enable and constrain action and make social life at least somewhat predictable and meaningful,"[104] something that North in a sports analogy calls "the rules of the game,"[105] The institutional arrangements are "sets of interrelated institutions."[106]

The institutional perspective was needed to account for the irrational behavior of the actors. Institutions help actors make more rational decisions without necessary cognitive efforts of the actors.[107] The firms, and especially marketing, need to recognize the properties of the service ecosystems and the institutional perspective to it. Adaptability, norms, and values as well as the governing principles can differ heavily depending on cultural and geographic context, which are crucial for competing successfully in an ecosystem environment.

The ecosystem idea also highlights the relational character of the S-DL: "Because actors are loosely coupled and nested within service ecosystems, they must continually invite other actors to engage with and exchange service. They do this by making compelling value propositions that result in transactions. Thus, relationships precede transactions rather than vice versa […]."[108]

Take Amazon as an example. Amazon is known and renowned for its radical customer orientation and for managing the relationship to the customers and their ecosystems. On the other hand, you might ask some suppliers using Amazon distributing their products (and in future may be services) about their opinion about Amazon. You can hear a completely different story. The service level for suppliers is poor, and the same is true for the management of the relationship between the suppliers and Amazon. This might turn to a major future issue for Amazon when the suppliers start to use their ecosystems in order to avoid using Amazon. The message here is that a company should not focus only on one actor (customer) and on one ecosystem but all ecosystems of the relevant stakeholders.

This relationship idea of the S-DL lays the foundation for the H2H orientation of H2H Marketing. Every business transaction is at the end determined by a Human-to-Human connection and forms one more hub in the company ecosystem. The establishment of such a service ecosystem should become a central task of marketing departments. In this way, a form of

---

[104] Vargo, S. L., & Lusch, R. F. (2017). *op. cit.*, p. 49.

[105] North, D. C. (1990). Institutions, Institutional Change, and Economic Performance: Political Economy of Institutions and Decisions, p. 4. Cambridge, United Kingdom: Cambridge University Press.

[106] Vargo, S. L., & Lusch, R. F. (2016). *op. cit.*, p. 11.

[107] Vargo, S. L., & Lusch, R. F. (2016). *op. cit.*

[108] Lusch, R. F., & Vargo, S. L. (2014). *op. cit.*, p. 167.

Table 2.3 Transitional concepts on the way from the G-DL to the S-DL

G-DL concepts	Transitional concepts	S-DL concepts
Goods	Services	Service
Products	Offerings	Experiences
Feature/attribute	Benefit	Solution
Value-added	Co-production	Co-creation of value
Profit maximization	Financial engineering	Financial feedback/learning
Price	Value delivery	Value proposition
Equilibrium systems	Dynamic systems	Complex adaptive systems
Supply chain	Value chain	Value creation network/ constellation
Promotion	Integrated marketing communications	Dialogue
To market	Market to	Market with
Product orientation	Market orientation	Service orientation

marketing is created that becomes more humane through the focus on human interaction on the one hand, and on the other hand, it creates progress and competitiveness through the pressure of having to deliver convincing value propositions without which other actors cannot be convinced. FlixBus is applying these principles since the start of the company. They are shaping the future of mobility. Many factors had helped Germany-based FlixMobility GmbH emerge as Europe's leading mobility provider. Its unique business model combined total service orientation and digital technology with a traditional transportation company. FlixBus became a complete mobility provider by diversifying also into railway services and was overcoming challenges faced by entering the US market.

2.3.4   The Practical Transition from G-DL to S-DL

Table 2.3[109] shows the transition phase that served as preparation and had to be overcome to get towards the S-DL.

The transition between the two views is more comprehensible from this table, as it proves difficult to explain the S-DL without relying on G-DL terminology. Additionally, the transitional concepts can serve as orientation and

---

[109] Adapted from "Service-dominant logic: reactions, reflections and refinements", by R. F. Lusch, & S. L. Vargo, 2006, *Marketing Theory*, 6(3), p. 286.

practical advice for companies that are still bound to the G-DL as to what a transition to the S-DL might look like.[110]

Since a few years, a selected number of companies have made the transition to establishing ecosystems around their offerings. One of the outstanding examples is the Intel ecosystem. Over the last 20 years, Intel has created a network with partners and stakeholders, thriving on stakeholders' mutual benefits, each of them contributing to the growth of the ecosystem. It all started with the personal computer but also included industrial customization, avionics, chemicals, transportation, etc. In every application where computer power was needed, Intel was involved. In many cases, the processes were embedded in machines and equipment, but the lines between the partners were blurred from hardware to software to services, which allowed the network to expand continuously and establish new types of partnerships. Subsequently, the Intel ecosystem got another boost through cloud applications where the reach was expanded spanning all around the globe, including satellite systems.

The Intel ecosystem not only includes industrial partners but also governments, research institutions, universities, and nonprofit organizations. The partners profit from their capabilities and expertise by collaborating with each other. Especially visible examples are the applications in the area of **Internet of Things** (**IoT**). Just consider a warehouse application where the organization of the storehouse itself requires cooperative intelligence on the designs, the constructions, the operation, and the in and out logistics. In many cases, an end-to-end innovation is required, which can only be handled by a cooperative ecosystem.

Artificial intelligence is now speeding up industries, research, and commerce around the globe. Intel is nurturing these developments from many angles in the ecosystem. Other innovations need to be integrated into the dynamic ecosystem, which must be scalable and hopefully sustainable to increase agility and improve ROI. SAP and IBM have also established their own ecosystems besides being part of the Intel one, so have Adobe and General Electric. The range and efforts of these companies are different, but their conscious effort to establish their own ecosystem is proof of our conceptual thinking.

---

[110] Kowalkowski, C. (2010). What does a service-dominant logic really mean for manufacturing firms? CIRP Journal of Manufacturing Science and Technology, 3(4), pp. 285–292. https://doi.org/10.1016/j.cirpj.2011.01.003

2.4   Digitalization

The ability to navigate the technologies disrupting industries and understand key principles of the transformation is crucial for survival. For companies it is essential to grab the opportunities exploring the nature and history of transformative technology. AOL, Blackberry, Commodore, Kodak, Netscape, and Nokia are negative example. Amazon and Google show to where continuous digital transformation can lead. Often, digitalization and digitization are used synonymously with digital transformation. They seem to be the current buzzwords, although the definition and understanding of the matter and its consequences vary. In its most simple form, digitization means the process of converting analogue data into digital data, e.g., converting information on paper into data. Digitalization implies the use of data in digital processes, and digital transformation is the application of data and processes in new business models. Big shifts can take place with the digital transformation, for example, the control of local facilities could now be monitored remotely, and whole supply chains can be integrated. A special term is Industry 4.0. It refers to the application of digital transformation in manufacturing and related applications. Big Data, Cloud Computing, and other terms are used as synonyms under digitalization in the political and economic discourse.[111]

2.4.1   Digitalization Changing the Modus Operandi

The mere transformation of information into digital form is not enough to call it digitalization. The deciding factor is that the digitally available information can now be processed by systems and machines, and it becomes *operational*, usable. The effect of digitalization is achieved through target-oriented use and networking of digitized information. The process opens up new spaces for companies, new business models, and the potential for new technological advancements and innovations that are waiting to be exploited. The coronavirus pandemic has accelerated this development enormously; within weeks major technology jumps could be noticed. In health offices and medical services, digital applications were applied. During lockdown period, most people conducted work from home and used online services as a daily matter. Even those who had avoided online use (banking, shopping, communication with

---

[111] Ross J.W., Beath C. M., Mocker M (2019). Designed for Digital: How to Architect Your Business for Sustained Success (Management on the Cutting Edge) MIT Press, 2019

family and friends) until now were forced to try it out, and many will stay with it even after the lockdown eases.

One of the biggest recipients to benefit from the lockdown is Netflix, the online streaming entertainment service and Zoom, the 2020 leader in enterprise video communications. Both applications experienced a tremendous growth in their membership number due to the fact that people were forced to stay at home and look for ways to entertain themselves. Even before the lockdown, for most of the younger population, watching movies or news on their smart phone or computer was the medium of choice. Consequently, the TV industry has experienced a revolution. Early television sets and transmissions were analog; high-frequency waves were modulated with images and sound. Next, signals were transmitted digitally with TV sets decoding them so that we could watch the content. Today, we have advanced to video-on-demand and streaming services. Besides Netflix, there are Amazon Prime, Apple TV, etc. and the conventional TV program providers, trying to stay relevant. Applications technology and customer interfaces are digitalized, and the business models are highly adaptable to individual needs.

Wolf and Strohschen summarize the concept of digitization in a precise definition: "We speak of digitization when analogue service provision is completely or partially replaced by service provision in a digital, computer manageable model."[112] We consider digitalization as the use of digital technologies in various forms in changing business models to provide new revenue and value-creating opportunities. There are challenges for companies resulting from digital change. Executives find themselves confronted with highly competitive and rapidly changing markets where digital innovation is imperative for staying relevant.[113] Thanks to ongoing commoditization, initially differentiating factors of the value proposition are now becoming standardized commodities, losing their differentiating effect.[114]

Furthermore, firms have to deal with losing control over customer relationships, and dealing with a new type of customer for whom the terminology ranges from the empowered *prosumer* and *digital native* that is part of

---

[112] Wolf, T., & Strohschen, J.-H. (2018). Digitalisierung: Definition und Reife - Quantitative Bewertung der digitalen Reife, p. 58. Informatik Spektrum, 41(1), pp. 56–64. https://doi.org/10.1007/s00287-017-1084-8. Translation from German to English.

[113] Ernst & Young (2011). The digitisation of everything: How organisations must adapt to changing consumer behaviour [Report]. Retrieved from https://www.ey.com/Publication/vwLUAssets/The_digitisation_of_everything_-_How_organisations_must_adapt_to_changing_consumer_behaviour/%24file/EY_Digitisation_of_everything.pdf

[114] Schlotmann, R. (2018). Digitalisierung auf mittelständisch: Die Methode "Digitales Wirkungsmanagement". Berlin, Germany: Springer.

Generation Y, to the *Homo Digitalis*, derived from Homo Oeconomicus.[115] While many technological changes caused by digitalization and the resulting need to adapt and respond are clearly visible for firm's executives, one variable is not taken into account adequately: the speed of these changes and its implications for the firms. The time customers need to adopt new technology is ever-decreasing. It took almost a century for telephones, which took 70 years to get to a 50% penetration of households, and almost three decades for the radio, at 28 years. In comparison, it took only 10 years for access to the Internet. Firms need to assume that this trend towards shorter adoption spans will continue and that new adoption rates may need to be considered in terms of weeks and months, not years or decades. This leaves them with heavy implications as ever more agility and fast-paced responsiveness will be needed to stay on top of the competition.

Additionally, digitalization needs to be addressed not only from an economic standpoint but also from a political and societal direction. For example, there is a clear imbalance between economic and social perspective. While technological advancement in industries is part of political agendas, necessary social considerations receive very little attention. Firms do not take topics like the universal basic income (UBI) proposed as remedy for the consequences of high unemployment rates caused by digitalization seriously. Unemployment rates have major economic consequences in society, like changes in customer behavior and varying levels of demand for goods and services.[116]

Additionally, a rethinking process for the role of machines and the relationship between people and machines is overdue. For the future, it will be necessary to find a proper balance between humaneness (*high-touch*) and technology (*high-tech*). On a small and big scale, as Naisbitt explained, we need to ask the question: Who is in charge? Does man control technology, or is it the other way around? The far-reaching consequences that digitalization brings are also evident in the terminology used in its context, as it is often regarded as a *megatrend*[117] or even *gigatrend*.[118]

[115] Backhaus, K., & Paulsen, T. (2018). Vom Homo Oeconomicus zum Homo Digitalis – Die Veränderung der Informationsasymmetrien durch die Digitalisierung. In M. Bruhn, & M. Kirchgeorg (Eds.), Marketing Weiterdenken: Zukunftspfade für eine marktorientierte Unternehmensführung (pp. 105–122). Wiesbaden, Germany: Springer Gabler.

[116] Precht, R. D. (2018). Jäger, Hirten, Kritiker: Eine Utopie für die digitale Gesellschaft (6th ed.). München, Germany: Goldmann.

[117] Naisbitt, J. (2015). Der Horizont reicht meist nur bis zum nächsten Wahltag. In Bundeszentrale für politische Bildung (Ed.), Megatrends?. Aus Politik und Zeitgeschichte, 65(31–32), pp. 3–6. Retrieved from https://www.bpb.de/apuz/209953/der-horizont-reicht-meist-nur-bis-zum-naechsten-wahltag-

[118] For a development to be considered a *gigatrend* it must influence all existing megatrends, on all areas of life and this on a global scale while having a half-life period of at least 30 years. See Linden, E., &

For the description of the development path of digitalization, a step model is used, which usually consists of two or three steps, depending on the author. For the illustration of the development steps of digitalization, we opted for a three-step model (see Fig. 2.11[119]), commonly used by various authors.[120] The stages are fundamental digital data processing, interconnected information and communication, and interconnected products and services. All stages can be distinguished between external and internal digitalization. In 1991, everything started with the establishment of the Internet and the first homepage at CERN, the European Organization for Nuclear Research.[121] The computers were stationary and automated data processing was the goal. One of the common applications was Enterprise Resource Planning (ERP). About 10 years later, mobile Internet came to life, and information and communication established the Web 2.0 applications. Internal social media was established, and Cloud Computing and Big Data application started to develop. In 2011, Industry 4.0 was created for external and internal industrial use in Germany. Smart phone apps and business models based on digital products and services became mainstream, and the dissemination of Industry 4.0 started in many industries. These solutions were building on existing computerized applications, but now with bidirectional connectivity huge benefits could be realized. These evolutionary phases are summarized in Fig. 2.11.

- *First Phase: Fundamentals of data processing*

The first phase lays the infrastructural foundation for digitalization and includes basic connectivity requirements and fundamental software and hardware to enable data transfer and process ability.[122]

- *Second Phase: Interconnected information and communication*

Building on the fundamental infrastructure from the first phase, the main milestone of the second phase is the internal and external interconnection and

---

Wittmer, A. (2018). Zukunft Mobilität: Gigatrend Digitalisierung [Monograph]. Retrieved from https://www.alexandria.unisg.ch/253291/

[119] The evolutionary steps are adapted from Saam et al. (2016). The illustration of the Industry 4.0 is adapted from Deloitte (2015) and Kagermann, Wahlster, & Helbig (2013).

[120] Schlick, J., Stephan, P., & Zühlke, D. (2012). Produktion 2020: Auf dem Weg zur 4. industriellen Revolution. IM: die Fachzeitschrift für Information Management und Consulting, 27(3), pp. 26–34. Retrieved from https://www.econbiz.de/Record/im-schwerpunkt-industrie-4-0-produktion-2020-auf-dem-weg-zur-4-industriellen-revolution-schlick-jochen/10010019258

[121] For more information visit the CERN website which documents the beginnings of the world wide web: http://info.cern.ch/

[122] Saam, M., Viete, S., & Schiel, S. (2016). *op. cit.*

EXTERNAL DIGITALIZATION INTERNAL DIGITALIZATION

STAGE 1: FUNDAMENTAL DIGITAL DATA PROCESSING

- STATIONARY INTERNET
- HOMEPAGE

- COMPUTER
- ERP
- AUTOMATED DATA PROCESSING

STAGE 2: INTERCONNECTED INFORMATION AND COMMUNICATION

- MOBILE INTERNET
- INTERNET APPLICATION USED FOR INFORMATION AND COMMUNICATION
- EXTERNAL SOCIAL MEDIA

- BIG DATA
- CLOUD COMPUTING
- INTERNAL SOCIAL MEDIA

STAGE 3: INTERCONNECTED PRODUCTS AND SERVICES

- BUSINESS MODELS BASED ON DIGITAL PRODUCTS AND SERVICES

- APPLICATIONS

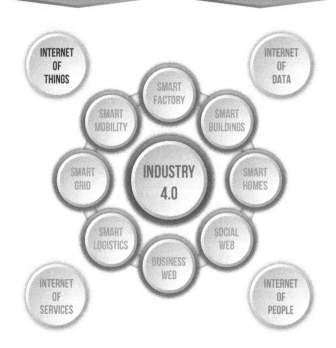

Fig. 2.11 Evolutionary steps of digitalization and the industry 4.0 environment

aggregation of data and communication. This phase has relevant strategic implementations for companies. There should be a company-wide implemented strategy for the digital transformation that leads all business units in the same direction. The holistic interconnection process of this phase should be used to break up organizational silos and to integrate business units coherently. Further, a successful interconnection is a necessary precondition for the next phase.[123]

- *Third Phase: Interconnected products and services*

Digitalization is seen as the enabler for the fourth industrial revolution.[124] Schlick argue that we are currently standing at the dawn of a new era, initiated by *cyber-physical systems* (CPS), "distributed, intelligent objects that are interconnected via Internet technologies. In the field of production technology, this can include, for example, individual process modules as well as plants and equipment or individual intelligent products." [125]

So, after the second phase of connected data, information, and communication, the maxim of the third phase is the interconnection of the physical and the digital (*cyber*) world. This development is expected to have disruptive consequences for the economy, creating new business models, destroying outdated ones, advances in the further monetization of data, and flexibility and efficiency gains in production.

Overall, industry development is getting closer towards the Industry 4.0 vision. Some firms already reached the third phase of digital evolution,[126] and steps in technological developments towards the *smart factory* and *smart service world* are being taken. Still, digital transformation is at its starting point,[127] and the potential of the mixing of the physical and digital world is far from being exhausted.[128] World leading electrical equipment providers like GE,

---

[123] Saam, M., Viete, S., & Schiel, S. (2016). *op. cit.*

[124] Kagermann, H., Wahlster, W., & Helbig, J. (2013). Deutschlands Zukunft als Produktionsstandort sichern: Umsetzungsempfehlungen für das Zukunftsprojekt Industrie 4.0 [Report]. Retrieved from https://www.bmbf.de/files/Umsetzungsempfehlungen_Industrie4_0.pdf

[125] Schlick, J., Stephan, P., & Zühlke, D. (2012). Produktion 2020: Auf dem Weg zur 4. industriellen Revolution, p. 27. IM: die Fachzeitschrift für Information Management und Consulting, 27(3), pp. 26–34. Retrieved from https://www.econbiz.de/Record/im-schwerpunkt-industrie-4-0-produktion-2020-auf-dem-weg-zur-4-industriellen-revolution-schlick-jochen/10010019258. Translated from German to English.

[126] Saam, M., Viete, S., & Schiel, S. (2016). *op. cit.*

[127] Lies, J. (2017). Die Digitalisierung der Kommunikation im Mittelstand: Auswirkungen von Marketing 4.0. Wiesbaden, Germany: Springer Gabler.

[128] Pfeiffer, S. (2015). Industrie 4.0 und die Digitalisierung der Produktion – Hype oder Megatrend? In Bundeszentrale für politische Bildung (Ed.), Megatrends?. Aus Politik und Zeitgeschichte, 65(31–32),

Siemens, ABB, Hitachi, and Shanghai Electric have taken up this challenge and lead the revolution. GE is providing a platform which enables all kinds of future solutions. Siemens wants to be a partner for the digital transformation. They support the flexibility of production process and integrate technologies of the future like AI, AR, VR, etc. in their solution offerings. By providing technologies and solutions for their customers, these companies believe that they ensure a competitive advantage.

The pace of technology change is tremendous and ever-accelerating. This implies the need for fast adaptations for the industry. An objective examination of firms' accomplishments by the consulting agency Pierre Audoin Consultants shows a sharp discrepancy and regional differences.[129] This trend study on the state of digital strategy in midsize to large firms[130] was conducted in the UK, Germany, and France. The findings showed that only a small share of the analyzed firms (28%) was pursuing a company-wide digital strategy, while most of the companies (72%) are still stuck in the early stages of digital transformation or are executing digital projects in some areas. However, they are without an underlying all-encompassing strategy. Interesting is the fact that most of the firms (69%) entrusted a central person with the key responsibility for all digitalization projects and efforts, while a small share of firms (only 14%) appointed a Chief Digital Officer (CDO). Most of the firms rely on the Chief Marketing Officer (CMO) or, in less common cases, the Chief Information Officer (CIO) to take care of the digital transformation. This indicates the responsibility that marketing departments have in this context.

Marketing must become aware of its importance in the digital transformation within the company and must act accordingly. To start with, it has incorporated this change into their mindset. This is the reason why we selected digitalization as one of the influencing factors in the conceptual framework of H2H Marketing. An outstanding example is the completely redesigned production line in Affalterbach, South Germany for Mercedes-AMG performance cars. In this facility, the superlative engine M 139 four-cylinder turbocharged engine is produced. The engine production is integrated assembly process with an intelligent network points which could be used as example for future industry applications. The basis of smart production is the

---

pp. 6–12. Retrieved from https://www.bpb.de/apuz/209955/industrie-4-0-und-die-digitalisierung-der-produktion

[129] Teknowlogy (2020). *IoT C&SI Survey 2020* [Study report]. Retrieved from https://75572d19-371f-4ade-aeb6-61dbca89834b.filesusr.com/ugd/f21868_2f8ab8213a00460f8777de2057430fb0.pdf

[130] Pierre Audoin Consultants (2015). Holistic Customer Experience in the Digital Age: A Trend Study for Germany, France and the UK [Whitepaper]. Retrieved from https://www.pac-online.com/holistic-customer-experience-digital-age

congenial interplay of innovative and digital technologies with the expertise of experienced assembly technicians. A sophisticated IT architecture forms the backbone of all processes. Bechtle AG—a strong IT partner supports the smooth operation of the central IT systems on-site with a tailor-made Business Operations Service.

2.4.2 Digitalization Affecting Marketing: Dematerialization and the Individualization of the Value Proposition

The weighing of value proposition, based on a known brand, design, or a special technology, is becoming more important. It is forcing companies to react and strengthen their value offerings. They also must think about new business models. Increasing commoditization is now becoming standard, while commodities are losing their differentiating effect. This trend can be noticed in many industries, in B2C as well as B2B.[131] In the travel industry, agencies giving personal service became commoditized by transparent comparisons of bookings through websites like Trivago and Booking.com. Similarly, retail banking sees its position threatened with the prolific use of online banking like Open Bank or N26. Due to easy accessibility of product characteristics and price comparisons through the abundance of information to customers, as well as competitors, value proposition in many sectors has changed. To counter the erosion of their differentiation positions, firms are investing their efforts into the shift from product to service and solution providers.[132] Companies that offer personalization options and add service layers to already existing products are the most successful in facing the commoditization tendency.

Customers today seeking information are no longer dependent on what the company provides. They can use social networks and search functions to become well-informed independently. They are recipients *and* senders at the same time by engaging in customer to customer interaction, informing others, and reviewing products and services.[133] Overall, there is a rising need for individualized, personal services, calling for a more individualized approach from the firm's side, as shown in Fig. 2.12.[134]

---

[131] Schlotmann, R. (2018). *op. cit.*

[132] Ernst & Young (2011). *op. cit.*

[133] Kotler, P., Kartajaya, H., & Setiawan, I. (2017). *op. cit.*

[134] Reinartz, W. (2018). Kundenansprache in Zeiten digitaler Transformation. In M. Bruhn, & M. Kirchgeorg (Eds.), Marketing Weiterdenken: Zukunftspfade für eine marktorientierte Unternehmensführung (pp. 123–138). Wiesbaden, Germany: Springer Gabler.

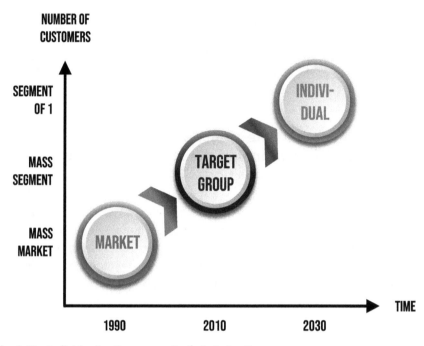

Fig. 2.12 Individualization as result of digitalization

This call can be answered successfully with the help of available data from the customers. The directions for marketing are clear: insights per person have to be generated, and the value proposition, content, and the access have to be tailored to the individual. This is economically feasible because the marginal costs of digital products tend towards zero. Even small-scale niche products can be made and sold profitably, while the nonphysical form of digital products and services also allow rapid market penetration of global markets. Digitalization furthermore is facilitating the trend towards products losing their physical form, which can already be observed at many points in everyday life, as shown in Fig. 2.13.[135]

In the process of dematerialization, products and services are transformed into software and apps. Current examples for this phenomenon are keys, identification documents, money, tickets (flights, cinema, train, etc.), etc.; there is no end in sight. When once physical things become apps and software, momentous results happen. No longer do only products and services

---

[135] Adapted from *Digitaler Darwinismus: Der stille Angriff auf Ihr Geschäftsmodell und Ihre Marke* (2nd. ed., p. 335), by R. T. Kreutzer, & K.-H. Land, 2016, Wiesbaden: Germany: Springer Gabler.

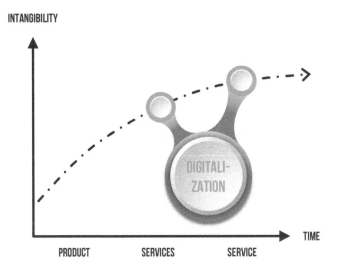

INTANGIBILITY

DIGITALI-
ZATION

TIME

PRODUCT   SERVICES   SERVICE

Fig. 2.13 Digitalization driving dematerialization

change, but complete value chains become obsolete.[136] The consequences of the "sharing economy," shifting focus from product-centricity towards service-centeredness for shared and more efficient use of resources (car sharing), aggravate the dematerialization process further.[137]

Additionally, deep, structural changes will take place within the course of the digital transformation, with the Internet of Things (IoT) being an essential driver of change. Land, in this context points out that the term IoT is somewhat misleading, because there will not be an Internet of *Things* but an Internet of *services*; he calls it a "world machine," a colossal infrastructure based on the communication of machines, products, and devices, all connected by transmitters and sensors. For firms that want to be successful inside of these structures, it is necessary to think in terms of software and services, not in physical products. [138]

Dematerialization affects marketing directly. One of the tasks of H2H Marketing is to compensate dematerialization of the value proposition by presenting it comprehensively, making it "tangible." With Virtual and Augmented

---

[136] Land, K.-H. (2018). Dematerialisierung: Die Neuverteilung der Welt in Zeiten der Digitalen Transformation und die Folgen für die Arbeitswelt. In C. Brüssel, & V. Kronenberg (Eds.), Von der sozialen zur ökosozialen Marktwirtschaft (pp. 153–166). Wiesbaden, Germany: Springer VS.

[137] Frey, A., Trenz, M., & Veit, D. (2017). The role of technology for service innovation in sharing economy organizations – a service-dominant logic perspective. In Proceedings of the 25th European Conference on Information Systems (ECIS), Guimarães, Portugal, June 5–10, 2017, pp. 1885–1901. Retrieved from https://aisel.aisnet.org/cgi/viewcontent.cgi?article=1120&context=ecis2017_rp

[138] Land, K.-H. (2018). *op. cit.*, p. 160.

Reality, new products and service can be demonstrated, making them tangible for the customer. Even better, technologies make it possible for firms to explain complex products and services not possible before and to support their own customer service in fieldwork, even when the intangibility is increasing.

2.4.3   Digitalization Affecting Marketing: New Customer Behavior

Today's customers manage to evade the influence of the firms, as brand values and brand communication cease to be the basis for purchasing decisions. Interaction and communication between customers, mainly excluding firms from the process, are becoming the relevant parameters for customers' decisions.[139] This transition has its starting point in the abundance of information available to customers. "Consumers now have real-time, mobile access to data that they previously relied on brands to provide them with."[140]

The classic buying process in the stationary retail trade usually implies that the customer first selects a provider. At the *Point-of-Sale*, which is matching with the *Point-of-Decision*, he then decides which product meets his needs best by getting an overview of the offered products and comparing them based on product information and, finally, decides on-site in favor of a certain product.[141]

The Internet has changed this traditional sequence. The customer now has access to an overwhelming variety of goods and services. Even more important, the customer has access to dynamically growing information about her human problem so that she gains insights far before she spends any time for searching products and services that might solve her problem. The decision-making process is based on more detailed product information, additional test reports, as well as product evaluations presented by other customers. All the information available paints a transparent and comparable picture of the product, from which he can make his decision. In addition, the customer can rely on emotional buying motives and allow the acceptance and popularity of products in his peer group (via social media) to influence the purchasing

[139] Kotler, P., Kartajaya, H., & Setiawan, I. (2017). *op. cit.*

[140] Ernst & Young (2011). *op. cit.*

[141] Heinemann, G., & Gaiser, C. W. (2016). SoLoMo – Always-on im Handel: Die soziale, lokale und mobile Zukunft des Omnichannel-Shopping (3rd ed.). Wiesbaden, Germany: Springer Gabler.

Fig. 2.14 The SoLoMo mindset

decision.[142] So effectively, the Point-of-Decision decouples itself from the Point-of-Sale. The customer today first selects a product as a possible solution of her human problem and subsequently chooses a supplier, not vice versa. Search engines, communication between customers, and effective networks play an important role in the decision-making process, which gains strategic importance for firms, while the Point-of-Sale becomes secondary.

The new Homo Digitalis shows a changed buying behavior in general. Heinemann[143] coined this behavior, *social*, *local*, and *mobile*, often abbreviated as *SoLoMo* (see Fig. 2.14[144]).

This means that people stay inside of the social media world, can be localized through the smartphone and other technologies, and use the smartphone that is "Always-On" as access to the Internet ecosystem. The relocation of the purchasing process into the digital world has a strong effect on the customer journey of the customers.

---

[142] Gehrckens, M., & Boersma, T. (2013). Zukunftsvision Retail – Hat der Handel eine Daseinsberechtigung? In G. Heinemann, K. Haug, M. Gehrckens, & dgroup (Eds.), Digitalisierung des Handels mit ePace: Innovative E-Commerce-Geschäftsmodelle unter Timing-Aspekten (pp. 51–76). Wiesbaden, Germany: Springer Gabler.

[143] Heinemann, G. (2014). SoLoMo - Always-on im Handel: Die soziale, lokale und mobile Zukunft des Shopping. Wiesbaden, Germany: Springer Gabler.

[144] Adapted from *SoLoMo – Always-on im Handel: Die soziale, lokale und mobile Zukunft des Omni-Channel-Shopping* (3rd ed., p. 65), G. Heinemann, & C. W. Gaiser, 2016, Wiesbaden, Germany: Springer Gabler.

Social, here, refers to the grown importance of social networks, where the majority of online users form digital communities, in which rating activities, discussions, answering questions, and sharing content are taking place. Consequently, more of the decision-making process is determined based on the opinions of others.[145] *Mobile* connectivity offers today's customers the possibility to instantly access all kinds of information in which they find enrichment and facilitation for their lives. Furthermore, an increasing share of the purchase preparation today is being done *mobile*, on-site. Customers use their smartphones at the Point-of-Sale to look up ratings, reviews, and other useful information to come to a purchasing decision, which may lead them to finally buy the product online. The last characteristic of the concept refers to the constant traceability of the digital users via Global Positioning System (GPS) and the benefits they derive from *location-based services*, such as the optimized local search for products or services.

Heinemann[146] describes the underlying *Always-In-Touch* mindset of the *smart natives*, similar to *digital natives*. They are heavy users with high affinity for technology and the Internet, based on four pillars: the technical prerequisite of the mindset, which is *Always-On*, lies in connectivity– a more open communication by always being in contact with other users from social network and online offers that are easily accessible at any time. *Always-In-Touch*, the centerpiece of the SoLoMo mindset, is the consequence of this prerequisite. Because the Internet and smartphones form an integral part of smart natives' lives, they attach great importance to intuitive handling, personalization, and easy access to useful functions via apps (*SoLoMo Usability*). Also, they expect information and online services to be available at any given moment, independent of time and place. Everyday life gets busier by filling previously media-free, unoccupied time with smartphone usage (*SoLoMo Efficiency*). Additionally, the smart native is constantly connected and engages in active communication with friends, colleagues, and other users from online communities, for example, via social media (*SoLoMo Communication*). Due to the fear of missing out on notifications and new content from his peers, he also tends to stay *Always-On*.[147] The SoLoMo Convergence "[...] describes the combination of different functions, contents and channels in a single device."[148] The smartphone nowadays covers issues from all areas of life, may it be work-related or private, for purchasing, and information or

---

[145] See also Kotler, P., Kartajaya, H., & Setiawan, I. (2017). *op. cit.*

[146] Heinemann, G. (2014). *op. cit.*

[147] Heinemann, G. (2014). *op. cit.*

[148] Heinemann, G. (2014). *op. cit.*, p. 56.

entertainment purposes. Facebook and WhatsApp are prevalent in the Western world, WeChat in China, and Yandex in Russia.

Modern marketing must take this mindset and the changed information and decision-making behavior of the smart natives into account. To achieve this, all purchasing behavior models developed so far should be used in conjunction with the new possibilities of digitalization in order to better understand people. Since 2018, when the Facebook- Cambridge Analytica data breach occurred, we know that users' personal data could be harvested and misused. Cambridge Analytica used without consent Facebook data and created personal, psychological profiles of voters by to be predominantly used for political advertising applied at Ted Cruz and Donald Trump campaigns.[149] So far, not sufficient legal regulation exist to curb these kind of anti-human activities. To many traditional companies, the digitalized world may seem threatening,[150] but it can also offer great chances for them to leverage as social media and online communities offer a rich source of valuable insights.[151]

2.4.4 Digitalization Affecting Marketing: New Relationship Between Supplier and Customer

Imagine the following example: You come back home from work, late in the evening and you notice a package at your doorstep. You pick it up and are surprised to see the Apple logo, since you did not order anything from them. Upon opening it, you see that there's the new Apple smartwatch model inside. You think to yourself that it actually could be a nice present for your technology-loving niece who turns 16 next week. After all, you would have looked for something similar for her, so in the end, you are pleased with the idea and decide to keep it.[152]

---

[149] Chan, R. (2019). The Cambridge Analytica whistleblower explains how the firm used Facebook data to sway elections. *Business Insider*. Retrieved from https://www.businessinsider.in/tech/news/the-cambridge-analytica-whistleblower-explains-how-the-firm-used-facebook-data-to-sway-elections/articleshow/71461113.cms

[150] See e.g. Kozinets, R. V. (2015). Netnography: Redefined. Los Angeles, CA: Sage.

[151] See also LaValle, S., Lesser, E., Shockley, R., Hopkins, M. S., & Kruschwitz, N. (2011). Big Data, Analytics and the Path From Insights to Value. MIT Sloan Management Review, 52(2), pp. 21–32. Retrieved from https://sloanreview.mit.edu/article/big-data-analytics-and-the-path-from-insights-to-value/

[152] The idea for this example stems from Backhaus, K., & Paulsen, T. (2018). Vom Homo Oeconomicus zum Homo Digitalis – Die Veränderung der Informationsasymmetrien durch die Digitalisierung. In M. Bruhn, & M. Kirchgeorg (Eds.), Marketing Weiterdenken: Zukunftspfade für eine marktorientierte Unternehmensführung (pp. 105–122). Wiesbaden, Germany: Springer Gabler. The authors used a similar example to illustrate the new relationship between customer and supplier.

This example shows an aspect of the changing role understanding of customer and supplier. The new relationship is characterized by an information asymmetry, a reversed knowledge advantage. With the help of digital information, acquisition, and processing (Big Data and Data Analytics), providers are able to gain profound insights into the latent needs and desires of their consumers in order to formulate offers that the consumer would not even have come up with herself.

Amazon provides a great service for the customers with its suggestion system. They do not send the product unsolicited, but they know preferences of their Prime customers through prior purchases and searches. Etsy has a similar approach but, in addition, builds on the entrepreneurial spirit of its sellers' community. Together, they create an artisan marketing hype on international scale. Spotify started in a similar fashion by giving unknown artists a platform for publicizing their songs. Today, Spotify has replaced radio stations for listeners who prefer to create their own music experience.

The consumer also profits from the increasing interconnectedness and transparency becoming an informed and empowered counterpart. The role of the customer changes as he is actively getting involved in the production process, making her a *prosumer*, a consumer, and producer at the same time, co-creating value with the firm. The consumer can take the role of a producer in many ways. She can support manufacturers in the innovation process by generating ideas, testing concepts and prototypes for them, and engaging as a lead user during the market launch (called *open innovation*). Alternatively, she can configure the final product according to her wishes (called *mass customization*).[153]

Both presented ways are considered *upstream participation*– collaborative activities before finishing the production process, where the consumer takes the role of a co-creator, while the firm is the main creative force to build a value proposition. In *downstream participation*, this role assignment gets turned around. The consumer takes the creator role, and the firm has only a supporting, co-creating function. In this case, customers take it upon themselves to make a product known and recommended; the value is defined and created during the use of the product by the clients, while the firm would actively participate in the benefits.

Apart from his interest in co-creation, the connected customer engages in open communication about the brand, commenting and reviewing the product, and often times turns into outspoken advocate or opponent of the brands.[154] Further, he can engage in self-service activities by taking over

---

[153] Heinemann, G., & Gaiser, C. W. (2016). *op. cit.*
[154] Kotler, P., Kartajaya, H., & Setiawan, I. (2017). *op. cit.*

operational tasks that traditionally lie in the company's domain: "Some pro-sumers will […] help other users with technical service issues of a particular product. These individuals can be very useful sources of product development ideas or can be incentivized as a low-cost provider of technical service to other consumers."[155]

Companies, on the other hand, can lose control over the formation of the public image about themselves and their performance. The new understand-ing of the customer's role means that companies will have to accept a customer-driven relationship rather than being able to control the relationship with the customer themselves. Due to these developments, loyal brand advocates that publicly praise and defend a brand become crucial for its public image (more on brand advocacy as effective tool to deal with the democratization of brands in Chap. 4).[156]

This leaves marketing with clear implications: co-creation of value is desir-able both for the company and the customer and should be enabled. A co-creation culture is needed as a differentiation factor in comparison to the competition and to foster the brand image, on which the customers exercise increasingly more control. Handing over control to the customer might seem like a frightening concept for companies, but marketing needs to find a way to use it in a positive way for strengthening customer engagement.

2.4.5   Digitalization for a Better Marketing

The core message to marketing for digital transformation is that it must not be corrupted by short-run corporate goals and should avoid getting reduced solely to the communication function. At the same time, marketing must acquire digital skills in order to not lose touch with better-educated customers (*Homo digitalis, prosumers*) and fall behind other departments in its own com-pany when it comes to digital competences.

Marketers need to understand the dynamics of the new connected custom-ers and firms and that "[c]onnectivity changes the key foundation of market-ing: the market itself."[157] In business, reality marketing has a key role in digital transformation, as it is mostly the CMO and his department who are entrusted with central responsibility for digitalization affairs. The question is, if it can live up to the expectations. Despite all digitalization advances, the human fac-tor must remain at the center of marketing's agenda. Apart from all the

---

[155] Ernst & Young (2011). *op. cit.*
[156] Kotler, P., Kartajaya, H., & Setiawan, I. (2017). *op. cit.*
[157] Kotler, P., Kartajaya, H., & Setiawan, I. (2017). *op. cit.*

euphoria about what can be digitalized, companies must not forget for what, for whom and why they do what they do. Only then can digitalization be used meaningfully for the benefit of people.[158]

In spring of 2020, triggered by the corona crisis, large online retailers like Amazon, Alibaba, MercadoLibre, and Flipkart expanded their market shares enormously. Out of the $4 trillion worldwide sales, they garnered for them more than 50% share. Traditional retailers tried to combine physical sales with online offerings to stay relevant. Specialists like Etsy, Glamour, Firebox, Indochino, BikesDirect, etc. offered specific product range and tried to increase their customers' interactions. Also in smaller countries like Australia, Vietnam, etc., online sales finally became part of the regular life.

Storyline

After the "Call for Adventure" in Chap. 1, we started our "Great Journey" in the present chapter. The first milestone in this journey has been the presentation of the H2H Marketing Model with two layers, related by a cause-effect correlation. The first layer consists out of the three influencing concepts. Influencing, because of their effect on marketing in general. The three remarkable parts of our Great Journey are Design Thinking as mindset, iterative and agile innovation process, and toolbox with tools that help companies to lift their problem understanding and their creativity to solve problems on a higher level. Design and marketing are going hand in hand with engineering when it comes to meaningful innovations. During this part of the journey, we discovered the core competencies needed to bring marketing back to the "front end of innovation," With the S-DL, we reached another milestone. The 11 fundamental premises represent the starting point. During the course of this stage, we discovered that S-DL has the substance to take over the role of a "grand theory" for future marketing thanks to its ability to integrate different and sometimes atomic trends and developments in marketing over the last decades. The remarkable takeouts of S-DL for H2H Marketing consist, out of a fundamental shift in the viewpoint of value creation with a tremendous change of the roles of customers and suppliers, the ever-increasing importance of networks or ecosystems and the shift from goods to services to service as the main basis of exchange. This stage ended with the presentation of observable transitions from G-DL to S-DL. We then spotted digitalization as the third and final influencing concept to H2H Marketing. We explained the term digitalization briefly in order to understand that it is more than an enabler for

---

[158] King, K. A. (2015). The Complete Guide to B2B Marketing: New Tactics, Tools, and Techniques to Compete in the Digital Economy. Upper Saddle River, NJ: Pearson Education.

using new communication channels. As the other two influencers (DT and S-DL), it affects the mindset needed in marketing to understand the importance of the ongoing digital transformation on the core: the market itself. Digitalization leads to individualization and dematerialization of the value proposition. It affects the customer behavior and mindset (SoLoMo) and requires new capabilities in marketing to handle the changing relationship to the customers as prosumer. Here, the discovery of the first level of the H2H Marketing Model ends, and we will step into the second level in the next chapter.

Questions

1. What are the three influencing factors or concepts of the H2H Marketing Model? What is the role of each of these three within the model?
2. What are the three components of H2H Marketing in the Model? Please explain them briefly. How are they interconnected?
3. What is the difference between H2H Process and the traditional marketing mix?
4. What is the so-called trifecta of innovation proposed by IDEO? What is the meaning for marketing?
5. What are the core competencies of marketing?
6. What are the major effects of the ongoing digitalization on H2H Marketing?
7. What are the consequences of increasing customer-to-customer interactions enabled by the digitalization to H2H Marketing?
8. What is a prosumer and how does the term deal with co-creation of value?
9. Why is engagement a key performance indicator for many companies when you analyze the relationship between customers and suppliers?

References

Achrol, R. S., & Kotler, P. (1999). Marketing in the network economy. *Journal of Marketing, 63*, 146–163. https://doi.org/10.2307/1252108.

Ahrendts, A. (2013). Burberry's CEO on turning an aging British Icon into a Global Luxury Brand. *Harvard Business Review*. Retrieved from https://hbr.org/2013/01/burberrys-ceo-on-turning-an-aging-british-icon-into-a-global-luxury-brand

Backhaus, K., & Paulsen, T. (2018). Vom Homo Oeconomicus zum Homo Digitalis – Die Veränderung der Informationsasymmetrien durch die Digitalisierung. In M. Bruhn & M. Kirchgeorg (Eds.), *Marketing Weiterdenken: Zukunftspfade für eine marktorientierte Unternehmensführung* (pp. 105–122). Wiesbaden: Springer Gabler.

Blatt, M., & Sauvonnet, E. (Eds.). (2017). *Wo ist das Problem?: Mit Design Thinking Innovationen entwickeln und umsetzen* (2nd ed.). München: Franz Vahlen.

Brown, T. (2008). Design thinking. *Harvard Business Review, 86*(6), 84–92. Retrieved from https://hbr.org/2008/06/design-thinking

Carlgren, L., Rauth, I., & Elmquist, M. (2016). Framing design thinking: The concept in idea and enactment. *Creativity and Innovation Management, 25*(1), 38–57. https://doi.org/10.1111/caim.12153.

Constantin, J. A., & Lusch, R. F. (1994). *Understanding resource management.* Oxford, OH: Planning Forum.

Deloitte. (2015). *Industry 4.0: Challenges and solutions for the digital transformation and use of exponential technologies* [Report]. Retrieved from https://www2.deloitte.com/tw/en/pages/manufacturing/articles/industry4-0.html

Elsbach, K. D., & Stigliani, I. (2018). Design thinking and organizational culture: A review and framework for future research. *Journal of Management, 44*(6), 2274–2306. https://doi.org/10.1177/0149206317744252.

Ernst & Young. (2011). *The digitisation of everything: How organisations must adapt to changing consumer behaviour* [Report]. Retrieved from https://www.ey.com/Publication/vwLUAssets/The_digitisation_of_everything_-_How_organisations_must_adapt_to_changing_consumer_behaviour/%24file/EY_Digitisation_of_everything.pdf

First Round Review. (2019). How design thinking transformed Airbnb from a failing startup to a billion dollar business. *First Round Review.* Retrieved from https://firstround.com/review/How-design-thinking-transformed-Airbnb-from-failing-startup-to-billion-dollar-business/

Frey, A., Trenz, M., & Veit, D. (2017). *The role of technology for service innovation in sharing economy organizations – A service-dominant logic perspective.* In Proceedings of the 25th European Conference on Information Systems (ECIS), Guimarães, Portugal, June 5–10, 2017, pp. 1885–1901. Retrieved from https://aisel.aisnet.org/cgi/viewcontent.cgi?article=1120&context=ecis2017_rp

Gassmann, O., & Schweitzer, F. (2014). Managing the unmanageable: The fuzzy front end of innovation. In O. Gassmann & F. Schweitzer (Eds.), *Management of the fuzzy front end of innovation* (pp. 3–14). Cham: Springer.

Gehrckens, M., & Boersma, T. (2013). Zukunftsvision Retail – Hat der Handel eine Daseinsberechtigung? In G. Heinemann, K. Haug, M. Gehrckens, & dgroup (Eds.), *Digitalisierung des Handels mit ePace: Innovative E-commerce-Geschäftsmodelle unter Timing-Aspekten* (pp. 51–76). Springer Gabler: Wiesbaden.

Gobble, M. M. (2014). Design thinking. *Research Technology Management, 57*(3), 59–61. https://doi.org/10.5437/08956308X5703005.

Grots, A., & Pratschke, M. (2009). Design thinking – Kreativität als Methode. *Marketing Review St. Gallen, 26*(2), 18–23. https://doi.org/10.1007/s11621-009-0027-4.

Gummesson, E. (1995). Relationship marketing: Its role in the service economy. In W. J. Glynn & J. G. Barnes (Eds.), *Understanding services management* (pp. 244–268). New York, NY: Wiley.

Haeckel, S. H. (1999). *Adaptive enterprise: Creating and leading sense-and-respond organizations*. Boston, MA: Harvard Business Press.

Hasso Plattner Institute of Design. (2019). *An introduction to design thinking: Process guide*. Retrieved from https://dschool-old.stanford.edu/sandbox/groups/designresources/wiki/36873/attachments/74b3d/ModeGuideBOOTCAMP2010L.pdf

Hasso-Plattner-Institut. (2019). *Die design thinking-Regeln*. Retrieved from https://hpi.de/school-of-design-thinking/design-thinking/hintergrund/design-thinking-prinzipien.html

Heinemann, G. (2014). *SoLoMo – Always-on im Handel: Die soziale, lokale und mobile Zukunft des Shopping*. Wiesbaden: Springer Gabler.

Heinemann, G., & Gaiser, C. W. (2016). *SoLoMo – Always-on im Handel: Die soziale, lokale und mobile Zukunft des Omnichannel-Shopping* (3rd ed.). Wiesbaden: Springer Gabler.

IDEO. (2019). *How to prototype a new business* [Blog post]. Retrieved from https://www.ideou.com/blogs/inspiration/how-to-prototype-a-new-business

Johansson-Sköldberg, U., Woodilla, J., & Çetinkaya, M. (2013). Design thinking: Past, present and possible futures. *Creativity and Innovation Management, 22*(2), 121–146. https://doi.org/10.1111/caim.12023.

Kagermann, H., Wahlster, W., & Helbig, J. (2013). *Deutschlands Zukunft als Produktionsstandort sichern: Umsetzungsempfehlungen für das Zukunftsprojekt Industrie 4.0* [Report]. Retrieved from https://www.bmbf.de/files/Umsetzungsempfehlungen_Industrie4_0.pdf

King, K. A. (2015). *The complete guide to B2B marketing: New tactics, tools, and techniques to compete in the digital economy*. Upper Saddle River, NJ: Pearson Education.

Kotler, P., Kartajaya, H., & Setiawan, I. (2017). *Marketing 4.0: Moving from traditional to digital*. Hoboken, NJ: Wiley.

Kowalkowski, C. (2010). What does a service-dominant logic really mean for manufacturing firms? *CIRP Journal of Manufacturing Science and Technology, 3*(4), 285–292. https://doi.org/10.1016/j.cirpj.2011.01.003.

Kozinets, R. V. (2015). *Netnography: Redefined*. Los Angeles, CA: Sage.

Kreutzer, R. T., & Land, K.-H. (2016). *Digitaler Darwinismus: Der stille Angriff auf Ihr Geschäftsmodell und Ihre Marke* (2nd ed.). Wiesbaden: Springer Gabler.

Land, K.-H. (2018). Dematerialisierung: Die Neuverteilung der Welt in Zeiten der Digitalen Transformation und die Folgen für die Arbeitswelt. In C. Brüssel & V. Kronenberg (Eds.), *Von der sozialen zur ökosozialen Marktwirtschaft* (pp. 153–166). Wiesbaden: Springer.

LaValle, S., Lesser, E., Shockley, R., Hopkins, M. S., & Kruschwitz, N. (2011). Big data, analytics and the path from insights to value. *MIT Sloan Management Review, 52*(2), 21–32. Retrieved from https://sloanreview.mit.edu/article/big-data-analytics-and-the-path-from-insights-to-value/

Liedtka, J. (2018). Why design thinking works. *Harvard Business Review, 96*(5), 72–79. Retrieved from https://hbr.org/2018/09/why-design-thinking-works

Lies, J. (2017). *Die Digitalisierung der Kommunikation im Mittelstand: Auswirkungen von Marketing 4.0*. Wiesbaden: Springer Gabler.

Lindberg, T., Meinel, C., & Wagner, R. (2011). Design thinking: A fruitful concept for IT development? In H. Plattner, C. Meinel, & L. Leifer (Eds.), *Design thinking: Understand – improve – apply* (pp. 3–18). Berlin: Springer.

Linden, E., & Wittmer, A. (2018). *Zukunft Mobilität: Gigatrend Digitalisierung* [Monograph]. Retrieved from https://www.alexandria.unisg.ch/253291/

Lusch, R. F., & Vargo, S. L. (2014). *Service-dominant logic: Premises, perspectives, possibilities*. Cambridge: Cambridge University Press.

McKinsey & Company. (2018). *Microsoft's next act* [Podcast]. Retrieved from https://www.mckinsey.com/industries/technology-media-and-telecommunications/our-insights/microsofts-next-act

Mower, S. (2017). How Christopher Bailey transformed burberry and redefined brand revivals in the 21st century. *Vogue*. Retrieved from https://www.vogue.com/article/burberry-christopher-bailey-legacy

Naisbitt, J. (2015). Der Horizont reicht meist nur bis zum nächsten Wahltag. In Bundeszentrale für politische Bildung (Ed.), Megatrends?. *Aus Politik und Zeitgeschichte, 65*(31–32), 3–6. Retrieved from https://www.bpb.de/apuz/209953/der-horizont-reicht-meist-nur-bis-zum-naechsten-wahltag

Nemko, M. (2017). *Marketing is evil: Marketers use many psychological ploys to make you buy what you shouldn't* [Blog post]. Retrieved from https://www.psychologytoday.com/us/blog/how-do-life/201701/marketing-is-evil

North, D. C. (1990). *Institutions, institutional change, and economic performance: Political economy of institutions and decisions*. Cambridge: Cambridge University Press.

Orton, K. (2017, March 28). *Desirability, feasibility, viability: The sweet spot for innovation* [Blog post]. Retrieved from https://medium.com/innovation-sweet-spot/desirability-feasibility-viability-the-sweet-spot-for-innovation-d7946de2183c

Pfeiffer, S. (2015). Industrie 4.0 und die Digitalisierung der Produktion – Hype oder Megatrend? In Bundeszentrale für politische Bildung (Ed.), *Megatrends?. Aus Politik und Zeitgeschichte, 65*(31–32), pp. 6–12. Retrieved from https://www.bpb.de/apuz/209955/industrie-4-0-und-die-digitalisierung-der-produktion

Pfoertsch, W. A., & Sponholz, U. (2019). *Das neue marketing-mindset: Management, Methoden und Prozesse für ein Marketing von Mensch zu Mensch*. Wiesbaden: Springer Gabler.

Pierre Audoin Consultants. (2015). *Holistic customer experience in the digital age: A trend study for Germany, France and the UK* [Whitepaper]. Retrieved from https://www.pac-online.com/holistic-customer-experience-digital-age

Prahalad, C. K., & Ramaswamy, V. (2000). Co-opting customer competence. *Harvard Business Review, 78*(1), 79–87. Retrieved from https://hbr.org/2000/01/co-opting-customer-competence

Precht, R. D. (2018). *Jäger, Hirten, Kritiker: Eine Utopie für die digitale Gesellschaft* (6th ed.). München: Goldmann.

Reinartz, W. (2018). Kundenansprache in Zeiten digitaler transformation. In M. Bruhn & M. Kirchgeorg (Eds.), *Marketing Weiterdenken: Zukunftspfade für eine marktorientierte Unternehmensführung* (pp. 123–138). Wiesbaden: Springer Gabler.

Reutemann, B. (2017). *Service design: Der Turbo für Ihr Business* [Presentation]. Retrieved from https://bernd-reutemann.de/wp-content/uploads/2017/02/Servicedesign.pdf

Robinson, P. K., & Hsieh, L. (2016). Reshoring: A strategic renewal of luxury clothing supply chains. *Operations Management Research, 9*, 89–101. https://doi.org/10.1007/s12063-016-0116-x.

Ross, J. W., Beath, C. M., & Mocker, M. (2019). *Designed for digital: How to architect your business for sustained success (Management on the Cutting Edge)*. MIT Press.

Saam, M., Viete, S., & Schiel, S. (2016). *Digitalisierung im Mittelstand: Status Quo, aktuelle Entwicklungen und Herausforderungen* [Research project]. Retrieved from https://www.kfw.de/PDF/Download-Center/Konzernthemen/Research/PDF-Dokumente-Studien-und-Materialien/Digitalisierung-im-Mittelstand.pdf

Schlick, J., Stephan, P., & Zühlke, D. (2012). Produktion 2020: Auf dem Weg zur 4. industriellen revolution. *IM: Die Fachzeitschrift für information management und consulting, 27*(3), 26–34. Retrieved from https://www.econbiz.de/Record/im-schwerpunkt-industrie-4-0-produktion-2020-auf-dem-weg-zur-4-industriellen-revolution-schlick-jochen/10010019258

Schlotmann, R. (2018). *Digitalisierung auf mittelständisch: Die Methode "Digitales Wirkungsmanagement"*. Berlin: Springer.

Scott, W. R. (2008). *Institutions and organizations: Ideas and interests*. Los Angeles, CA: Sage.

See Edman, K. W. (2009). *Exploring overlaps and differences in service dominant logic and design thinking*. In her contribution to the First Nordic Conference on Service Design and Service Innovation she compared DT and S-DL and demonstrated the overlap. Available under http://www.ep.liu.se/ecp/059/016/ecp09059016.pdf

Sheth, J. N., & Parvatiyar, A. (2000). The evolution of relationship marketing. In J. N. Sheth & A. Parvatiyar (Eds.), *Handbook of relationship marketing* (pp. 119–148). Thousand Oaks, CA: Sage.

Sinek, S. (2009). *Start with why: How great leaders inspire everyone to take action*. New York: Penguin.

Sisodia, R. S., Sheth, J. N., & Wolfe, D. (2014). *Firms of endearment: How world-class companies profit from passion and purpose* (2nd ed.). Upper Saddle River, NJ: Pearson Education.

Teknowlogy. (2020). *IoT C&SI Survey 2020* [Study report]. Retrieved from https://75572d19-371f-4ade-aeb6-61dbca89834b.filesusr.com/ugd/f21868_2f8ab8213a00460f8777de2057430fb0.pdf

Vargo, S. L., & Lusch, R. F. (2004). Evolving to a new dominant logic for marketing. *Journal of Marketing, 68*(1), 1–17. https://doi.org/10.1509/jmkg.68.1.1.24036.

Vargo, S. L., & Lusch, R. F. (2008). Service-dominant logic: Continuing the evolution. *Journal of the Academy of Marketing Science, 36*(1), 1–10. https://doi.org/10.1007/s11747-007-0069-6.

Vargo, S. L., & Lusch, R. F. (2016). Institutions and axioms: An extension and update of service-dominant logic. *Journal of the Academy of Marketing Science, 44*(1), 5–23. https://doi.org/10.1007/s11747-015-0456-3.

Vargo, S. L., & Lusch, R. F. (2017). Service-dominant logic 2025. *International Journal of Research in Marketing, 34*(1), 46–67. https://doi.org/10.1016/j.ijresmar.2016.11.001.

Verganti, R. (2009). *Design-driven innovation: Changing the rules of competition by radically innovating what things mean.* Boston, MA: Harvard Business Press.

Wilken, R., & Jacob, F. (2015). Vom Produkt- zum Lösungsanbieter. In K. Backhaus & M. Voeth (Eds.), *Handbuch Business-to-Business-Marketing: Grundlagen, Geschäftsmodelle, Instrumente des Industriegütermarketing* (2nd ed., pp. 147–164). Wiesbaden: Springer Gabler.

Wolf, T., & Strohschen, J.-H. (2018). Digitalisierung: Definition und Reife – Quantitative Bewertung der digitalen Reife. *Informatik Spektrum, 41*(1), 56–64. https://doi.org/10.1007/s00287-017-1084-8.

3

H2H Mindset: The Basis

Should not marketing be *for* the people and *not against* them? Every marketer can make a conscious choice to work for a better world or its own benefit. Promotion of a Human-to-Human (H2H) Marketing means that we have a basis for understanding the human to be the center and not as the means to a goal. The H2H Marketing Model that we reference to represents the effects and implications that the factors Design Thinking, Service-Dominant Logic, and digitalization can have on marketing if they are directed to solve human issues. A handful of companies like Airbnb, Bristol-Meyer Squibb, Cigna, Microsoft, Patagonia, Salesforce, Telenor, and Whole Foods Market have implemented the new approach already, and others have started working on it. Some countries and regions are also applying aspects of it, such as the Digital Village initiative of India's Prime Minister Modi, or the CoLab Digital Region supported by the Bertelsmann Foundation.

The basis of H2H Marketing is the H2H Mindset. It is the first requisite, has normative character, and defines the grounding of the new concept. It is a fundamental requirement for the second component of strategic side (H2H Management) and the third component with its operational side (H2H Process) for eventual success. This mindset should not only be shared by employees of marketing departments and other executives; it should be anchored deep inside the organization; we will first have a look at the term *mindset* itself and then examine an already existing marketing mindset found in market and customer orientation. H2H Marketing sees marketing itself as a mindset.

Looking for a proper definition of "mindset," two characteristics appear to be evident: firstly, a filter function determining how we perceive the world

© The Author(s), under exclusive license to Springer Nature Switzerland AG 2021
P. Kotler et al., *H2H Marketing*, https://doi.org/10.1007/978-3-030-59531-9_3

around us and what we expect from ourselves and others. Secondly, a behavior control function influencing the behavior towards others and ourselves[1] based on the perception of the world resulting from the filter function.[2] The business coach Svenja Hofert proposes a definition, which combines both functions and will serve as a definition in the H2H Marketing approach. She states:

> The mindset is a person's changing logic of thought that triggers [her] actions or non-actions and is co-determined by [her] environment. It is the attitude of the mind that leads to something being (not) perceived, seen, heard, understood, felt, analyzed, interpreted, communicated in a certain way—and from this non-action being derived.[3]

The definition displays that a mindset is modifiable, not necessarily static but rather shapeable. Stanford professor Carol Dweck, in this context, presented the distinction between *fixed mindset* and *growth mindset*.[4] She describes that a fixed mindset is found in "people who view talent as a quality they either possess or lack," while someone with a growth mindset "enjoy[s] challenges, strive[s] to learn, and consistently see[s] potential to develop new skills."[5] With this distinction, she makes clear that people can change their mindset if they are willing to do so and that it is advantageous for companies to have employees with a growth mindset. Hofert, in this context, speaks of an *agile mindset*. Important to mention is that the idea of an absolute growth mindset is not realistic; it is a common misconception Dweck rectifies by pointing towards the mixed nature of the mindset, always consisting of a fixed share and a growth share, only differing in the proportional distribution of both. The individual mindset depends on the context and in a business context. This implies that a company with its normative management can affect the mindset of its employees.

This concept of the growth mindset, together with Hofert's definition is taken as the basis for the mindset understanding of H2H Marketing. Mindset, thus, is understood as thinking and acting logic that determines how

---

[1] See e.g. Brooks, R., & Goldstein, S. (2008). The Mindset of Teachers Capable of Fostering Resilience in Students. Canadian Journal of School Psychology, 23(1), pp. 114–126. https://doi.org/10.1177/0829573508316597

[2] Schulz, M. (2011). New Mindsets for Service-Orientated Marketing: Understanding the Role of Emotions in Interpersonal Relationships [Doctoral thesis]. Retrieved from https://ourarchive.otago.ac.nz/handle/10523/1928

[3] Hofert, S. (2018). Das agile Mindset: Mitarbeiter entwickeln, Zukunft der Arbeit gestalten, p. 8. Wiesbaden, Germany: Springer Gabler. Translated from German to English.

[4] Dweck, C. S. (2006). Mindset: The new psychology of success. New York, NY: Random House.

[5] How Companies Can Profit from a "Growth Mindset", Para. 1. (2014). Harvard Business Review. Retrieved from https://hbr.org/2014/11/how-companies-can-profit-from-a-growth-mindset

individuals or people as a collective in organizations perceive the world and which actions they derive from their perception. The mindset can be changed under the condition that people or organizations have the willingness for constant self-reflection and allow its resulting changes to take place. If a mindset is anchored in the organizational and cultural basis of a company, it can usually be observed in artifacts, visible products of the thinking and action logic. The mindset of organizations should be managed by exemplifying and implementing it with integrity and consistent actions.

3.1 Market Orientation as Traditional Marketing Mindset

With companies already having established customer and market orientation, a mindset for marketing has been established.[6] When hearing the term *marketing thinking*, a common association is "putting the customer first." While customer orientation focuses strictly on the customer, market orientation adds the perspective of the firm and its competitors. Market-oriented perspective stands in contrast to resource orientation, the importance of which can be shown with the concept of *core competencies*, a concept that is central not only to resource but also to market-oriented corporate management and showcases that there is not necessarily a contradiction between the two views. The difference lies only in the direction it is viewed from. The *Resource-Based View* (RBV first looks for strategically relevant competencies inside the firm and then checks whether these competencies can be turned into customer value. The *Market-Based View* (MBV) on the other hand defines the needed competencies from the perspective of the market and, from this, derives consequences for the company. In conclusion, in the MBV, the market defines how a strategically superior position *should* be reached, while in the RBV, the own resources determine how this position *can* be reached.[7]

An interesting approach to this issue can be found in the work of Matzler, Stahl, and Hinterhuber, who propose an integrative model called the

---

[6] Kumar, V., Jones, E., Venkatesan, R., Leone, R. P. (2011). Is Market Orientation a Source of Sustainable Competitive Advantage or Simply the Cost of Competing? Journal of Marketing, 75(1), pp. 16–30. Retrieved from https://www.researchgate.net

[7] Nolte, H. (1998). Aspekte ressourcenorientierter Unternehmensführung. In H. Nolte (Ed.), Aspekte ressourcenorientierter Unternehmensführung (pp. III-VIII). München, Germany: Rainer Hampp. Retrieved from http://hdl.handle.net/10419/116857

Customer-Based View (CBV), adding the *Value-Based View* (VBV), in an attempt to combine the three perspectives.[8]

The VBV gives priority to the interests of the equity investors and customers– maximizing the value of the company and the customers become key objectives for corporate management. The model of Matzler et al. is based on the assumptions that the company value is a function of customer satisfaction and that the ability to create customer value is determined by the resources a company is equipped with and the efficiency with which it uses them. The core competencies that are necessary for this can only be financed if the shareholders are willing to do so due to the development, i.e., positive development of the company value, thus integrating the VBV. The causal relationships between the three perspectives are shown in Fig. 3.1.[9]

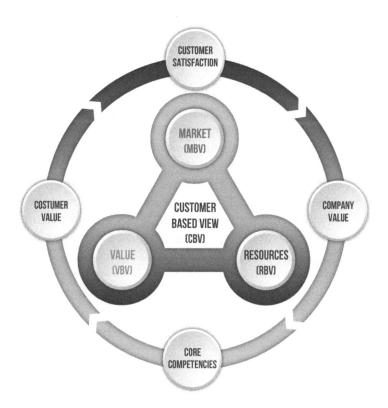

Fig. 3.1 The integrative model of the customer-based view

[8] Matzler, K., Stahl, H. K., & Hinterhuber, H. H. (2009). Die Customer-based View der Unternehmung. In H. H. Hinterhuber, & K. Matzler (Eds.), Kundenorientierte Unternehmensführung: Kundenorientierung- Kundenzufriedenheit - Kundenbindung (6th ed., pp. 4–31). Wiesbaden, Germany: Gabler.

[9] Adapted from Matzler, K., Stahl, H. K., & Hinterhuber, H. H. (2009). *op. cit.*, p. 7.

The integration of value and the idea that customer value depends on the application of core competencies fits perfectly into the S-DL used in H2H Marketing. The concept should not be confused with the shareholder value model. It postulates that superior shareholder value only can be realized based on customer satisfaction and that the shareholder value has to be invested partly into the development of core competencies in order to co-create customer value.

An example of the CBV model could be a company decides to increase the development of new knowledge and skills. The resulting new knowledge and skills enable the firm to provide superior customer value resulting in competitive advantage. Optimally, this competitive advantage is then transformed into above-average return on capital, which then would attract and provide enough financial resources for the exploitation of new opportunities and development of new skills and knowledge.[10]

Duerr Group, one of the world's leading mechanical and plant engineering firms, implements and mastered the CBV, even though it could be not aware of the existence of this concept. Megtec and Universal were founded in the USA and had similar structure in terms of the company's size and revenues to Duerr, were merged into Duerr Group, and follow the same principles initiatively. Duerr is providing its customers outstanding knowledge and skills. This led to superior market position and is strongly correlated to better customer value proposition. Consequently, Duerr provided its stockholder great returns, and its stakeholder benefited from the core competencies and the business attitude.

Consequently, the CBV not only ties together two opposing views, but it also shows a possible way of how the influence of customer orientation on the company value can be operationalized and thus measured via the customer satisfaction as an indicator:

> In the customer-based view [...], resources and specific skills are sources of economic rents when they lead to unique and valuable offers that are recognizable to customers. [...] Enterprises must be able to [...] develop competencies and skills in a company-wide learning process in order to create higher value for the customer than their competitors.[11]

While the MBV prioritizes the market and the RBV puts emphasis on the firm and its resources, the CBV integrates those differing perspectives in an

---

[10] Matzler, K., Stahl, H. K., & Hinterhuber, H. H. (2009). *op. cit.*
[11] Matzler, K., Stahl, H. K., & Hinterhuber, H. H. (2009). *op. cit.*, p. 27.

innovative way. While it integrates the views on a conceptual level, it needs clear instructions for how the relationship between the different stakeholders should be managed. For this purpose, the SPICE Stakeholder Model introduced by Sisodia et al.[12] in their book *Firms of Endearment* can serve as guidance. In this model, all stakeholder groups are interdependent. There is not only a bond between the firm and its stakeholders; the stakeholders are among themselves connected (see Fig. 3.2[13]).

Sisodia et al.[14] see the successful alignment of the interests of all parties as the ultimate goal for a sustainable, endearing business.

A brilliant example of the understanding of the interconnectedness of stakeholder relationships is the Declaration of Interdependence by Whole Foods Market. Businesses like Whole Foods Market understand that with interdependent stakeholder groups, sustainable success is only possible through collaborative efforts, which helps their partner grow and creates a competitive advantage. This guiding principle of creating value together as a team rather than at the expense of each other corroborates the idea of the CBV, and together they represent the foundation for the understanding that underlies the H2H Mindset.

Fig. 3.2 The SPICE stakeholder model

[12] Sisodia, R. S., Sheth, J. N., & Wolfe, D. (2014). *op. cit.*
[13] Adapted from Sisodia et al. (2014). *op. cit.* With quotation marks indicated direct quotes are taken from the respective chapters that they are attributed to in the Figure.
[14] Sisodia, R. S., Sheth, J. N., & Wolfe, D. (2014). *op. cit.*

This approach is also consistent with the Service-Dominant Logic. Although the S-DL would argue that the firms alone cannot create value for the customer, its FP4 stating that "operant resources are the fundamental source of strategic benefit"[15] is in congruence with the statement of Matzler stressing the importance of development of knowledge and skills for obtaining and maintaining competitive advantage[16] (for excerpts of the declaration, see Fig. 3.3[17]).

One of the facilitating companies for the development of Customer-Based View (CBV) application is HubSpot from Boston. HubSpot is a developer and marketer of software products for inbound marketing, sales, and customer service. Marketing, sales, and service software can help companies grow because "good for business" should also mean "good for the customer." They offer a marketing hub, which grows traffic, convert leads, and proves ROI with all-in-one marketing software and provides all the tools necessary to run complete inbound marking campaigns. They also have a Sales Hub for every part of the sales process, which includes a full suite of sales tools for the team to shorten deal cycles and increase close rates. In addition, they offer a Service Hub and customer relations service management, which turn happy customers into growth. They helped companies like the video stream application Zoom, VooV, and DingTalk to flourish. Similar software solutions are provided by Google, which applied them in various companies. FitBit, the health-tracking solution is one of them.

Industrial markets see similar developments. SKF from Sweden is a great case for a company on the way to becoming a solution provider. At the end of the 1990s, there were three major competitors in Europe, SKF, INA, and FAG in the rolling bearing market. At that time, SKF was a pioneer in industrial business, set to become a solution provider for the operators of stored machines and systems. The company has consistently become more reliable as the solution partner to industry on all questions rotation developed. Sune Karlsson as CEO in the late 1990s bestowed on the service sector a strong and sustainable growth spurt, which was supported by several significant acquisitions of service companies. SKF industrial services is expanding today to a far greater extent than other industrial companies and receives from the senior management the necessary strategic and operational support.[18]

---

[15] Vargo, S. L., & Lusch, R. F. (2016). *op. cit.*, p. 8.

[16] Matzler, K., Stahl, H. K., & Hinterhuber, H. H. (2009). *op. cit.*

[17] Excerpts are taken from the Whole Foods Market Website. Retrieved from https://www.wholefoods-market.com/mission-values/core-values/declaration-interdependence

[18] See Pfoertsch, W. A., & Sponholz, U. (2019). *op. cit.*

Whole Foods Market
Declaration of Interdependence
Our Purpose is to Nourish People and the Planet

Whole Foods Market is a dynamic leader in the quality food business. We are a purpose-driven company that aims to set the standards of excellence for food retailers. We are building a business in which high standards permeate all aspects of our company. Quality is a state of mind at Whole Foods Market. We recognize the interdependence among our stakeholders - those who benefit from or are impacted by our company. Our success is optimized by a win-win strategy, and all of our stakeholders are simultaneously benefitting.

[...]

We Satisfy and Delight Our Customers

Our customers are the lifeblood of our business and our most important stakeholder. We strive to meet or exceed their expectations on every shopping experience. We deliver outstanding customer service through our knowledge, skill, enthusiasm and operational excellence. We continually experiment and innovate to offer a better customer experience. We create store environments that are inviting, fun, unique, comfortable, attractive, nurturing and educational. Our stores are community meeting places where people can join their friends and make new ones.

[...]

We Practice Win-Win Partnerships With Our Suppliers

We are part of an interdependent business ecosystem. There are tens of thousands of suppliers that we depend on to create an outstanding retail shopping experience for our customers. We view our trade partners as allies in serving our stakeholders. We treat them with respect, fairness and integrity - expecting the same in return. We listen compassionately, we think carefully and we always seek win-win relationships with everyone engaged in our business.

[...]

We Care About Our Communities and the Environment

We serve and support a local experience. The unique character of each store is a direct reflection of a community's people, culture and cuisine. We celebrate and strengthen each community through employment, investment in local non-profits and a conscious commitment to our local producers. We leverage our foundations to broaden our community impact. We champion nutritional education for children, food access in underserved areas and microcredit for the poorest of the poor. We practice and advance environmental stewardship. We balance our needs with the needs of the rest of the planet so that the Earth will continue to flourish for generations to come. Our industry-leading quality standards support sustainable agriculture, animal welfare and ocean preservation. We are committed to reduced packaging, composting and water and energy conservation.

[...]

Fig. 3.3 Excerpts of the declaration of interdependence by whole foods market

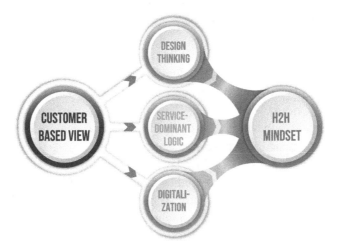

Fig. 3.4 The development process of the H2H mindset

Thinking about market orientation as an already existing mindset, one may ask why there would be a need for a new mindset. The answer is found in the influencing factors of the H2H Marketing Model: the H2H Mindset is the product of an already existing mindset in the shape of market orientation integrated into the CBV, adapted to the new developments of Design Thinking, the S-DL, and digitalization (see Fig. 3.4).

This "modernization" (as shown in Fig. 3.4) of the mindset has its starting point in the integrated model of the CBV and the stakeholder view expansion of the SPICE model, which is then amplified by taking into account the three influencing factors of the H2H Marketing Model and the imperative for changes in the mindset that they imply.

3.2 The H2H Mindset Explained

3.2.1 Human-Centeredness

Customer orientation is a cornerstone of traditional marketing. The Customer-Based View (CBV) goes one step further. In the model of the CBV, customer satisfaction receives significant attention as it is considered the prerequisite for increases in company value.[19] Another point is that economic actors are interdependent, which is repeatedly expressed in the works of Vargo and Lusch on

---

[19] Matzler, K., Stahl, H. K., & Hinterhuber, H. H. (2009). *op. cit.*

the S-DL through *co-creation of value* or *reciprocal service-for-service exchange*.[20, 21, 22]

In the H2H orientation of H2H Marketing, customers are not seen as abstract elements but are rather taken for what they are– human beings.[23] Human beings make the decisions with all their rational and irrational behavior, emotions, needs, and wishes. This makes it necessary to put oneself in their position and inevitably think inside a human-centered frame. People must not be degraded to a passive role as recipients.

Human-centeredness in H2H Marketing is quintessential to the whole approach. Design Thinking and the H2H Process have their starting points in a *human* problem (*H2H problems*). A person with the H2H Mindset has internalized that his actions and thoughts are oriented towards the meaningfulness for himself and others. Additionally, with a human focus, marketing can confront a "dehumanization" process caused by digitalization and automation. Digitalization may provide an abundance of data and easily accessed information, but adequate use and interpretation are only possible with human involvement. Here are two examples.

- *Human-centeredness in concrete terms: a positive example*

A product manager of a bicycle company suspects that it is the lack of comfort that causes few people in the city to use their bicycles for their daily needs. The development team undergoes an empathetic change of perspective and examines the problems from the users' point of view. The team finds out that it is the traffic jam problem in the city above all that prevents people from shopping in the city center and causes them to use the car to get to the supermarkets, which have big parking facilities outside of the city. Because of this habit, people don't consider bicycles as alternative means of transportation for their routine shopping experience. The human-centered approach and the resulting findings have successfully contributed to avoiding waste of resources by identifying the real problem and not paying development costs for improved comfort as a response to the initial hypothesis that the lack of comfort of the bicycles is the problem.

- *Human-centeredness in concrete terms: a negative example*

A product developer is working on a new bicycle for people living in big cities. It is, above all, the inadequate ergonomics of the current bicycles that

[20] Vargo, S. L., & Lusch, R. F. (2008). *op. cit.*

[21] Vargo, S. L., & Lusch, R. F. (2016). *op. cit.*

[22] Vargo, S. L., & Lusch, R. F. (2017). *op. cit.*

[23] See e.g. Kotler, P., Kartajaya, H., & Setiawan, I. (2010). Die neue Dimension des Marketings: Vom Kunden zum Menschen (P. Pyka, Trans.). Frankfurt, Germany: Campus.

the developer sees as the reason for low use of bicycles in urban traffic. He assigns the development department with the design of a new, more comfortable model of the bicycle to remedy this problem. In this consideration, people are only analyzed from an ergonomic point of view, and the problems people actually have with hurdles in urban transport are not taken into account.

3.2.2 Service Orientation

The H2H Mindset emphasizes the importance of service orientation in that S-DL, where service means using your own knowledge and skills to the benefit of others.[24] It thus goes beyond the traditional concept of services, since not only services but also products, software, brands, etc. are used as a vehicle transporting knowledge and skills from one person to another. On the contrary, a strict product mindset was identified as a common obstacle on the way from a product to a platform and service provider.[25]

Service orientation following the S-DL has a strong collaborative and integrative character. S-DL unifies the many forms and specializations of marketing, integrating, for example, B2C, B2B, A2A, and Service Marketing, as well as Customer Experience Management, Customer Relationship Management, and digital marketing- an integrative impulse strongly advocated also by H2H Marketing. All these forms have their right to coexist and provide valuable suggestions on how to design marketing for a specific context, something Gummesson addresses when he says: "The time now seems ripe for integration, for focusing on the commonalities—but to remain contextually grounded, keeping the specificity of practical application and change in sight."[26]

A further impetus for collaboration and a stronger focus on co-production and co-creation of value is provided by digitalization connecting everything and everyone, empowering customers in their role. Engaging with customers should be viewed as a dialogue among equals and not from a superior firm perspective that considers the customer to be inferior.[27] Service orientation also influences the way innovation is thought:

---

[24] See e.g. Vargo, S. L., & Lusch, R. F. (2004). *op. cit.*

[25] Zhu, F., & Furr, N. (2016). Products to Platforms: Making the Leap. Harvard Business Review, 94(4), pp. 72–78. Retrieved from https://hbr.org/2016/04/products-to-platforms-making-the-leap

[26] Gummesson, E. (2011). 2B or not 2B: That is the question, p. 190. Industrial Marketing Management, 40(2), pp. 190–192. https://doi.org/10.1016/j.indmarman.2010.06.028

[27] Payne, A. F., Storbacka, K., & Frow, P. (2008). Managing the co-creation of value. Journal of the Academy of Marketing Science, 36(1), pp. 83–96. https://doi.org/10.1007/s11747-007-0070-0

We argue that the S-D logic premise that all economies are service economies and postulate that all businesses are service business liberates marketers to think of innovation in new and innovative ways [...]. That is, innovation is not defined by what firms produce as output but how firms can better serve.[28]

Therefore, the motivation of serving the customer in the best possible way with own knowledge and skills forms a fundamental part of the H2H Mindset. Here are two more examples.

- *Service orientation in concrete terms: a positive example*

The sales representative of a small firm offering production services to customers who want to produce small electronic items visits a possible client who wants to know if the firm can offer her a specific product that she has in mind. Unfortunately, the representative's firm does not have the necessary machinery to fulfill the needs of the customer. Nevertheless, she remembers that a former cooperation partner (with which the firm had partnered in previous projects) does have the needed machinery. The salesman refers the customer to the former cooperation partner, pointing out that his own firm is not in a position to provide the requested services, whereby, doing so, she used her knowledge about the production facilities of the other firm to the benefit of the customer, resulting in a three-way win for everyone.

- *Service orientation in concrete terms: a negative example*

The sales representative, when asked if her firm could produce the product the client is thinking about, assures the client that the production is feasible with the machinery the firm currently has. Although the salesperson is not entirely sure about this, she remembers producing a somewhat similar product some months ago. Six weeks later, after many hours of work that already went into production planning, the sales man's boss angrily confronts her informing her that the firm lacks the needed machinery. The salesman has to call the customer to tell her the disappointing news, and the customer, as expected, is very annoyed. The sales representative, in an attempt to save face, comes up with excuses and keeps quiet about the machinery of the cooperation partner, resulting in a three-way loss for everyone.

---

[28] Vargo, S. L., & Lusch, R. F. (2008). *op. cit.,* p. 4f. Journal of the Academy of Marketing Science, 36(1), pp. 1–10. https://doi.org/10.1007/s11747-007-0069-6

3.2.3   Agility and Experimentalism

As discussed before, digitalization has dramatically increased the speed of change, and it will continue to do so into the future. For companies, this means that they need new management principles, organizational structures, and processes. Above all, people need new skills and abilities in order to keep pace with the speed of digitalization. Repercussions of the changes can be seen in the delegation of tasks. They get less and less delegated to individuals and are handled by self-organizing teams able to tackle the risen complexity of the tasks. High autonomy of employees is increasingly considered a must, due to increasing speed of change. There is simply not enough time for complex decision-making processes with many approval loops and outdated employee role models seen in flat hierarchies. Employees in this context have more freedom of decision and can find more purpose in their work than before, which on the other hand, goes along with higher personal responsibility and willingness to adapt to changes.[29]

An *agile mindset*, as introduced by Hofert, can form the basis for these developments. "An agile mindset is flexible and always capable of updating itself when new information and experiences make it necessary. The more agile a person's mindset is, the more effectively it can act in different situations."[30] In her work, Hofert proposes four statements that show the basic assumptions underlying the agile mindset. These assumptions are flexible and open for elaborations- the reader may add own ideas to the list:[31]

- "Digitalization demands flexibility from us."
- "Flexibility means that everyone must take responsibility."
- "Small organizational units (teams) are more flexible than larger ones."
- "Without strict hierarchical structures, people can be more innovative."

A person with an agile mindset perceives change as something fundamentally positive and not threatening. This mindset is characterized by the courage to embrace the "trial and error" motto, making mistakes and learning from them, an approach deeply rooted in the iterative Design Thinking process and expressed in the H2H mindset characteristic *experimentalism*. The following example gives us a good look at this.

---

[29] Bathen, D., & Jelden, J. (2014). *op. cit.*
[30] Hofert, S. (2018). *op. cit.*, p. VIIf.
[31] For the following see Hofert, S. (2018). *op. cit.*, p. 20.

- *Agility and experimentalism in concrete terms: a positive example*

In the evening, a customer service employee calls his firm's call center and says that he is currently at the assembly line at a customer's site. The customer urgently needs a replacement for a machine element that had broken down just at the time the service employee arrived. The call center informs her that the needed machine parts will not be available before the weekend and that the customer will have to wait until Monday. The service employee then checks if he maybe can repair the machine element that needs to be replaced in order to at least bridge the time until the spare part arrives. Since no serious consequential damage is to be expected if the attempt fails, and the production manager agrees with the cost calculation, he puts his plan into action. After the weekend, he asks the production manager whether the repaired element did its job and the spare part had arrived. Content with the result, the production manager affirms that the service employee had done a great job. In a creative and experimental way, the customer service employee provided a fast and direct solution to the customer's problem, acting autonomously and responsibly.

- *Agility and experimentalism in concrete terms: a negative example*

After being told by the call center that the spare part will not be available for at least 3 more days, the service employee informs the production manager that he cannot help her today and that he will need to wait until Monday. Although the production manager expresses rather desperately that the downtime of the machine in question would result in financial and organizational difficulties for the company, the customer service employee insists, showing total lack of empathy, that his hands are tied here and that the customer must understand that he cannot do anything for her other than order the spare part.

3.2.4 Empathic Interest in Other Perspectives

Change in perspective is an essential element to the H2H Marketing understanding, as was laid out before. Instead of only examining a problem from his own point of view, several perspectives should be taken into account, a way of thinking inherent to Design Thinking and the H2H Process (more on that in Chap. 6).

In Design Thinking, this means that the *design challenge* should be viewed from a variety of different points in order to consciously decide on a perspective under which the problem should first be solved, as illustrated in the Double-Diamond model (for recap see Chap. 2.1) with its alternating phases of divergence and convergence. In the S-DL, this change of perspective is also required by permanently switching between Market-Based View (MBV) and Resource-Based View (RBV) to clarify what knowledge and skills the own company has (RBV) that neither customers nor competitors have (MBV), as previously discussed.

The change of perspective in H2H Marketing involves the observation and analysis of a problem from various perspectives, namely, from those of all stakeholders. Regarding the sequence, it is important to always start from the perspective of the user or the bearer of the problem. For this change of perspective to succeed, an employee with H2H Mindset must be equipped with enough empathy to understand the problem. The stimulation of empathy, especially in an emotional sense, is a decisive element when it comes to developing solutions that are desirable for the user and profitable and technically feasible for the provider.[32]

For a positive and negative example, we refer to the case of the product development of a bicycle, used to illustrate the *human-centeredness* characteristic, because it also serves for the demonstration of what it means to do an empathic change of perspective.

3.3 H2H Mindset Inside the H2H Marketing Model

As the basis for H2H Marketing, we saw that having an H2H Mindset means the following:

- To consider in all thoughts and actions the good of the people involved and their sense of purpose, and to remember that value cannot be created unilaterally but can only be offered in the form of a value proposition
- To act in a service-oriented way, using skills and knowledge for the benefit of others
- Being adaptable, reflective, recognizing arising problems and changes, and contributing quickly and pragmatically their solution solving
- To listen empathetically to the people involved and to understand their situation

---

[32] Brown, T. (2008). *op. cit.*

Figure 3.5 summarizes the consequences that the three influencing factors of the H2H Marketing Model have for the H2H Mindset and how these consequences manifest in the character traits of the H2H Mindset.

It is important to recall that the H2H Mindset is an individual state of mind, which is context-based by individual experiences a human being made throughout his life, and which is a personality trait based on the personal motivation to change or grow. Companies can influence the H2H Mindset of their employees through two major means:

1. Pay attention to the H2H Mindset of new employees during the recruiting process. The task is to find out whether a potential employee has the personality trait to grow his personal mindset. Furthermore, the company should check with a test like the NEO Personality Inventory[33] whether a potential employee already has characteristics of the H2H Mindset.
2. Develop and establish a corporate culture (or corporate mindset) that enables existing employees to live their H2H Mindset. Refer to the CBV Model (Fig. 3.1) and the SPICE model (Fig. 3.2).

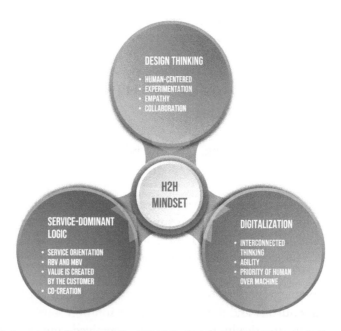

Fig. 3.5 Determining factors of the H2H Mindset inside the H2H marketing model

---

[33] Costa, P. T., & McCrae, R. R. (2008). The Revised NEO Personality Inventory (NEO-PI-R). London, UK: SAGE.

Practically, this means that companies who want to use H2H Marketing have to have both: employees with H2H Mindset and a corporate culture, which enables and facilitates the employees to use this mindset for the implementation of the H2H Marketing.

The aspects we examined do not stand alone but are to be regarded as interconnected. It is a mindset that is not only beneficial for the marketing department but for every employee who wants to master the challenges of digitalization. The core message is that the more there are people who have the H2H Mindset, the better H2H Marketing can be implemented. Putting the human at the center of attention in the H2H Mindset is a critical prerequisite for the success of the following strategic and operative sides of H2H Marketing.

In recent years, a few companies have applied some of these principles, one example being Panera Bread. The key ingredient to Panera Bread's company culture is caring, which means that management cares about success of community, individuals, and its employees' futures. Their concern for employees is seen in the better than competitive compensation and benefits. Panera's 2000 plus bakery cafes in the USA and Canada are all devoted to "delivering fresh, authentic artisan bread served in a warm environment by engaging associates." Panera has the highest level of customer loyalty among quick-casual restaurants and is consistently at the top of rankings for best casual dining brand and customer service. Furthermore, Panera donates its entire stock of unsold bread and baked goods to local hunger relief agencies and charities. They also have "Panera Cares" cafes that aim to fight hunger by allowing customers to pay what they can.

Another example from Denmark would be Novo Nordisk. The pharmaceutical company was founded in 1923 in the small town of Bagsvaerd, close to Copenhagen. Novo Nordisk's overriding purpose is to "defeat diabetes," which includes preventing, treating, and ultimately curing the disease. It has offices in 79 countries and markets its products in more than 185 countries. The company is renowned for its commitment to ethics and quality and a culture built on respect and accountability. Novo Nordisk was an early adopter of the "triple bottom line" approach to business and has strived to create value for all its stakeholders. The "Novo Nordisk Way" describes "who we are, where we want to go and how we work." The company uses senior employees as "facilitators" who travel around the world looking at its operations to ensure that they adhere to the "Novo Nordisk Way" and to share best practices across the company.

Let us add another company with another focus—Inditex, from Spain. Founded by Amancio Ortega in 1975, Inditex has become the largest textile company in the world. It has more than 7400 locations in 96 countries with a turnover of $30 billion in 2019. Its retail stores operate under brands such as Zara, Bershka, Oysho, Pull&Bear, Stradivarius, Uterqüe, Zara Home, and Massimo Dutti. It designs and produces almost all of its products and ships them directly to stores twice a week, thus staying in step with fashion trends straight from the catwalk. In 2001, the company adopted a "social strategy" that includes dialogues with all key stakeholders, an internal code of conduct, and social audits of all suppliers. Their overriding aim is to create beautiful, ethical, quality products and to create fashion that is "right to wear."

A case study which combines all determining factors of Human-to-Human Mindset is Good Kitchen (Det Gode Køkken) in Holstebro, Denmark: in this case, all three factors DT, SD-L, and D are directed to the empathetic interests of the customer. The Good Kitchen is a part of the food services from Holstebro Municipality, Denmark, to the local senior citizen living at home. They solved in an innovative way one of the big welfare challenges with the rapidly growing number of seniors: How do we ensure that senior citizens can still eat what they want when the local authority delivers the food when they are no longer able to cook their own food?

With a design-driven innovation process that involves senior citizens, drivers, kitchen staff and management teams, programmers, and designers, the issue was solved. They came up with a user-friendly digital tablet-based ordering system which ensures the drivers can easily obtain and deliver orders for senior citizens in the municipality. With the new perspective, a create solutions based on human-centeredness was found. These aspects are character traits of Human-to-Human Mindset, and, thus, "The Good Kitchen" case also reflects the same character traits in all the three approaches. More details could be found in our Case Study Collection publication.

Storyline

After traveling the "Great Journey" with the elements Design Thinking, Service-Dominant Logic, and digitalization of our level-one H2H Marketing Model, we have entered the phase of "brave action" in our story. The story starts with the hero "H2H Mindset" which acts on an individual as well as on a corporate level. On the corporate level, we have shown that the H2H Mindset is a further development of the integrated model of the Customer-Based-View and the SPICE Stakeholder Model. In the next stage, we focused on the four explicitly mentioned characteristics of the individual H2H Mindset, and the first brave action of this hero ends with the H2H Mindset in the H2H Marketing Model. In the next chapter, the next hero is waiting: the H2H Management Approach.

Questions

1. What are the foundational characteristics of the term "mindset" according to H2H Marketing?
2. How are the mindset of individuals (employees) and organizations (employing companies) interconnected? Which one is manageable? How would you manage it?
3. What are the four characteristic elements of the individual H2H Mindset? Please find positive and negative examples from your own experience.
4. What means service orientation for you personally, and why is it important to differentiate service orientation in the sense of S-DL from service orientation (in the sense of customer service orientation)?
5. How can companies implement an agile mindset in their organization? Do you find real examples in the field that already set their employees an example of an agile mindset?
6. What are the attributes of the H2H Mindset driven by Design Thinking, S-DL, and digitalization (remember the first level of the H2H Marketing Model)? Why is the willingness to collaborate and to co-create so important for the H2H Mindset?

References

Bathen, D., & Jelden, J. (2014). *Marketingorganisation der Zukunft* [Report]. Retrieved from https://www.marketingverband.de/marketingkompetenz/studien/marketingorganisation-der-zukunft/

Brooks, R., & Goldstein, S. (2008). The mindset of teachers capable of fostering resilience in students. *Canadian Journal of School Psychology, 23*(1), 114–126. https://doi.org/10.1177/0829573508316597.

Brown, T. (2008). Design thinking. *Harvard Business Review, 86*(6), 84–92. Retrieved from https://hbr.org/2008/06/design-thinking

Costa, P. T., & McCrae, R. R. (2008). *The revised NEO personality inventory (NEO-PI-R)*. London: Sage.

Dweck, C. S. (2006). *Mindset: The new psychology of success*. New York, NY: Random House.

Gummesson, E. (2011). 2B or not 2B: That is the question. *Industrial Marketing Management, 40*(2), 190–192. https://doi.org/10.1016/j.indmarman.2010.06.028.

Hofert, S. (2018). *Das agile Mindset: Mitarbeiter entwickeln, Zukunft der Arbeit gestalten*. Wiesbaden: Springer Gabler.

How Companies Can Profit from a "Growth Mindset". (2014). *Harvard Business Review*. Retrieved from https://hbr.org/2014/11/how-companies-can-profit-from-a-growth-mindset

Kotler, P., Kartajaya, H., & Setiawan, I. (2010). *Die neue Dimension des Marketings: Vom Kunden zum Menschen* (P. Pyka, Trans.). Frankfurt: Campus.

Kumar, V., Jones, E., Venkatesan, R., & Leone, R. P. (2011). Is market orientation a source of sustainable competitive advantage or simply the cost of competing? *Journal of Marketing, 75*(1), 16–30. Retrieved from https://www.researchgate.net

Matzler, K., Stahl, H. K., & Hinterhuber, H. H. (2009). Die customer-based view der Unternehmung. In H. H. Hinterhuber & K. Matzler (Eds.), *Kundenorientierte Unternehmensführung: Kundenorientierung–Kundenzufriedenheit–Kundenbindung* (6th ed., pp. 4–31). Wiesbaden: Gabler.

Nolte, H. (1998). Aspekte ressourcenorientierter Unternehmensführung. In H. Nolte (Ed.), *Aspekte ressourcenorientierter Unternehmensführung* (pp. III–VIII). München: Rainer Hampp. Retrieved from http://hdl.handle.net/10419/116857

Payne, A. F., Storbacka, K., & Frow, P. (2008). Managing the co-creation of value. *Journal of the Academy of Marketing Science, 36*(1), 83–96. https://doi.org/10.1007/s11747-007-0070-0.

Pfoertsch, W. A., & Sponholz, U. (2019). *Das neue marketing-mindset: Management, Methoden und Prozesse für ein Marketing von Mensch zu Mensch.* Wiesbaden: Springer Gabler.

Schulz, M. (2011). *New mindsets for service-orientated marketing: Understanding the role of emotions in interpersonal relationships.* Doctoral thesis. Retrieved from https://ourarchive.otago.ac.nz/handle/10523/1928

Sisodia, R. S., Sheth, J. N., & Wolfe, D. (2014). *Firms of endearment: How world-class companies profit from passion and purpose* (2nd ed.). Upper Saddle River, NJ: Pearson Education.

Vargo, S. L., & Lusch, R. F. (2004). Evolving to a new dominant logic for marketing. *Journal of Marketing, 68*(1), 1–17. https://doi.org/10.1509/jmkg.68.1.1.24036.

Vargo, S. L., & Lusch, R. F. (2008). Service-dominant logic: Continuing the evolution. *Journal of the Academy of Marketing Science, 36*(1), 1–10. https://doi.org/10.1007/s11747-007-0069-6.

Vargo, S. L., & Lusch, R. F. (2016). Institutions and axioms: An extension and update of service-dominant logic. *Journal of the Academy of Marketing Science, 44*(1), 5–23. https://doi.org/10.1007/s11747-015-0456-3.

Vargo, S. L., & Lusch, R. F. (2017). Service-dominant logic 2025. *International Journal of Research in Marketing, 34*(1), 46–67. https://doi.org/10.1016/j.ijresmar.2016.11.001.

Zhu, F., & Furr, N. (2016). Products to platforms: Making the leap. *Harvard Business Review, 94*(4), 72–78. Retrieved from https://hbr.org/2016/04/products-to-platforms-making-the-leap

4

H2H Management: Putting Trust and Brand in Focus

Trust has become the ultimate currency for marketing in today's world. In this chapter, we will focus on the strategic level of H2H Marketing, by putting special emphasis on trust management. Then we will illustrate the new thinking in brand management, basing both into the new theoretical framework – the H2H Marketing Model. This has implication for the new marketing in general and for developing a human-centered mindset. It enables the strategic and operative implementation of H2H Marketing.

Today, we are living in a *Reputation Economy*[1] where trust is the lead instrument for doing business (see also Ted Talk How to build and rebuild trust | Frances Frei). The world is experiencing emotional, polarizing debates, with trust in governments declining dramatically in recent years. In a chaotic world of turmoil, people searching for guidance and orientation are increasingly looking towards companies and their leaders for guidance. Leading companies and their CEOs are expected not only to navigate business topics but also to address social, economic, and political issues. Company brand plays a special role because it can serve as a trust anchor, as a point of orientation. It can contribute to establishing a trusting relationship between companies and customers, which is a top priority H2H Marketing.

Strategic H2H Marketing is divided into the two main pillars: trust management and brand management. They give companies the tools to create trust through various levers such as brand activism (outgrowth of CSR), Customer Experience Management, reputation management, and trust management.

---

[1] Sarkar, C., & Kotler, P. (2018). Brand Activism: From Purpose to Action (Kindle edition). n.p.: IDEA BITE PRESS. Retrieved from www.amazon.com

© The Author(s), under exclusive license to Springer Nature Switzerland AG 2021
P. Kotler et al., *H2H Marketing*, https://doi.org/10.1007/978-3-030-59531-9_4

Trust has a positive impact on many different areas and is the breeding ground for loyalty and brand advocacy, essentials in the connectivity age where companies have lost direct control over their brands.

There is still an immense discrepancy between the promises made by companies in comparison with actual performance meeting expectations. Edelman[2] in their 2019 *Trust Barometer Special Report: In Brands We Trust* found that 53% of respondents stated "[e]very brand has a responsibility to get involved in at least one social issue that does not directly impact its business," while only 21% of respondents agreed with the statement "brands I use keep the best interests of society in mind." Consequently, this chapter is intended to provide companies with tools and approaches on how trust can be fostered but also to act as a wake-up call for companies (see Fig. 4.1[3]).

In the retail sector, trusted brands are able to get stronger, because their trust management is very focused. In 2019, Walmart revenues were larger than $500 billion, and Aldi, Ikea, and Amazon are outperforming their local peers. In the last 50 years, Aldi has created a "whole-being branding concept" that offers products with no frills and low prices".[4] Their branding approach is based in the passionate belief that without own brand identity, there is no long-term brand destiny.

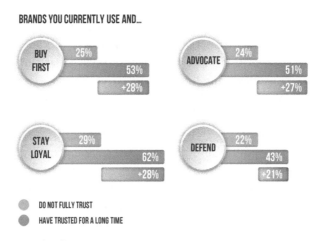

BRANDS YOU CURRENTLY USE AND...

BUY FIRST — 25% / 53% / +28%

ADVOCATE — 24% / 51% / +27%

STAY LOYAL — 29% / 62% / +28%

DEFEND — 22% / 43% / +21%

DO NOT FULLY TRUST

HAVE TRUSTED FOR A LONG TIME

Fig. 4.1 The rewards of trust

[2] Edelman. (2019). 2019 Edelman Trust Barometer Special Report: In Brands We Trust? [Report], p. 13. Retrieved from https://www.edelman.com/sites/g/files/aatuss191/files/2019-06/2019_edelman_trust_barometer_special_report_in_brands_we_trust.pdf

[3] Taken from Edelman. (2019). *op. cit.*, p. 11.

[4] Aaker, D. A., & McLoughlin, D. (2010). *Strategic Market Management: Global Perspectives.* Chichester, United Kingdom: Wiley.

4.1   H2H Trust Management

4.1.1   The Big Trust Crisis: An Opportunity for Companies to Thrive

"We're in a full-blown trust crisis".[5] This statement is not only a personal opinion; it can be backed by reliable data. In 2020, the Edelman Trust Study found the sharpest decline in general trust in the USA ever measure.[6] 56% believe that capitalism in today's form is not the right economic system.[7]

The corona crisis improved the trust position of traditional media and many governments around the world. The phenomenon of disinformation is not new, but distribution of media has changed radically due to new technologies, so that the role of "gatekeeper" that professional journalist should have by conducting fact checks has weakened. Furthermore, today's public not only acts as mere consumers of information but are actively involved as information producers, e.g., with blog posts or social media. Similar to developments in branding, we can also speak of democratization in the area of information production.

With such developments, it does not come as a surprise that the "loss of truth," with 59% of respondents agreeing, was identified as main consequence of the downward trend of trust in media in the 2018 Edelman Trust Study. These societal changes in trust are accompanied by rising accountability from employers and expectations for businesses to lead the change. Building trust is the highest valued expectation (69% of respondents) people have for CEOs, while "64% [...] say that CEOs should take the lead on change rather than waiting for government to impose it".[8] In 2019 this figure rose even further, from 64% to currently 76%. 71% of employees agreeing that CEOs should take a clear stand on employee-driven, as well as industry issues, political events, and national crises.

The employer is seen as a "trusted partner for change," which verifies the importance of firms getting active on societal, political, and economic issues. The newest data shows that trusting a company to do the right things ranks

---

[5] Sarkar, C., & Kotler, P. (2018). *op. cit.*, THE TRUST CRISIS section, Para. 7.

[6] Edelman. (2018). 2018 Edelman Trust Barometer: Global Report [Report], p. 6. Retrieved from https://www.edelman.com/sites/g/files/aatuss191/files/2018-10/2018_Edelman_Trust_Barometer_Global_Report_FEB.pdf

[7] Edelman. (2020). *2020 Edelman Trust Barometer: Global Report* [Report], p. 12. Retrieved from https://cdn2.hubspot.net/hubfs/440941/Trust%20Barometer%202020/2020%20Edelman%20Trust%20Barometer%20Global%20Report-1.pdf

[8] Edelman. (2018). *op. cit.*, p. 29.

among the top five buying criteria with 81% of consumers surveyed expressing its importance.[9] This demand for commitment needs to be recognized by firms. Those who embrace these developments by actively engaging in brand activism can reap strategic and economic benefits from it, while others that stay quiet may suffer negative consequences. "In a highly polarized world, it's no longer good enough to be neutral".[10]

4.1.2   H2H Trust Management in Practice

Rebranding may be needed for a company to stay alive, but it is not always successful.[11] Yahoo disappeared despite great efforts of rebranding. After lagging behind, their attempts to catch up didn't convince customers that they could be trusted again. Sometimes, it needs time and substantial investments to stay current and earn the trust of the customers again. BP (British Petroleum) tried to make their rebranding move to Beyond Petroleum, but the disaster of Deep Horizon impeded their effort, and the transition will take some time for British Petroleum.

A successful rebranding example is Mastercard, which is worldwide number two in the global credit card market. Although Mastercard is a hard-core money transaction business, they chose to adopt the slogan "money isn't everything" and launched their campaign "Priceless…there are some things that money can't buy. For everything else, there is MasterCard." With that clever move, Mastercard distinguished itself from their big rival, Visa, as a more "human" company and doubled their transaction volume. Now, Mastercard is timely working on a "world beyond cash" to adapt to the new digitalized shopping world. The company is ranked very high in diversity and training of its employees and reputed to be a good company to work for. The future will show how Mastercard can keep up its brand trust by applying the H2H Trust Management concept. Raja Rajamannar, Chief Marketing and Communications Officer at Mastercard is working on this diligently since 2013 and knows that brand building never stops, particularly in coronavirus times.

Trust management in H2H Marketing can provide solutions for current developments. Figure 4.2 shows the cause and effect relationships between

---

[9] Edelman. (2019). *op. cit.*, p. 8.

[10] Sarkar, C., & Kotler, P. (2018). *op. cit.*, Preface, para. 5.

[11] Interesting Case studies are in: Gaiser, B., Linxweiler, R., Brucker, V. Ed. (2005). Praxisorientierte Markenführung – Neue Strategien, innovative Instrumente und aktuelle Fallstudien, Germany: Gabler, Wiesbaden.

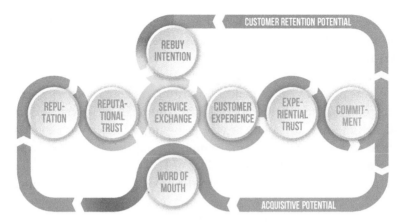

Fig. 4.2 Cause and effect model for integrated trust management

brand activism (see Sect. 4.1.3), reputation, reputational trust, service exchange, customer experience, experiential trust, commitment, rebuy intention, and word of mouth as key variables of H2H Trust Management. Pfoertsch and Sponholz developed this model, which adapts and integrates several existing models and consistent empirically proved impacting factors on reputational and experiential trust.[12] These empirically proved factors are for reputational trust: brand image, company's size, and industry to which the company belongs. For experiential trust, these are communication behavior, conflict handling, cooperation, and solution orientation of the people directly involved in the customer experience. In addition, there are activities of the supplying company like relationship investments, customer integration, and the use of value-based pricing that impact experiential trust. Finally, customer satisfaction plays a key role in experiential trust. All these factors represent an action framework which helps the companies to reinforce trust in their brand. We added brand activism as an updated version of Corporate Social Responsibility (CSR) initiatives to the original model.

Three of all these concepts and factors are of special interest and will be examined in the course of this chapter: brand activism, Customer Experience Management, and reputation management (see Fig. 4.2).

H2H Trust Management is based on a trust concept consisting of four parts: trust propensity, affective trust, reputational trust, and experiential trust. It is also based on the realization that only experiential and reputational trust can be "managed." For this reason, the following chapter on trust management will highlight the relevant mechanisms for strengthening

---

[12] See Pfoertsch, W. A., & Sponholz, U. (2019). *op. cit.*

reputational trust through CSR and an integrated reputation management model and experiential trust through CXM.

As a response to customers firms are required to make societal progress happen and Corporate Social Responsibility needs to be rethought drastically. We are going to have a look at how firms, by doing good for society, can also do good for their shareholders. In the context of "democratization of the brand," reputation management also gains importance. With more touchpoints to handle than ever (both online and offline), Customer Experience Management presents an essential pillar of H2H Marketing and will receive additional attention (in Chap. 5) with the introduction of the Omnichannel concept.

4.1.3   Brand Activism: Rethinking CSR

To consistently place people at the center of entrepreneurial activity means actively addressing their problems. For this, it is not enough to perceive Corporate Social Responsibility (CSR) as a compulsory exercise. It is not sufficient any longer to do good only for not looking bad. Far too long, CSR was used for publicly proclaiming and showcasing. A broad range of superficial assistance to social projects was given. This outdated approach to CSR may have worked in the past but is not suited for today's world.[13]

In 2018, *brand activism* was presented as a mature development of CSR to respond to new customer demands: "Brand Activism consists of business efforts to promote, impede, or direct social, political, economic and/or environmental reform with the desire to improve society".[14] The integration of brand activism into H2H Trust Management follows the idea of strengthening reputation through activism for the good of society. At the same time, brand activism fits into our H2H Marketing Model because of its correlation to H2H Brand Management.

This kind of new thinking is urgently needed as research indicates that 66% of the American consumers surveyed consider it "important for brands to take public stands on social and political issues […]",[15] with social media being the medium of choice to demonstrate the firm's position on these issues.

[13] Kotler, P., Hessekiel, D., & Lee, N. R. (2013). GOOD WORKS!: Wie Sie mit dem richtigen Marketing die Welt - und Ihre Bilanzen - verbessern (N. Bertheau, Trans.). Offenbach, Germany: GABAL.

[14] Sarkar, C., & Kotler, P. (2018). *op. cit.*, BRAND ACTIVISM: A WORKING DEFINITION section, para. 8.

[15] Sprout Social. (2017). Championing Change in the Age of Social Media: How Brands Are Using Social to Connect With People on the Issues That Matter [Report], p. 3. Retrieved from https://media.sprout-social.com/pdf/Sprout-Data-Report-Championing-Change-in-the-Age-of-Social-Media.pdf

Generation Z members are demanding even more. They are "a group of early adopters, digital natives and energized advocates".[16] From 2020, the demographic group of Gen Z will make up for four out of ten consumers, and it is this group that has the highest propensity (94%) to consider brand activism activities crucial and, more than previous generations, perceive companies as a collaboration partner to bring about change.[17]

These developments come with an imperative for firms to act, which may trouble marketers and executives. But once understood, the new dynamics of brand activism can open a way to connect with the customers inside their communities, an area as discussed in the O-Zone model (in Fig. 4.18) usually completely out of the firm's reach. It gives brands the opportunity to engage in purpose and meaning-driven dialogue with customers, which comes with a major benefit – the interaction takes place in a social, non-intrusive way, fully in line with the *Permission Marketing* approach by Seth Godin.[18] As the Sprout study shows: "Brands have an invitation from their audiences to get involved and the space to do it via social […]".[19] The 2017 Cone Communications CSR study takes it even one step further declaring that firms do "not only [have] the invitation, but the mandate to step up to solve today's most complex social and environmental issues".[20] Moreover, with social media, there are various ways of getting started with brand activism (see Fig. 4.3[21]).

Marketers should ask themselves, "Does my firm live up to its mandate?" and "Is my firm actively engaged in activities that foster the greater good?" Some firms may experience a strong desire to get started but fear the consequences of brand activism going wrong.[22] For those in doubt of brand activism, a look at the risk-reward ratio may be of help. Sprout Social found that the rewards for the brand outweigh the risk, as it was discovered that when consumers' personal beliefs align with what brands are saying, 28% will publicly praise a company. When individuals disagree with the brand's stance, 20% will publicly criticize a company".[23] Therefore, clear positioning on

---

[16] Cone Communications. (2017). 2017 Cone Gen Z CSR Study: How to Speak Z [Report], Move over Millenials, Here Comes Gen Z section, para. 1. Retrieved from http://www.conecomm.com/research-blog/2017-genz-csr-study

[17] Cone Communications. (2017). *op. cit.*, p. 2.

[18] Godin, S. (2007). *op. cit.*

[19] Sprout Social. (2017). *op. cit.*, p. 2.

[20] Cone Communications. (2017). *op. cit.*, p. 35.

[21] Sprout Social. (2017). *op. cit.*, p. 15.

[22] Sarkar, C., & Kotler, P. (2018). Sprout Social. (2017). *op. cit.*, p. 2.

[23] Sprout Social. (2017). *op. cit.*, p. 4.

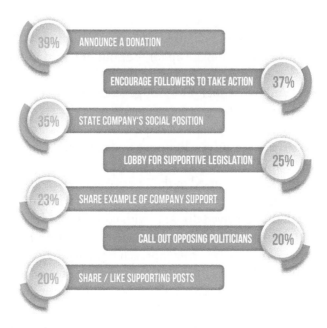

Fig. 4.3 Most effective ways for brands to take a stand on a specific cause on social media

critical issues can serve as an effective driver of brand advocacy, since research indicates that positive brand advocacy will outweigh the negative.

Even negative advocacy can culminate in a positive result for the brand as the critique may trigger brand advocates that otherwise might have remained dormant.[24] Moreover, with the connectivity that social media provides, firms have excellent ways to get started with brand activism.

Brand activism puts focus not on vision statements but concrete action. The term "activism" might indicate short-term thinking. We use it more in the sense of social involvement. Firms should look for *wicked problems* to tackle, putting human needs and desires at the center of attention.[25] Customers will recognize and remunerate companies focusing on helping society and enable firms to thrive with the trust they gain along the way.[26] As a positive example, we can bring up The Body Shop again, with its emphasis on natural ingredients and no animal testing. They are working towards a worldwide ban on animal-tested cosmetics. Even traditional companies like Unilever are

---

[24] Kotler, P., Kartajaya, H., & Setiawan, I. (2017). *op. cit.*

[25] Rittel, H. W. J., & Webber, M. M. (1973). Dilemmas in a General Theory of Planning. Policy Sciences, 4(2), pp. 155–165. https://doi.org/10.1007/BF01405730

[26] Kotler, P., Hessekiel, D., & Lee, N. R. (2013). *op. cit.*

increasing positive social impact and are leading in sustainability efforts. Some of them co-developed a circular business model that creates an infinite process circle for using resources most efficiently. Ernst & Young (EY) pledged to support "inclusive capitalism" to redirect investments into assets in better directions. Besides Ernst & Young, many other examples can be found in the publication brand activism.[27]

4.1.4   Optimizing Results with Customer Experience Management

The well-cited article "Welcome to the experience economy"[28] describes the evolution from a service to an experience economy in which the customer experience receives increasing attention as commoditization of goods and services is leading to the erosion of business models. Now, more than 20 years later, good Customer Experience Management (CXM) is more critical than ever. With new channels online and offline, and the connected customer constantly switching between them, the customer experience has become more complex and dependent on a growing number of influencing factors.[29] Effective CXM is crucial for fostering experiential trust, one of the manageable trust components.

We should first define customer experience (CX) since it is quite an ambiguous term. "Customer Experience is the cumulative perception and reflection of all experiences from the single or multiple interactions of the customer with the contact points of a provider over the period of one or more exchange processes [...]".[30] Mapping the whole customer journey along all touchpoints and channels can provide clarification for marketers to understand the complex CX better. Following the 5As framework (Aware, Appeal, Ask, Act, Advocate) introduced previously, several digital and physical touchpoints along the customer path can be identified. Figure 4.4 provides an overview of typical touchpoints.[31]

---

[27] Sarkar, C., & Kotler, P. (2018). *op. cit.*

[28] Pine, II, B. J., & Gilmore, J. H. (1998). Welcome to the Experience Economy. Harvard Business Review, 76(4), pp. 97–105. Retrieved from https://hbr.org/1998/07/welcome-to-the-experience-economy

[29] Heinemann, G., & Gaiser, C. W. (2016). *op. cit.*

[30] Mayer-Vorfelder, M. (2012). Basler Schriften zum Marketing: Vol. 29. Kundenerfahrungen im Dienstleistungsprozess: Eine theoretische und empirische Analyse, p. 71. Wiesbaden, Germany: Gabler. Translation from German to English.

[31] The touchpoints have been adapted from Hansen (2018). The 5A Customer Path concept is taken from Kotler et al. (2017).

The constant switching and interplay between on- and off-line channels and touchpoints that are controlled by the firm and those that lie outside of the firm's influence sphere creates demanding challenges for firms who want to provide a seamless experience across all channels and touchpoints.[32] The touchpoints shown in Fig. 4.4 display the shifts in customer behavior that leads to the new customer path. For example, individual purchasing decisions increasingly are being determined based on the opinion of others, which manifests in the touchpoints of the *ask* phase, e.g., web communities and reviews/ratings, where "the customer path changes from individual to social".[33]

There is a great example for a B2B social media touchpoint enhancement. In 2013, Volvo Trucks placed a YouTube ad using Jean Claude Van Damme, a Belgian actor and retired martial artist, best known for his martial arts action films. The video demonstrated the precision of Volvo's new dynamic steering system by having the actor perform his epic leg split, a stunt he is widely

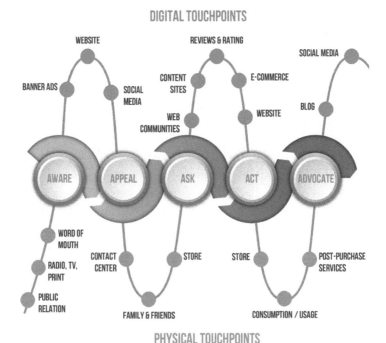

Fig. 4.4 Physical and digital touchpoints along the 5A customer path

[32] Heinemann, G., & Gaiser, C. W. (2016). *op. cit.*
[33] Kotler, P., Kartajaya, H., & Setiawan, I. (2017). *op. cit.*, p. 63.

known for. This video elevated Volvo to a brand icon on YouTube.[34] The company was able to improve its brand image and accelerate sales in the years to follow. Many truck drivers and truck owners who watched the video to see Van Damme became extremely interested in the precision driving solution of Volvo trucks. This is a very good example of the flexibility between physical and digital customer touchpoints. Potential customers use the enhanced transparency of brands that the Internet provides to revise product and service offerings thoroughly. This transforms the structure of the customer journey from a linear path into a customer cycle with iterative feedback loops.[35] This is reflected in the 5A customer path that is not necessarily linear. Steps may get skipped.

For example, a customer might *act* out of an impulse without researching deeper, thus skipping the *ask* phase, while others might *advocate* a brand without actually buying it (e.g., luxury cars). The path can also take the form of a loop when customers jump back to previous steps as is depicted in Fig. 4.5.[36] The figure shows the concept of a spiral consumer decision journey introduced by Court et al.[37] in an article published in the McKinsey Quarterly,

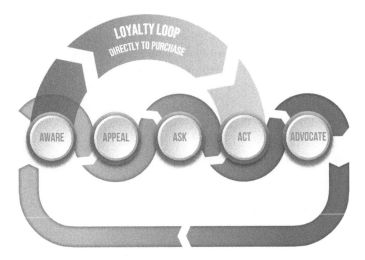

Fig. 4.5 The spiral consumer decision journey

[34] Volvo Trucks (2013). *Volvo Trucks - The Epic Split feat. Van Damme (Live Test)* [YouTube video]. Retrieved from https://www.youtube.com/watch?v=M7FIvfx5J10

[35] Heinemann, G. (2014). *op. cit.*

[36] The spiral form of the decision journey with the traditional and loyalty loop has been adapted from Court, Elzinga, Mulder, & Vetvik (2009). The 5A Customer Path concept is adapted from Kotler et al. (2017).

[37] Court, D., Elzinga, D., Mulder, S., & Vetvik, O. J. (2009). The consumer decision journey. McKinsey Quarterly, 3, pp. 1-11. Retrieved from https://www.mckinsey.com/business-functions/marketing-and-sales/our-insights/the-consumer-decision-journey

where the customer path starts with an initial set of brands, which then undergo active evaluation. To make for a consistent image, the consumer decision journey by Court was combined with the 5A customer path. After having decided which brand to buy, the post-purchase experience takes places.

Amazon is undoubtedly a great example for extensive post-purchase support. Since the post-purchase experiences are the most memorable part of the overall brand experience, Amazon follows up every purchase with emails and banners and product placements. IBM can be cited as a good industrial example. When they serve large companies or government institutions, they assign a customer relationship manager and have all digital interactions being adapted to the new business relationship situation. Starbucks rewards loyalty with referral programs using physical cards and digital interaction.

The circular decision journey has a peculiarity similar the 5A customer path. It does not cling to the classic funnel structure. It includes feedback loops that can even lead to expansion along the path instead of solely narrowing the options like a funnel. An example of this is the expansion of the initially considered set of brands after having evaluated other brands. To keep in mind is how crucial the interconnectedness of all steps is. A pleasant experience with a brand after the purchase including usage/consumption, post-purchase services can create advocates, which in turn publicly praise and defend the brand through positive word of mouth. Finally, it influences the probability of being in the initial consideration set of brands.[38] Marketers must identify the customer touchpoints and the channels used in order to create an integrated across channels and consistent experience and allocate resources where they are needed most.

4.1.5   Build a Strong Reputation

Reputation has gained significance in the past years, especially due to unprecedented transparency[39] and the lack of trust crisis that firms, governments, and media alike are suffering.[40] The Reputation Institute in its 2019 RepTrak® 100 study assesses the situation as follows: "[…] companies are on trial in the

[38] Court, D., Elzinga, D., Mulder, S., & Vetvik, O. J. (2009). *op. cit.*

[39] Wüst, C. (2012). Corporate Reputation Management – die kraftvolle Währung für Unternehmenserfolg. In C. Wüst, & R. T. Kreutzer (Eds.), Corporate Reputation Management: Wirksame Strategien für den Unternehmenserfolg (pp. 3-56). Wiesbaden, Germany: Springer Gabler.

[40] Sarkar, C., & Kotler, P. (2018). *op. cit.*

WHEN A COMPANY IS DISTRUSTED...

57% 15%

15% WILL BELIEVE POSITIVE INFORMATION
AFTER HEARING IT 1-2 TIMES

57% WILL BELIEVE NEGATIVE INFORMATION
AFTER HEARING IT 1-2 TIMES

WHEN A COMPANY IS TRUSTED...

51% 25%

51% WILL BELIEVE POSITIVE INFORMATION
AFTER HEARING IT 1-2 TIMES

25% WILL BELIEVE NEGATIVE INFORMATION
AFTER HEARING IT 1-2 TIMES

Fig. 4.6   Trust protecting the reputation

court of public opinion. It's a time of 'reputation judgment day' when companies are scrutinized on all aspects of their company—ethics, leadership, values, and beyond".[41]

In the "reputation economy," reputation and trust gained from taking on "the biggest and most urgent problems facing society"[42] are an essential condition for success. Trust and reputation cannot be viewed separately, as recent analysis[43] shows. The Edelman Trust Barometer study found that trust serves as a protective shield against reputational damage, by softening the impact of bad news while boosting positive reaction to good news (see Fig. 4.6).

These findings point towards a clear assessment of the importance of building trust and reputation. Reputation has crucial strategic significance and is a task for the upper management where it should form a part of the overarching business strategy.

In current literature sources, there is no consensus on a uniform definition of reputation and the demarcation from other areas, such as brand management. It is imprecise, as reputation management relies on similar concepts such as the identity as the starting point and the images that stakeholders have as the basis for the resulting reputation.[44] Image and reputation in this context

[41] Reputation Institute. (2019). Winning Strategies in Reputation: 2019 German RepTrak® 100 [Report], p. 5. Retrieved from https://insights.reputationinstitute.com/website-assets/2019-germany-reptrak

[42] Sarkar, C., & Kotler, P. (2018). *op. cit.*, BRAND ACTIVISM: A WORKING DEFINITION section, para. 11.

[43] Adapted from Edelman (2011). 2011 Edelman Trust Barometer: Global Report, p. 35.

[44] Wüst, C. (2012). *op. cit.*

need to be distinguished clearly: "[…] whereas image reflects what a firm stands for, reputation reflects how well it has done in the eyes of the marketplace".[45]

Reputation is the aggregation of the stakeholders' images that result from congruencies and discrepancies between expectations and the firm's offerings. Furthermore, images are more volatile as they are easily influenced by external factors, while managing reputation as the evaluated sum of all images requires a long-term commitment. Depending on the stakeholders, images of the same firm can vary substantially. While an armaments manufacturer may be an excellent firm in economic terms, thus a good image in the eyes of financial analysts, the public image of the firm and its products may be the opposite. However, what exactly determines excellent reputation management? For H2H Marketing we use the following description given by Cornelia Wüst:

> The central task of a systematic reputation management is, therefore, to build, maintain and protect the good reputation of a company synergistically with the identity, the brand and the image in the desired form, to achieve a positive attitude towards the company and its services, across all stakeholders, integrated and evaluated in the strategic, operational and financial goals of an organization.[46]

She describes proactive "expectation management considering the relevant shareholders and is therefore subject to a permanent change process"[47] as the core of reputation management. Therefore, firms should identify the exact stakeholders, their needs, expectations, and influence on the overall reputation to understand them and take actions to meet their demands.

For this purpose, the persona concept[48] can be of good use, creating a stereotypical persona for each stakeholder group. In the form of a persona, firms can condense target groups of a service or product and stakeholder groups into concrete exemplary avatars that take into account the social environment, expectations, and desires of the different stakeholders. The concept is not scientifically grounded but is rather a useful method for better

---

[45] Weiss, A. M., Anderson, E., & MacInnis, D. J. (1999). Reputation Management as a Motivation for Sales Structure Decisions, p. 75. Journal of Marketing, 63(4), pp. 74-89. https://doi.org/10.1177/002224299906300407

[46] Wüst, C. (2012). *op. cit.*, p. 16.

[47] Wüst, C. (2012). *op. cit.*, p. 16.

[48] Adlin, T., & Pruitt, J. (2009). Putting Personas to Work: Using Data-Driven Personas to Focus Product Planning, Design, and Development. In A. Sears, & J. A. Jacko, Human-Computer Interaction: Development Process (1st ed., pp. 95-120). Boca Raton, FL: CRC Press.

understanding customers and other stakeholder groups.[49] "Although there is no common understanding in literature about the utilization of personas, all methodological approaches pursue the objective of obtaining a deeper understanding of users".[50]

In line with the S-DL, the exploration of the background of the personas can help to understand how the stakeholder groups co-create value with the firm. "Effective personas are based on the kind of information you can't get from demographics, survey data, or suppositions, but only from observing and interviewing individual people in their own environments".[51] Getting this crucial context information can help in active expectation management and can be translated into the integrated reputation management model (shown in Fig. 4.7).

In the model, the starting point is the identity values, in the forms of norms and actions of the company that is communicated to the stakeholders via communication specialists. Communication plays a decisive role in the process, and it is recommended to organize it "[...] a stakeholder relations team whose permanent task is to translate external expectations into internal measures and processes. Stakeholder management thus becomes a strategic task of corporate management".[52]

In summary, it can be said that reputation management is communication and expectation management of internal and external stakeholders and shapes reputation over a long period of time. Reputation needs values, norms, morals, and ethics as a basis for which the H2H Mindset provides guidance to help to translate these values and norms into words and deeds that put focus on action, not on mere words.[53] And although reputation is difficult to measure and quantify in money terms, it definitely has an impact on the goodwill of a firm and therefore on its actual market value. "A good reputation acts like a magnet. It attracts us to those who have it".[54] This magnet effect on different

---

[49] Häusling, A. (2016). Serie Agile Tools. Personalmagazin, 10, pp. 36-37. Retrieved from https://www.haufe.de/download/personalmagazin-102016-personalmagazin-381028.pdf

[50] Schäfer, A., & Klammer, J. (2016). Service Dominant Logic in Practice: Applying Online Customer Communities and Personas for the Creation of Service Innovations, p. 259. Management, 11(3), pp. 255-264. Retrieved from https://econpapers.repec.org/article/mgtyoumng/v_3a11_3ay_3a2016_3ai_3a3_3ap_3a255-264.htm

[51] Adlin, T., & Pruitt, J. (2009). *op. cit.*, p. 98.

[52] Wüst, C. (2012). *op. cit.*, p. 40.

[53] Sarkar, C., & Kotler, P. (2018). *op. cit.*

[54] Fombrun, C. J., & Van Riel, C. B. M. (2004). Fame & Fortune: How Successful Companies Build Winning Reputations, p. 3. Upper Saddle River, NJ: Pearson Education.

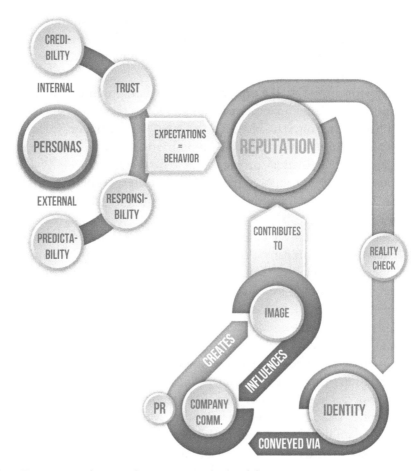

Fig. 4.7 Integrated reputation management model

stakeholders (as shown in Fig. 4.8[55]) can explain the economic value-creating function of reputation. For example, a good reputation will have positive consequences for the firm's ability to raise capital from investors, which then can be used for creating real economic value through innovations and investment into market growth.

4.2   H2H Brand Management

H2H Marketing follows a highly integrative and collaborative approach. Consequently, the brand cannot be viewed separately but rather integrated into the subsystem of H2H Marketing. In the B2B Brand Management

[55] Fombrun, C. J., & Van Riel, C. B. M. (2004). *op. cit.*, p. 5.

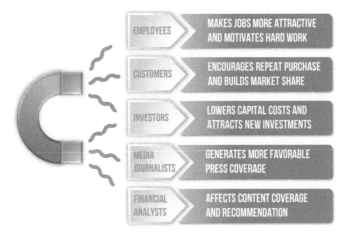

Fig. 4.8   Reputation as a magnet for stakeholders

publication, we defined it as "holistic brand approach." Now, the impact of the three influencing factors of H2H Marketing Model on the H2H Brand Management will be explored, and concrete strategic and operative tools will be presented to face today's challenges in brand management.

The future of marketing and brand management is human-centric. In *Marketing 3.0*[56] human-centric marketing was introduced. Today, this is still considered the next evolutionary step after customer-centric marketing. The human-centric orientation is growing in importance in increasingly "inhuman" times, characterized by artificial intelligence, automation, robotics, etc., and brands need to adapt to this by becoming more human. "Human-centric marketing [...] is still the key to building brand attraction in the digital era as brands with a human character will arguably be the most differentiated".[57]

The newly proposed H2H Brand Management combines three components: holistic brand management constitutes the starting point to which the two pillars *Brand-formative Design (BFD)* and *Collaborative Branding (CB)* are added. Because BFD is a new multi-dimensional communicative means, integrating and creating feelings, emotions, associations or wants with consumers are an integrated part CB helps how a company can mobilize consumers' resources, engaging them in creative and innovation processes (as illustrated in Fig. 4.9).

The holistic brand management had and still has the task to create a consistent and authentic brand on a regional, national, international, and global

---

[56] Kotler, P., Kartajaya, H., & Setiawan, I. (2010). *op. cit.*
[57] Kotler, P., Kartajaya, H., & Setiawan, I. (2017). *op. cit.*, p. 109f.

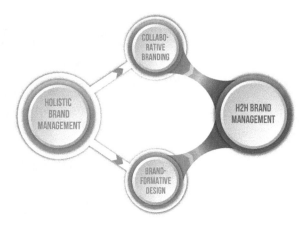

Fig. 4.9   The development process of H2H brand management

scale and to adapt dynamically to new environmental requirements in order to stay relevant as a brand. On this level, the company must strategically determine the *brand identity* and its value propositions to differentiate itself from the competition in the eyes of the customer, generating a *brand image*.

H2H Brand Management is closely linked to the H2H Process, constantly integrating and reacting to human insights, value propositions, content, customer access, and trust. At the operational level, the goal is the consistent implementation of the brand identity in collaboration with the customers and the integrated networks and communities. This co-creation of the brand is one of the essential innovations incorporated into H2H Marketing.

Furthermore, companies need to adjust to the new networked world where the control over the perception of the brand only partially lies in their hands while the word of mouth from friends and family or online community rating systems (the *f-factor*) is becoming increasingly important for purchasing decisions and brand perception.[58] The third component is the brand-characterizing design where products, services, and experiences are designed from the perspective of the brand, taking into account product, customer, and context details.

4.2.1   Holistic Brand Management

When defining what a brand actually is, results are manifold. Following the classic definition of the American Marketing Association, it is described as "a

---

[58] Kotler, P., Kartajaya, H., & Setiawan, I. (2017). *op. cit.*

name, term, sign, symbol, or design, or a combination of these, that identifies the maker or seller of a product or service".[59] Other definitions range from a brand being a promise or an emotional intangible concept of experiences to the sum of perceptions connected to a product or a firm.[60] For this work, we will integrate both definitions and consider a brand as, "[...] a bundle of functional and non-functional benefits, the design of which from the point of view of the target groups of the brand, differentiates itself sustainably from competing offers".[61] This adds the *inside-out* view (brand identity orientation) to the *outside-in* view (brand image orientation). With this definition we combine the supplier view (*brand identity*) with the customer view (*brand image*), the intended benefits with the actual public perception of the brand. Thus, the brand becomes a customer-centric value proposition.

To understand the identity-based brand approach that goes back to Meffert and Burmann,[62] a look at its principles is needed. The identity-based concept goes beyond the outside-in view. Instead of only finding customer needs and orienting the firm accordingly, the inside-out perspective, which analyzes the self-image of the brand from the point of view of all internal target groups, is also integrated. This self-image is the *brand identity*, consisting of the attributes that in the eyes of the internal target groups are characteristic to the brand. Opposite to the brand's identity is the *brand image* as illustrated in Fig. 4.10.[63]

The brand identity can be actively developed and formed, the brand image, on the other hand, emerges time-delayed and only indirectly as a consequence of the brand identity management. The first step in creating a strong brand is the creation of a *brand promise*, condensing the brand identity to tangible, comprehensible statements about its utility. It should fulfil two functions: *customer needs (brand needs)* and a differentiation from the competition.

Under *brand behavior*, the product and service provision of the brand are understood as the behavior of brand representatives in direct contact with customers and all other contacts with the customer, e.g., advertisement.

---

[59] Kotler, P., & Armstrong, G. (2010). Principles of Marketing (13th ed.), p. 255. Upper Saddle River, NJ: Pearson.

[60] Kotler, P., & Pfoertsch, W. A. (2006). B2B Brand Management. Berlin, Germany: Springer.

[61] Burmann, C., Halaszovich, T., Schade, M., & Hemmann, F. (2015). Identitätsbasierte Markenführung: Grundlagen - Strategie - Umsetzung - Controlling (2nd ed.), p. 28. Wiesbaden, Germany: Springer Gabler. Translation from German to English.

[62] Meffert, H., & Burmann, C. (1996). Identitätsorientierte Markenführung. In H. Meffert, H. Wagner, & K. Backhaus (Eds.), Arbeitspapier Nr. 100 der Wissenschaftlichen Gesellschaft für Marketing und Unternehmensführung e.V. Münster, Germany: Wissenschaftliche Gesellschaft für Marketing und Unternehmensführung.

[63] Burmann, C., Halaszovich, T., Schade, M., & Hemmann, F. (2015). *op. cit.,* p. 30.

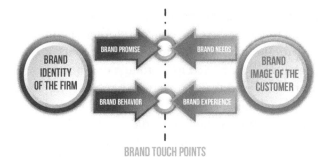

Fig. 4.10 Brand identity and brand image in the identity-based branding concept

Inversely, the customer's *brand experience*, which is the interactions between customer and brand, is reflected in the resulting *brand image*.

For the here proposed brand management to be successful, a high brand authenticity is needed to deliver brand experiences that fulfil the customer's needs across all touchpoints. This means that the brand promise that was given and the actual brand behavior need to be in line. Otherwise, a bad brand image and word of mouth are to be expected. When defining the brand identity, the firm has to consider four constitutive characteristics, which are shown in Table 4.1.[64]

The four constitutive characteristics were derived from analyzing the identity concept of individuals, which is comparable to the brand identity concepts proposed in the identity-based branding. For brands, this means that differentiation from other brands, the relational interaction, is a prerequisite

Table 4.1 Characteristics of identity and its implications for brand management

Characteristic	Implications
Reciprocity	The brand identity only develops in comparing the own brand with other brands: Being in relation with others and differentiating oneself
Continuity	Maintaining the essential defining brand characteristics over time
Consistency	Avoidance of contradictions in brand appearance at all brand touchpoints and in the behavior of executives and employees of the brand. Ongoing coherent coordination of the essential brand characteristics
Individuality	Uniqueness of essential identity features compared to competing brands

[64] The original table is in German and has been translated to English. Adapted from Burmann, C., Halaszovich, T., Schade, M., & Hemmann, F. (2015). *op. cit.,* p. 36.

for building or changing a brand (*reciprocity*). Individuals search for *continuity* and tend to stick to essential characteristics over a long period of time. The same holds true for brands. Further, *consistency* is crucial; the internal identity and the outer image need to be coherent – "walk your talk." *Individuality* on a personal level is determined in biological and sociological uniqueness. For brands, it is a conscious effort to achieve an individual brand perception. This is done either by underlining single, individual characteristics or by offering an individual combination of characteristics that would not necessarily be considered individual.[65]

In addition, meaningful brand characteristics must be considered when the company defines its brand identity. According to H2H Brand Management, relating the brand to the solution of a human problem (H2H problem) is the best way to create a meaningful brand identity. The overarching brand strategy goals are derived from this process, and a specific value proposition for the customer is the result. The value proposition, as well as all operations on the brand touchpoints, should be permeated by the H2H Mindset. The value proposition of the brand could stand in contrast to its intended brand behavior, which then influences the customer-perceived brand image in the eyes of the customer. This image must be constantly reevaluated, depending on the brand experience on the touchpoints, as well as through brand usage. It must prove to fulfil the brand needs that initiated the interaction between the customer and the brand. In this process (see Fig. 4.11), the brand serves as a mediator between the intended identity of a company and the brand image of the customer. The brand identity results from the vision and mission, corporate goals, value proposition, and operations of a company. The customer

Fig. 4.11   The relationship between firm, brand, and the customer

---

[65] Burmann, C., Halaszovich, T., Schade, M., & Hemmann, F. (2015). *op. cit.*

absorbs this through his perception and the experiences made with the brand and translates this into the use of the brand to meet his needs.

In the case of discrepancies between image and identity, adjustments must be applied to maintain consistency. An essential function of H2H Marketing is to build a brand that provides orientation and safety to stakeholders as an anchor in an increasingly dynamic, networked world. This is grounded on the understanding of customer processes and the resulting opportunities to gain insights that inspire and convince customers emotionally and cognitively, something we call *digital anthropology*.[66] In this sense, H2H Brand Management is the ultimate form of communicative interaction.

4.2.2   Factor S-DL: Development of a New Brand Logic

Parallel to the change from G-DL to S-DL thinking, branding has also experienced a shifting logic.[67] Branding is at present considered a collaborative, co-creation process.[68] The evolution of brand logic over time can be seen in Fig. 4.12.[69]

Branding in its early years was highly goods and output-oriented, and brands served as identifiers for customers to recognize goods visually. The customer had a passive role, as a mere recipient of *value-in-exchange*, the embedded brand value in the goods sold; thus together with the brand, he remained an operand resource – "resources on which an operation or act is performed to produce an effect".[70]

In the 1930s until the 1990s, brands became functional and symbolic images, from which customers gained knowledge about the brand's capability to fulfil their utilitarian or symbolic needs. Brands focused not only on the functional (external) but also the symbolic (internal) benefits for the customers. This was arguably needed to achieve differentiation from competitors whose offerings were becoming increasingly similar. Brands were considered

---

[66] Kotler, P., Kartajaya, H., & Setiawan, I. (2017). *op. cit.*

[67] Merz, M. A., He, Y., & Vargo, S. L. (2009). The evolving brand logic: a service-dominant logic perspective. Journal of the Academy of Marketing Science, 37(3), pp. 328-344. https://doi.org/10.1007/s11747-009-0143-3

[68] Rossi, C. (2015, May 27-29). Collaborative Branding [Conference paper]. Paper presented at the MakeLearn & TIIM Joint International Conference, Bari, Italy. Retrieved from https://www.researchgate.net/publication/282763907_COLLABORATIVE_BRANDING

[69] For the excursus on the evolving brand logic, if not noted differently see Merz, M. A., He, Y., & Vargo, S. L. (2009). op. cit. The shown figure is adapted from Merz et al. (2009). The Age of Transcendence notion is based on Sisodia et al. (2014).

[70] Vargo, S. L., & Lusch, R. F. (2004). Evolving to a New Dominant Logic for Marketing, p. 2. Journal of Marketing, 68(1), pp. 1-17. https://doi.org/10.1509/jmkg.68.1.1.24036

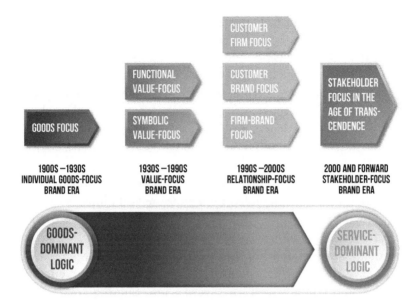

Fig. 4.12 The evolving brand logic

to be operant resources, which could be seen separately from the product offering. Customers remained operand resources *to* which the goods were branded. In the 1990s to 2000, the relationship-focus brand, "the general focus of branding switched from the brand image as the primary driver of brand value to the customer as a significant actor in the brand value creation process".[71] External customers and internal employees were now seen as participants in the increasingly interactive co-creation of the brand. Thinking shifted from viewing customers as operand resources, i.e., passive recipients to being considered as operant resources, active co-creators of brand value. This led to the determination that brand value changed from value-in-exchange to value-in-use perception of the customers.[72] Abolishing the value-in-exchange perspective also had implications for strategic marketing. While before the Point-of-Sale received major attention, service and relationship building came into the spotlight, with brand value determined in-use *after* the purchase. This created the effect that "the *time logic* of marketing exchange becomes open-ended".[73]

---

[71] Merz, M. A., He, Y., & Vargo, S. L. (2009). *op. cit.*

[72] Merz, M. A., He, Y., & Vargo, S. L. (2009). *op. cit.*

[73] Ballantyne, D., & Aitken, R. (2007). Branding in B2B markets: Insights from the service-dominant logic of marketing, p. 364. Journal of Business & Industrial Marketing, 22(6), pp. 363-371. https://doi.org/10.1108/08858620710780127

Furthermore, a change from output orientation to process orientation took place. Firms' employees were identified internal customers and as important drivers in the value co-creation, not only as makers of the physical product but also as service. Brands were now a promise to external customers with internal customers playing a crucial role.[74] This internal customer perspective and the resulting focus on service are in congruency with the S-DL, "S-D logic [...] suggests that it is the service experiences of customers that most commonly impact on brand value, through brand awareness and brand memory".[75]

With the upcoming movement towards a network perspective, the dyadic relationship concept gets replaced by *network* relationships, connecting the firm with brand communities and other stakeholders and *social* relationships between customers or other stakeholders (see Fig. 4.13[76]).

Now that we have established that brands are co-created, what implications does this have from an S-DL point of view? Today's brands are identifying, informative, and symbolic and have social interaction function. The various kinds of services brands offered to customers can be distinguished[77]:

- **The brand as a service for facilitating information processing**
  This kind of service is based on the identifying as well as the information function of brands. Products marked with a brand can be identified and distinguished more easily from other goods. This function has its origins in the time of strong product focus following the G-DL. S-DL constitutes a service to the customer, facilitating information processed during the purchasing process. In this context, the brand also offers an information function. Customers with previous experiences can use their knowledge (operant resource) to simplify information gathering and processing faced with complex market offerings.[78]

- **The brand as a service to influence the customer's self-concept**
  This kind of service goes back to the symbolic aspect of the brand, which can emerge from the firm's marketing measures or be determined by external

---

[74] Merz, M. A., He, Y., & Vargo, S. L. (2009). *op. cit.*

[75] Ballantyne, D., & Aitken, R. (2007). *op. cit.*, p. 367.

[76] Adapted from Merz, M. A., He, Y., & Vargo, S. L. (2009). *op. cit.*, p. 337.

[77] For the following see Drengner, J., Jahn, S., & Gaus, H. (2013). Der Beitrag der Service-Dominant Logic zur Weiterentwicklung der Markenführung. Die Betriebswirtschaft, 73(2), pp. 143-160. Retrieved from https://www.academia.edu/12178909/Der_Beitrag_der_Service-Dominant_Logic_zur_Weiterentwicklung_der_Markenf%C3%BChrung

[78] Drengner, J., Jahn, S., & Gaus, H. (2013). *op. cit.*

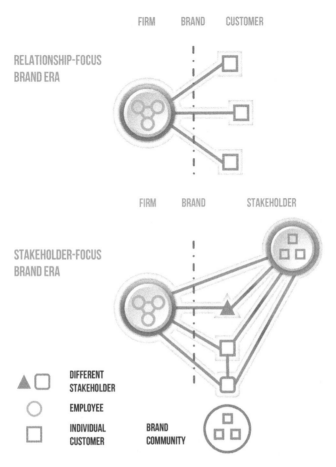

Fig. 4.13 From dyadic (1990s–2000) to network relationships (2000 and forward)

actors, the customers, the media, other organizations, etc. These co-created associations go beyond the functional value into the internal symbolic needs of the customers.[79] The symbolic function is best seen in luxury goods. A customer buys a luxury car, not primarily for the functional benefit of transportation but rather for the symbolic association of the brand that the customer wants to transfer onto herself.[80]

- **The brand as a service for building and maintaining social relationships**
  With the network perspective, brands now have a social interaction function, bringing customers together in different community groups. This can

---

[79] Merz, M. A., He, Y., & Vargo, S. L. (2009). *op. cit.*
[80] Drengner, J., Jahn, S., & Gaus, H. (2013). *op. cit.*

range from classic brand communities, where people share the same pleasure for a brand, to anti-brand communities, which collectively oppose a brand, to non-brand-focused communities, which shuns brands altogether. Thus, the brand's service in terms of the S-DL lies in creating opportunities for the customers to socially interact and build relationships, whatever they may be.

At the beginning of this chapter, the concept of identity-based brand management, connecting the self-concept of the firm with the perspective of the customers, was introduced. In S-DL brand logic, this identity-based model needs to undergo adaptations, because it "implicitly treats the brand as an asset fully controllable by the firm".[81] It does not acknowledge the influence of the customers and their socio-cultural environment; it considers the customers only as an operand resources. Ballantyne and Aitken confirm this by pointing out that the identity-based approach "ignores the value-in-use derived from a product by a customer over time, and also the word-of-mouth communicative effects generated from within brand communities." Additionally, there is an impetus for further developing identity, as the brand image is considered "dynamically constructed through social interaction".[82]

We support the work from Jan Drengner[83] that proposes a holistic way of viewing brand management in accordance with the S-DL. On one side, the brand is seen as part of a firm's value proposition; on the other side, it is seen as the socio-cultural context and interaction space of brands and customers that determine *brand meaning*. Under brand meaning, in this context, we understand it as the sum of individual experiences, associations, feelings, and behavior that generates a mental projection with an underlying meaning in the mind of the customer.[84, 85] As such, "brand meanings are socially constructed and in the public domain"[86].

To take these new considerations into account, we introduce a concept based on the S-DL that we call socio-culturally integrated brand management (shown in Fig. 4.14[87]), in which not the *brand image* is of interest, as in the identity-based model, but rather the *brand meaning*.

---

[81] Drengner, J., Jahn, S., & Gaus, H. (2013). *op. cit.*, p. 144.

[82] Ballantyne, D., & Aitken, R. (2007). *op. cit.*, p. 365.

[83] Drengner, J., Jahn, S., & Gaus, H. (2013). *op. cit.*

[84] Sherry, J. F. (2005). Brand Meaning. In A. M. Tybout, & T. Calkins (Eds.), Kellogg on Branding: The Marketing Faculty of The Kellogg School of Management (pp. 40-69). Hoboken, NJ: Wiley.

[85] Tarnovskaya, V., & Biedenbach, G. (2018). Corporate rebranding failure and brand meanings in the digital environment. Marketing Intelligence and Planning, 36(4), pp. 455-469. https://doi.org/10.1108/MIP-09-2017-0192

[86] Ballantyne, D., & Aitken, R. (2007). *op. cit.*, p. 365.

[87] Adapted from Drengner, J., Jahn, S., & Gaus, H. (2013). *op. cit.*, p. 154.

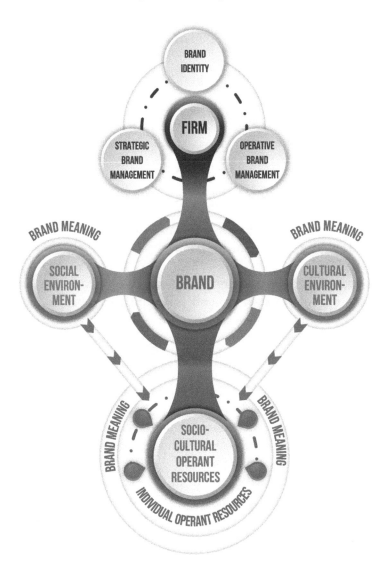

Fig. 4.14 Socio-culturally integrated brand management based on the S-DL

The brand identity in its intended meaning is still the starting point. The brand must offer a value proposition to the customers, who by using their operant resources attribute meaning to it. Customers with a similar socio-cultural background use similar operant resources to create value out of the value propositions. This may attribute coinciding meanings to a brand. The

Fig. 4.15 From informational to dialogical: new ways of communication

brand meaning is thus influenced by the socio-cultural environment, *co-created* under use of the customers' resources and *individually* determined.[88]

This implies boundaries in possibilities to influence brand meaning. Advertisement may have its limits when it comes to creating brand meaning, whereas trusted sources such as word of mouth coming from friends, colleagues, or family are considered more reliable. In times of co-created brand meaning, new forms of communication are needed (see Fig. 4.15[89]).

"We think it limiting to consider interaction and communication as separate processes. Any form of interaction between buyer and supplier acts as a source of brand meaning [...]".[90] In a service-dominant branding logic where customers are not passive receivers of one-way persuasive communication but, rather, interactive, co-creating resource integrators, communicational and dialogical interaction along all brand touchpoints should be embraced to successfully co-create brand meaning.[91]

H2H Marketing thus takes the identity-based holistic brand management as its foundation, which then is expanded to include the findings of the S-DL. Brand identity should be designed and communicated in a reasonable way. It should also be clear that the brand image, respectively, brand meaning, is co-created taking into account the social-cultural context of the customers. Thereby, the brand becomes a service and fulfils a variety of functions.

[88] Drengner, J., Jahn, S., & Gaus, H. (2013). *op. cit.*
[89] Ballantyne, D., & Aitken, R. (2007). *op. cit.*, p. 367.
[90] Ballantyne, D., & Aitken, R. (2007). *op. cit.*, p. 367.
[91] See also Drengner, J., Jahn, S., & Gaus, H. (2013). *op. cit.*

4.2.3   Factor Digitalization: The New Customer Path in the Connectivity Age

In the last chapter, we talked about the changes in customer behavior and the relationship between firm and customer caused by increased interconnectedness. With the rise of digital channels, customers can constantly switch between online and offline channels (*channel hopping*) and are not easy to trace. Since customers' expectations are also changing, firms look to multi- or Omnichannel approaches to make a consistent customer experience across all touchpoints possible.

For customers, digital advancement has two consequences. Firms have the possibility to overwhelm customers with endless outbound marketing communication by sending emails, tailored online ads, etc. On the other hand, customers utilize more ways to search for information and are active via inbound marketing. They block intrusive communication measures and comb through a vast number of resources to find transparent information. A commoditization transforms value proposition models in many sectors. At the same time, the overexposure to stimuli overstrains customers and makes them look for other sources they can trust which they find in friends, colleagues, and family.[92] With these new developments comes a new customer path, as shown in Fig. 4.16.

In the pre-connectivity era, the understanding of people's buying process was characterized by the 4 As: Customers become *aware* of a brand; then develop an *attitude* towards it, either positive or negative; decide how to *act*

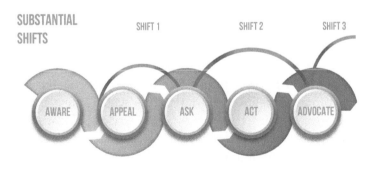

Fig. 4.16   The new customer path in the connectivity era

---

[92] Kotler, P., Kartajaya, H., & Setiawan, I. (2017). *op. cit.*

with purchase decision; and, finally, consider if they should buy again, *act again*. The 4A model is a typical funnel-shaped process, since with every step, the number of customers decrease.[93]

With connectivity, fundamental shifts in customer behavior took place, which created the need for a new customer path, the 5 As (already shown in Sect. 4.1.4), to adequately map the buying process.[94] Let's have a look at these particular shifts:

Shift 1: Liking or disliking a brand (the *attitude*) used to be defined individually, while today, the social context of the individual becomes a deciding factor. In the connectivity era, the initial *appeal* of a brand is influenced by the community surrounding the customer to determine the final attitude. Many seemingly personal decisions are actually social decisions.

Shift 2 represents the changed meaning of loyalty and the target setting companies derive from it. While loyalty before was seen in the repurchase of a brand, in the connectivity era, loyalty is ultimately defined as the willingness to advocate a brand.

Shift 3 is found in the growing connectedness among customers ask-and-advocate relationships, which rely on other customers to find out more about specific brands. The feedback they get positively or negatively affects the appeal of the brand.

These three shifts lead us to the new customer path consisting of the 5 As. The path starts with the *aware* phase, in which customers know a brand as a result of past experience, marketing communications, and/or the advocacy of others. In the *appeal* phase, the customer then processes these impressions and develops attraction towards certain brands. He then tries to find out more in the *ask phase* about the brands he is attracted to by, for example, getting into contact with other customers or studying online reviews. If convinced, the customer may take the next step with *act*. This does not only include the purchase of the product but also other interaction such as filing a complaint in case of a negative experience or post-purchase services. The advocate level is the last phase and is considered the highest goal in modern marketing by the creators of the 5A approach (for a more detailed overview of the 5 A customer path, see Fig. 4.17).

The high valuation of brand advocacy stems from customers increasingly turning to their social environment for information, rather than to the firms.

---

[93] Kotler, P., Kartajaya, H., & Setiawan, I. (2017). *op. cit.*
[94] Kotler, P., Kartajaya, H., & Setiawan, I. (2017). *op. cit.*

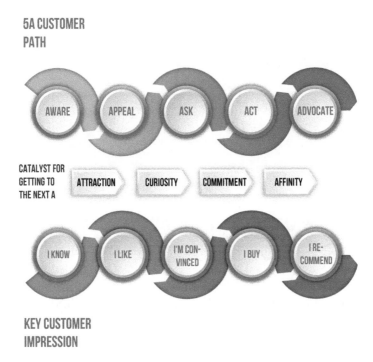

Fig. 4.17 The 5A customer path in detail

The increasing digitalization is reinforcing this effect. In a world of increasing volatility, uncertainty, complexity, and ambiguity (VUCA) brands serve more and more as trust anchors. The increasing digitalization leads to less and less direct contacts between employees of the branding companies and the customers. A humanized brand takes over this role of direct contact in a digitalized world. The effects of typical outbound marketing measures are declining,[95] which is partly due to a typical paradox in today's marketing. While customers today are more informed than ever, distraction, thanks to connectivity, is also at a record high. As the attention span and the time customers have for decisions decrease, while decisions to be made are manifold, they turn to the ones they trust for advice, which comes with substantial loss of control on the company side.[96]

This process is described as the "democratization of branding," essentially paraphrasing the Scott Cook quotation given at the beginning of the chapter, as they go on to state: "Technology-driven empowerment of consumers, such as the production of brand meaning by (micro) blogging, interaction in social

---

[95] Halligan, B., & Shah, D. (2018). *op. cit.*
[96] Kotler, P., Kartajaya, H., & Setiawan, I. (2017). *op. cit.*

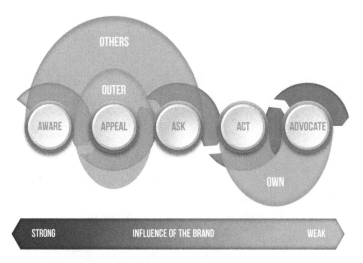

Fig. 4.18 The o-zone

networks or producing and disseminating brand advocacy, leads to new power relationships in both the commercial and non-commercial realms of branding".[97] Already in 2010, it had recognized the mode of action and the importance of brand advocacy inside social networks.

The influence that firms can have on brand communities and interpersonal communication is limited, which is why the loyal advocates of a brand come into play. When questions about a brand arise, there should be brand advocates stepping in to have a positive influence on the brand image and purchase decisions. Brand advocacy, another term for *word of mouth*, can be *active*, but only in rare cases, customers actively promote a brand. Otherwise, it can be *prompted*, by triggering. The two main triggers for prompted advocacy are negative brand advocacy or questions by others. In the light of this, negative advocacy from so-called brand haters is not to be considered a necessarily bad thing, as it can help activate advocates that might have remained inactive.[98]

Going all the way towards brand advocacy, each step of the customer path is situated in different spheres of influence (indicated in Fig. 4.18), a concept introduced as the *O-Zone*.

Getting closer to the personal center of the customer towards his *own* influence sphere, the influence of the brand diminishes. In the *outer* sphere, the firms are still in charge, managing the communication and touchpoints with

[97]Kemming, J. D., & Humborg, C. (2010). Democracy and nation brand(ing): Friends or foes?, p. 193. Place Branding and Public Diplomacy, 6(3), pp. 183-197. Retrieved from https://www.researchgate.net/publication/47378882_Democracy_and_nation_branding_Friends_or_foes

[98]Kotler, P., Kartajaya, H., & Setiawan, I. (2017). *op. cit.*

the customer. Entering the *others'* zone, communities and social contacts of the customers (*the f-factor*) are the deciding factors in influencing customers. Conversations inside communities, reviews, and rating systems, as well as advice from family and friends, are driving the purchase decision, resulting in a loss of influence on the side of the firm. The *own* influence is characterized as "a result of past experience and interaction with several brands, personal judgment and evaluation of the brands, and ultimately individual preference towards the chosen brand(s)"[99] and is thus beyond any direct control of the firm.

The three spheres are interconnected and interact with each other. For example, a brand does an excellent job on its *outer* influence sphere by providing a convincing experience, which results in positive word of mouth to others that consequently affects the personal brand assessment and preferences of the customer herself.

Firms have a certain influence on the aware and ask phases, which lie at the intersection of the *others'* and *outer* sphere, as well as exclusive influence on the brand appeal, while act and advocate are outside of the direct reach of the brand's influence. Brands, therefore, must focus on the outer and partially the others' sphere to affect the customers positively.[100] Along the way from awareness to advocacy, there are catalysts that marketers can leverage to break up bottlenecks between the steps:

- **First Catalyst: Increasing Attraction**

  Various approaches are viable to improve a brand's appeal. Brands with a human touch can make a brand more appealing to customers, since they are not perceived as robots without feelings but "a person with mind, heart and human spirit." In concordance with what the S-DL dictates, brands should treat customers as an operant resource on an equal footing, as "equal friends".[101]

  In addition to that, *brand activism*, meaning, taking a clear stand on current social, political, environmental, or economic issues, can strongly affect the brand appeal. Further focus should lie on the differentiation from competitors, for example, by offering customization or exceptional experiences, as Kotler et al. conclude: "The more bold, audacious, and unorthodox the differentiation is, the greater the brand's appeal is".[102]

---

[99] Kotler, P., Kartajaya, H., & Setiawan, I. (2017). *op. cit.*, p. 67.
[100] Kotler, P., Kartajaya, H., & Setiawan, I. (2017). *op. cit.*
[101] Kotler, P., Kartajaya, H., & Setiawan, I. (2017). *op. cit.*, p. 81.
[102] Kotler, P., Kartajaya, H., & Setiawan, I. (2017). *op. cit.*, p. 83.

- *Second Catalyst: Optimizing Curiosity*

Curiosity is the result of a discrepancy between the current and the desired state of knowledge. The true potential of creating curiosity lies in offering interesting information without being too revealing and thus demystifying the brand.[103] An effective way to do so is found in *Content Marketing* which will be discussed in the next chapter (see Chap. 5).

- *Third Catalyst: Increasing Commitment*

At this point, the customers may be convinced of a brand, but there is still a way to go until the actual purchase takes place. For this to happen, firms need to provide a seamless experience along all touchpoints. As customers are constantly switching between online and offline channels,[104, 105] an integrating approach towards channel management is necessary, which can be found in Omnichannel Marketing (more on that in Chap. 5.5).

- *Fourth Catalyst: Increasing Affinity*

To successfully transition from the sole purchasing act to turning customers into loyal advocates, firms need to engage with their customers beyond the typical touchpoints. This can mean building a rewards and loyalty program and interaction on social media or using gamification to get into closer contact. Without question, the post-purchase phase is where, for customers, the moment of truth arrives[106]: Does the product or service I purchased stand up to the pre-purchase promises given by the brand? The answer to the question has a strong effect on whether the customer develops an affinity towards a brand.

To conclude: There is an enormous increase in the importance of the customers' social context in purchasing decisions, whereby brands have to give up a part of their power. This makes it all the more important for companies to leverage phenomena and tools like word of mouth, brand advocacy, and brand communities in order to benefit from these developments. The loss of control is a wake-up call for marketers, showing that it is no longer they who sit in the driver's seat. Or in the form of a subtler hint, "Brand management should rather be a guiding activity, not a controlling one".[107]

---

[103] Kotler, P., Kartajaya, H., & Setiawan, I. (2017). *op. cit.*
[104] Haderlein, A. (2012). Die digitale Zukunft des stationären Handels: Auf allen Kanälen zum Kunden. München, Germany: mi-Wirtschaftsbuch.
[105] Heinemann, G. (2014). *op. cit.*
[106] See e.g. Vargo, S. L., & Lusch, R. F. (2016). *op. cit.*
[107] Rossi, C. (2015, May 27-29). *op. cit.*, p. 1886.

4.2.4   Factor Design Thinking: Brand-Formative Design

This subchapter puts emphasis on the interrelation of design and the brand. Usually, design is analyzed separately without recognizing the effect that convincing design can have on brands. As Of in his work on what he calls *Brand-formative Design* (BFD) lays out,[108] design can have a differentiating function, especially in the eyes of the commoditization trend let loose by digitalization. Therefore, design can contribute to building a competitive advantage by offering differentiation and thus have strategic importance. He concludes: "Design can be a tool to create uniqueness, to communicate values, to entertain, to simplify selections and to create consumer satisfaction".[109] In this short statement, the parallels to the functions of a brand and the inseparability of both become evident. Delightful and refreshing design of products, services, and the whole customer experience can have strong positive effects on brand management. "[J]ust one moment of unexpected delight from a brand is all it takes to transform a customer into the brand's loyal advocate".[110]

As was seen in the Design Thinking chapter, there is ambiguity in the somewhat subjective term *design*. The strict separation of marketers and designers is visible in the different understanding and practical approach to design and in the claims over its control that both parties express together with others, for example, engineers.[111] While traditional designers may focus on physical or aesthetic aspects of a product, H2H Marketing adopts a broader perspective. In an experience-oriented society searching for meaning, the focus lies increasingly on the design of meaningful experiences rather than on the exclusively physical design of objects.

In the spirit of Design Thinking, interdisciplinary convergence is needed. "Marketers must acquire a better understanding of the design process and designers must acquire a better understanding of the marketing process".[112] Design products, or services, touchpoints, etc., need to be understood as "objects in the context of subjects".[113] A visual representation of the contextual incorporation of design is given in Fig. 4.19.[114]

---

[108] For the following see Of, J. (2014). Brand Formative Design: Development and Assessment of Product Design from a Future, Brand and Consumer Perspective [Doctoral thesis]. Retrieved from http://d-nb.info/1053319665

[109] Of, J. (2014). *op. cit.,* p. 3.

[110] Kotler, P., Kartajaya, H., & Setiawan, I. (2017). *op. cit.,* p. 59.

[111] Of, J. (2014). *op. cit.*

[112] Kotler, P., Rath, G. A. (1984). DESIGN: A POWERFUL BUT NEGLECTED STRATEGIC TOOL, p. 19. Journal of Business Strategy, 5(2), pp. 16-21. https://doi.org/10.1108/eb039054

[113] Of, J. (2014). *op. cit.,* p. 77.

[114] Adapted from Of, J. (2014). *op. cit.,* p. 84.

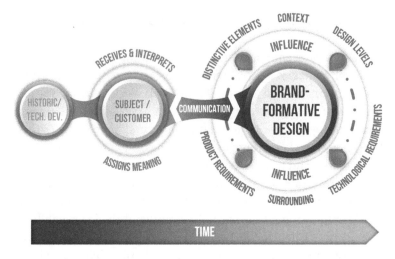

Fig. 4.19 Relationships between product, person, and context in brand-formative design

The subject in this model refers to the recipients (consumers) of the designed object (product, service, etc.), which is evaluated differently depending on the specific context. What is noteworthy is the perfect coherence between Of's model and the S-DL. The design does not in itself contain value but is received by the consumers, interpreted by using their knowledge and is finally assigned an individual meaning. Value creation in the S-DL is contextual *value-in-context* and experiential[115]; the same goes for design. The effectiveness and the meaning of design are closely tied to its context.[116] For example, the design of a gold-plated chandelier may be considered appropriate in a castle or a luxurious mansion but may appear absurd and pretentious in other circumstances. Also, the time factor is an important part of the context. A design which 20 years ago was considered outstanding may not evoke the same positive reactions today.[117]

In the spirit of accepting customers as collaborating partners and moving the human being into the center of marketing, firms may also actively involve them in the design process of *co-designing*. For this, firms need to determine the role of the customer in the design process, at which stages he will be involved, and how big his scope of design shall be. While Jan Of[118] focuses mainly on the customer's involvement in the physical design consisting of

---

[115] Vargo, S. L., & Lusch, R. F. (2016). *op. cit.*

[116] Of, J. (2014). *op. cit.*

[117] Of, J. (2014). *op. cit.*

[118] Of, J. (2014). *op. cit.*

packaging, logo, colors, etc., companies can consider at which other design points customers can be involved to better meet their preferences.

The work on BFD shows the importance that design has in the context of brand management that needs to be taken into account by marketers and people of other disciplines. As a practical recommendation, the iconic ten principles of good design by world-renown designer Dieter Rams can be helpful[119]:

1. "Good design is innovative."
2. "Good design makes a product useful."
3. "Good design is aesthetic."
4. "Good design makes a product understandable."
5. "Good design is unobtrusive."
6. "Good design is honest."
7. "Good design is long-lasting."
8. "Good design is thorough down to the last detail."
9. "Good design is environmentally-friendly."
10. "Good design is as little design as possible."

Following these recommendations, allowing co-creation in the design process, as well as understanding the contextual nature of design meaning will help marketers create a positive outcome from the interaction between design and the brand.

4.3   Branding in H2H Marketing

H2H Brand Management builds on the Customer-Based Brand Equity Approach[120] which is still relevant and key to brand management. Because of the impacting factors of the H2H Marketing Model, it has to be adapted today (see Fig. 4.20):

1. The brand purpose as the key component of the brand identity has to be related to the human problem a company can solve authentically. The capabilities of the company that enable it to solve such a problem are key for the brand positioning process. Brand meaning is key to the brand iden-

---

[119] For the following see Vitsœ. (n.d.). The power of good design: Dieter Rams's ideology, engrained within Vitsœ. Retrieved from https://www.vitsoe.com/gb/about/good-design

[120] Keller, K.L., Apéria, T., Georgson, M., 2008. Strategic brand management: A European perspective. Pearson Education.

Fig. 4.20 H2H brand management inside the H2H marketing model

tity. The promise and the proof to solve such problems load the brand with meaning for the involved and hopefully engaged stakeholders.

2. The brand personality has to be humanized and emotionalized to facilitate brand identity for the stakeholders.
3. The brand identity must be made dynamic by monitoring cultural changes and adapting the identity to these trends accordingly.
4. Companies must co-create the brand meaning with their customers and other authors from the outer zone. Brand communities (the f-factor and the O-Zone) have to be established and integrated into brand management and communication.
5. The brand communication has to be adapted from information to dialogue.
6. Trust, experience, and engagement have to be established as key performance indicators in brand management and have to be controlled continuously.
7. Companies should establish brand characterizing design as another dimension in the research and development process.

To overcome the big trust crisis, brand must be related to the authentic, human, and emotional promise of a company and/or product to solve a human problem effectively. This can be done either alone or even more authentically, together with other partners as a collaborate network. Only then, all stakeholders will trust a brand. The brand will become a trust anchor in a more and more destabilized environment. With the management approaches of CRM, CXM, CSR, reputation, service, and, finally, brand management, companies can develop and keep the trust they need to keep the brand relevant through the entire customer journey and help the customer to make their decisions. Companies need to keep their reputation management effective and create success stories with continuous reference streams as a magnet for all stakeholders. Liqui Moly is a traditional German brand from southern Germany, which could be used as an outstanding example. The company specializes in the production of fuel additives, lubricants, and motor oils and turned a commodity product supplied by huge international suppliers like ExxonMobil, British Petroleum, Chevron, or the most profitable company Aramco into a branded icon. With its full range, the company covers almost every wish of a motor enthusiast and is distribution to customers all over the world by OTV International. Liqui Moly oils and lubricants are used in cars, two-wheelers, commercial vehicles, construction machinery, boats, or garden tools. Whether for industrial, commercial, or private use, Liqui Moly products improve the service life of engines and units. The brand Liqui Moly has established very close relationship with all stakeholders through human-oriented management. Therefore, the brand is awarded almost annually as Germany's most popular engine oil brand. The company's products are highly regarded by both professionals and private users. They have a very strict code of compliance and show visible engagement for responsibility in and for the society (in German "sichtbares Engagement für gesellschaftliche Verantwortung"). The product solutions ensure that wear and tear on the engine has little effect and that its mileage is guaranteed for years at a high level.

A holistic brand management which considers collaborative brand and brand characterizing design is the foundation for this kind of success. With the change from G-DL to S-DL, brand logic also evolved and created a human-oriented focus which includes all stakeholders of the firm in the relevant ecosystems. From there on, brands are socio-culturally interpreted in dialogical way of communication. Digitalization opened up new means of connectivity and created new consumer paths.

The new H2H Brand Management which incorporates Design Thinking, the Service-Dominant Logic, and digitalization give marketers of today a powerful tool to be more meaningful and relevant for the stakeholders. The future of H2H Brand Management is human-centric built on brand-characterized design and acting from a customer's point of view. Together with the "humanized brand personality," it becomes more human.

The Service-Dominant Logic added the co-creation of the brand meaning and the networking perspective and makes the brand to operant resource. With digitalization, new customer journey and multidirectional communication is possible to form the brand into a trust anchor. Following these recommendations, allowing co-creation in the design process, as well as understanding the contextual nature of design meaning will help marketers create a positive outcome from the interaction between design and the brand.

In our daily lives, we want to be surrounded by trust-worth brands. Yet, in the corporate world, only very few executives act accordingly. Many don't know about the concept, and only some are able to know how to apply it. Its best application of H2H Brand Management could be found in the concept of B2B2C branding,[121] mostly known as Ingredient Branding. It is an effective and proven strategy that assists B2B companies to step out of the shadows of anonymity and become visible to the end consumer. Brands that are well-known today have exemplified that with the help of Ingredient Branding differentiation.[122] Ingredient Brands can distance themselves from competitors and enabling revenue and profitability growth. Large companies such as Intel, Huawei, and Microsoft have gained a competitive advantage. Also smaller companies like Gore Textiles, Schott Glass, and Recaro Seating applied the Ingredient Branding principle successfully and contributed immensely to their current success.

Aditya Birla Group is applying Ingredient Branding in their cellulose division Birla Cellulose with the Brand Liva and newly Livaeco. The Aditya Birla Group developed a playbook to create more H2H Brands within their group and reorient their corporate efforts for more human-oriented business. They wanted to create clarity about what Ingredient Branding is, which mechanisms it follows, and which advantages and disadvantages its application brings with it. Second, they wanted to deliver criteria to judge whether Ingredient Branding is a suitable strategy for its different businesses and, third, provide a clear step-by-step process how to put the theory into practice and accelerate the growth and profitability. Once implemented

[121] Pfoertsch, W., Beuk, F., Luczak, Ch. (2007). Classification of Brands: The case for B2B, B2C and B2B2C; Proceedings of the Academy of Marketing Studies, Volume 12, Number 1 Jacksonville, USA.

[122] Oliva, R., Srivastava, R., Pfoertsch, W., Chandler, J. (2009). Insights on Ingredient Branding, ISBM Report 08-2009, Pennsylvania State University, University Park, PA. USA.

successfully, Ingredient Branding Management becomes important to maintain a favorable market position and provide human-oriented offerings.[123]

Storyline

In this chapter, we got to know the second brave action of H2H Marketing–H2H Management. After a short introduction to the recent trust crisis, we learned about different approaches to manage trust as the central currency with which customers pay the offering companies. Brand activism is a first mean to manage trust. It represents a further development of the CSR concept and can be used to move from "green washing" to "walk the talk." With brand activism companies can integrate all essential stakeholders including the society and our planet into their goal and value system. Activism indicated that companies have to execute actions that serve these stakeholders significant and perceivable. From the definition of the term "trust," we learned that only experiential and reputational trusts are manageable. Customer Experience Management and reputation management are therefore the logical approaches to managing both types of trust. We walked along the 5 As customer path and discovered the importance to design and manage the experience at each and every touchpoint along this journey. We identified the importance of proactive expectation management for the reputation management. We then turned our attention to H2H Brand Management and realized that the CBBE approach must be further developed based on the findings of Design Thinking, Service-Dominant Logic, and digitization in order to serve as an anchor of trust for people. From S-DL we take out that branding is democratized in a way that the branding company does not have the power anymore to build the brand meaning alone. Brand meaning has to be co-created. There are several takeaways from digitalization for brand management. We have seen that there are three major shifts in the customer journey caused by the increasing connectivity of the customers. Another one is the O-Zone concept with the insight that companies can influence the outer- and others-zone but not the own-zone. We identified several catalysts to break up bottlenecks between the single stages of the O-Zone. Finally, we got to know the Brand-formative Design concept, which is heavily affected by Design Thinking. This concept helps to integrate design and marketing in the formation of brand meaning by designing customer experiences that fits to the context and needs of the customers. In the next chapter, we will step into the third brave action: the H2H Process.

---

[123] For detailed introduction, please see: Kotler, P., & Pfoertsch, W. A. (2010). Ingredient Branding - Making the Invisible Visible, Germany: Springer Publishing, Heidelberg.

Questions

1. What is the key target of holistic H2H Management?
2. What are the four types of trust? Which of them are manageable?
3. What are wicked problems and why should firms look for them to tackle them?
4. What is the meaning of the 5 As framework? Which phases out of the five are heavily impacted by the engagement of other players than the supplier and the customer? Why should you differentiate digital and physical touchpoints along the customer journey?
5. What is the persona concept and how does it fit into reputation management? What for can you use it when you look on Fig. 4.7?
6. What are the characteristics of brand identity and its implications for brand management?
7. What do we mean by "democratization of branding"?

References

Adlin, T., & Pruitt, J. (2009). Putting personas to work: Using data-driven personas to focus product planning, design, and development. In A. Sears & J. A. Jacko (Eds.), *Human-computer interaction: Development process* (1st ed., pp. 95–120). Boca Raton, FL: CRC Press.

Ballantyne, D., & Aitken, R. (2007). Branding in B2B markets: Insights from the service-dominant logic of marketing. *Journal of Business & Industrial Marketing, 22*(6), 363–371. https://doi.org/10.1108/08858620710780127.

Burmann, C., Halaszovich, T., Schade, M., & Hemmann, F. (2015). *Identitätsbasierte Markenführung: Grundlagen – Strategie – Umsetzung – Controlling* (2nd ed.). Wiesbaden: Springer Gabler.

Cone Communications. (2017). *2017 Cone Gen Z CSR study: How to Speak Z* [Report]. Retrieved from http://www.conecomm.com/research-blog/2017-genz-csr-study

Court, D., Elzinga, D., Mulder, S., & Vetvik, O. J. (2009). The consumer decision journey. *McKinsey Quarterly, 3,* 1–11. Retrieved from https://www.mckinsey.com/business-functions/marketing-and-sales/our-insights/the-consumer-decision-journey

Drengner, J., Jahn, S., & Gaus, H. (2013). Der Beitrag der Service-Dominant Logic zur Weiterentwicklung der Markenführung. *Die Betriebswirtschaft, 73*(2), 143–160. Retrieved from https://www.academia.edu/12178909/Der_Beitrag_der_Service-Dominant_Logic_zur_Weiterentwicklung_der_Markenf%C3%BChrung

Edelman. (2011). *2011 Edelman trust barometer: Global report* [Report]. Retrieved from https://www.slideshare.net/EdelmanInsights/2011-edelman-trust-barometer

Edelman. (2018). *2018 Edelman trust barometer: Global report* [Report]. Retrieved from https://www.edelman.com/sites/g/files/aatuss191/files/2018-10/2018_Edelman_Trust_Barometer_Global_Report_FEB.pdf

Edelman. (2019). *2019 Edelman trust barometer special report: In brands we trust?* [Report]. Retrieved from https://www.edelman.com/sites/g/files/aatuss191/files/2019-06/2019_edelman_trust_barometer_special_report_in_brands_we_trust.pdf

Fombrun, C. J., & Van Riel, C. B. M. (2004). *Fame & fortune: How successful companies build winning reputations.* Upper Saddle River, NJ: Pearson Education.

Gaiser, B., Linxweiler, R., & Brucker, V. (Eds.). (2005). *Praxisorientierte Markenführung – Neue Strategien, innovative Instrumente und aktuelle Fallstudien.* Wiesbaden: Gabler.

Godin, S. (2007). *Permission marketing.* London: Simon & Schuster.

Haderlein, A. (2012). *Die digitale Zukunft des stationären Handels: Auf allen Kanälen zum Kunden.* München: mi-Wirtschaftsbuch.

Halligan, B., & Shah, D. (2018). *Inbound-Marketing: Wie Sie Kunden online anziehen, abholen und begeistern* (D. Runne, Trans.). Weinheim: Wiley-VCH.

Hansen, N. L. (2018, January 25). *Dear CxO... Just focus on the customer journey!* [Blog post]. Retrieved from https://www.linkedin.com/pulse/dear-cxo-just-focus-customer-journey-nicolaj-l%C3%B8ve-hansen/

Häusling, A. (2016). Serie agile tools. *Personalmagazin, 10*, 36–37. Retrieved from https://www.haufe.de/download/personalmagazin-102016-personalmagazin-381028.pdf

Heinemann, G. (2014). *SoLoMo – Always-on im Handel: Die soziale, lokale und mobile Zukunft des Shopping.* Wiesbaden: Springer Gabler.

Heinemann, G., & Gaiser, C. W. (2016). *SoLoMo – Always-on im Handel: Die soziale, lokale und mobile Zukunft des Omnichannel-Shopping* (3rd ed.). Wiesbaden: Springer Gabler.

Kemming, J. D., & Humborg, C. (2010). Democracy and nation brand(ing): Friends or foes? *Place Branding and Public Diplomacy, 6*(3), 183–197. Retrieved from https://www.researchgate.net/publication/47378882_Democracy_and_nation_branding_Friends_or_foes

Kotler, P., & Armstrong, G. (2010). *Principles of marketing* (13th ed.). Upper Saddle River, NJ: Pearson.

Kotler, P., Hessekiel, D., & Lee, N. R. (2013). *GOOD WORKS!: Wie Sie mit dem richtigen Marketing die Welt – und Ihre Bilanzen – verbessern* (N. Bertheau, Trans.). Offenbach: GABAL.

Kotler, P., Kartajaya, H., & Setiawan, I. (2010). *Die neue Dimension des Marketings: Vom Kunden zum Menschen* (P. Pyka, Trans.). Frankfurt: Campus.

Kotler, P., Kartajaya, H., & Setiawan, I. (2017). *Marketing 4.0: Moving from traditional to digital.* Hoboken, NJ: Wiley.

Kotler, P., & Pfoertsch, W. A. (2006). *B2B brand management.* Berlin: Springer.

Kotler, P., & Rath, G. A. (1984). Design: A powerful but neglected strategic tool. *Journal of Business Strategy, 5*(2), 16–21. https://doi.org/10.1108/eb039054.

Mayer-Vorfelder, M. (2012). *Basler Schriften zum Marketing: Vol. 29. Kundenerfahrungen im Dienstleistungsprozess: Eine theoretische und empirische Analyse.* Wiesbaden: Gabler.

Meffert, H., & Burmann, C. (1996). Identitätsorientierte Markenführung. In H. Meffert, H. Wagner, & K. Backhaus (Eds.), *Arbeitspapier Nr. 100 der Wissenschaftlichen Gesellschaft für Marketing und Unternehmensführung e.V.* Münster: Wissenschaftliche Gesellschaft für Marketing und Unternehmensführung.

Merz, M. A., He, Y., & Vargo, S. L. (2009). The evolving brand logic: A service-dominant logic perspective. *Journal of the Academy of Marketing Science, 37*(3), 328–344. https://doi.org/10.1007/s11747-009-0143-3.

Of, J. (2014). *Brand formative design: Development and assessment of product design from a future, brand and consumer perspective.* Doctoral thesis. Retrieved from http://d-nb.info/1053319665

Oliva, R., Srivastava, R., Pfoertsch, W., & Chandler, J. (2009). *Insights on ingredient branding, ISBM Report 08–2009.* Pennsylvania State University, University Park, PA.

Pfoertsch, W., Beuk, F., & Luczak, Ch. (2007). Classification of brands: The case for B2B, B2C and B2B2C. *Proceedings of the Academy of Marketing Studies, 12*(1). Jacksonville, USA.

Pfoertsch, W. A., & Sponholz, U. (2019). *Das neue marketing-mindset: Management, Methoden und Prozesse für ein Marketing von Mensch zu Mensch.* Wiesbaden: Springer Gabler.

Pine, II, B. J., & Gilmore, J. H. (1998). Welcome to the experience economy. *Harvard Business Review, 76*(4), 97–105. Retrieved from https://hbr.org/1998/07/welcome-to-the-experience-economy

Reputation Institute. (2019). *Winning strategies in reputation: 2019 German RepTrak® 100* [Report]. Retrieved from https://insights.reputationinstitute.com/website-assets/2019-germany-reptrak

Rittel, H. W. J., & Webber, M. M. (1973). Dilemmas in a general theory of planning. *Policy Sciences, 4*(2), 155–165. https://doi.org/10.1007/BF01405730.

Rossi, C. (2015, May 27–29). *Collaborative branding* [Conference paper]. Paper presented at the MakeLearn & TIIM Joint International Conference, Bari, Italy. Retrieved from https://www.researchgate.net/publication/282763907_COLLABORATIVE_BRANDING

Sarkar, C., & Kotler, P. (2018). *Brand activism: From purpose to action* (Kindle edition). n.p.: IDEA Bite Press. Retrieved from www.amazon.com

Schäfer, A., & Klammer, J. (2016). Service dominant logic in practice: Applying online customer communities and personas for the creation of service innovations. *Management, 11*(3), 255–264. Retrieved from https://econpapers.repec.org/article/mgtyoumng/v_3a11_3ay_3a2016_3ai_3a3_3ap_3a255-264.htm

Sherry, J. F. (2005). Brand meaning. In A. M. Tybout & T. Calkins (Eds.), *Kellogg on branding: The marketing faculty of the Kellogg school of management* (pp. 40–69). Hoboken, NJ: Wiley.

Sisodia, R. S., Sheth, J. N., & Wolfe, D. (2014). *Firms of endearment: How world-class companies profit from passion and purpose* (2nd ed.). Upper Saddle River, NJ: Pearson Education.

Sprout Social. (2017). *Championing change in the age of social media: How brands are using social to connect with people on the issues that matter* [Report]. Retrieved from https://media.sproutsocial.com/pdf/Sprout-Data-Report-Championing-Change-in-the-Age-of-Social-Media.pdf

Tarnovskaya, V., & Biedenbach, G. (2018). Corporate rebranding failure and brand meanings in the digital environment. *Marketing Intelligence and Planning, 36*(4), 455–469. https://doi.org/10.1108/MIP-09-2017-0192.

Vargo, S. L., & Lusch, R. F. (2004). Evolving to a new dominant logic for marketing. *Journal of Marketing, 68*(1), 1–17. https://doi.org/10.1509/jmkg.68.1.1.24036.

Vargo, S. L., & Lusch, R. F. (2016). Institutions and axioms: An extension and update of service-dominant logic. *Journal of the Academy of Marketing Science, 44*(1), 5–23. https://doi.org/10.1007/s11747-015-0456-3.

Vitsœ. (n.d.). *The power of good design: Dieter Rams's ideology, engrained within Vitsœ.* Retrieved from https://www.vitsoe.com/gb/about/good-design

Volvo Trucks. (2013). *Volvo trucks – The Epic Split feat. Van Damme (Live Test)* [Youtube video]. Retrieved from https://www.youtube.com/watch?v=M7FIvfx5J10

Weiss, A. M., Anderson, E., & MacInnis, D. J. (1999). Reputation management as a motivation for sales structure decisions. *Journal of Marketing, 63*(4), 74–89. https://doi.org/10.1177/002224299906300407.

Wüst, C. (2012). Corporate reputation management – die kraftvolle Währung für Unternehmenserfolg. In C. Wüst & R. T. Kreutzer (Eds.), *Corporate reputation management: Wirksame Strategien für den Unternehmenserfolg* (pp. 3–56). Wiesbaden: Springer Gabler.

5

Rethinking Operative Marketing: The H2H Process

The classic 4P marketing mix has guided marketing thinking for many years. In the world of digitalization with newly restructured relationships and changed forms of communication, it may no longer be appropriate for today's business challenges.[1] The H2H Marketing presented here with its flexible iteration process brings new possibilities for a hyper-competitive world, in which outbound orientation and marketing measures without customer focus have ceased to have a positive impact.[2]

One of the fundamental differences to the previous marketing mix is the processing character of the strategic and operative marketing and the explicitly necessary iterations between the process phases. Furthermore, the process is based on the S-DL principle of integration.[3] Digital marketing, Content Marketing, Service Marketing, B2C and B2B Marketing, brand and marketing mix, as well as communicative and physical channels in the form of the Omnichannel concept all form part of it. Finally, based on the influencing factors of the H2H Marketing Model, phases and new focal points that are not or only implicitly incorporated into the 4P marketing mix are included in the process. In the following, it will be explained in detail how the H2H Process ties into the H2H Marketing Model and which new focal points are derived for its phases. It will be concluded by looking into the details of the individual phases of the iterative process.

[1] Constantinides, E. (2006). The Marketing Mix Revisited: Towards the twenty-first Century Marketing. Journal of Marketing Management, 22(3/4), pp. 407–438. https://doi.org/10.1362/026725706776861190

[2] Halligan, B., & Shah, D. (2018). *op. cit.*

[3] Vargo, S. L., & Lusch, R. F. (2004). *op. cit.*

© The Author(s), under exclusive license to Springer Nature Switzerland AG 2021
P. Kotler et al., *H2H Marketing*, https://doi.org/10.1007/978-3-030-59531-9_5

5.1   Serving H2H

The introduction into the process will start with an examination of the traditional 4P marketing mix and its shortcomings, opening up space for new innovative approaches. In the analysis of the evolution of the marketing mix, five conceptual successors (4Cs by Lauterborn, SIVA, SAVE, 5Cs by Hall, and the 5Es by Pfoertsch) will be examined to showcase how drastic course changes in marketing have shaped the way of implementing operative marketing. These depicted evolutionary steps then culminate in the H2H Process, which is built upon functioning principles taken from the newer approaches, as well as newly integrated elements such as the co-creation concept of the S-DL and the iterative approach behind Design Thinking. As presented in Fig. 5.1, the evolution starts with the traditional 4P marketing mix.

The term *marketing mix* was coined by Neil H. Borden and derived from the notion of the marketer as a "mixer of ingredients," one who is "constantly engaged in fashioning creatively a mix of marketing procedures and policies in his efforts to produce a profitable enterprise".[4] In his article *The Concept of the Marketing Mix*, he constructed a set of 12 elements that should be included in a manufacturer-oriented marketing mix. Jerome McCarthy then combined these elements creating a simple construct based on four variables: the 4Ps.[5]

5.1.1   Evolution of the Marketing Mix

More than 50 years have passed since the introduction of the McCarthy marketing mix, a long time in which its application for decades yielded reliable results for marketers.[6] Many companies applied the concept and trained their people: McDonalds, Coca Cola, Pepsi, and other small- and medium-sized companies. However, as we will see in the following, drastic developments and reorientations in the marketing world have deemed the 4Ps inappropriate for today's marketers, as it stems from a time in which, as Robert Lauterborn puts it, "The marketing world was very different. Roaring out of World War II with a cranked-up production system ready to feed a lust for better living,

---

[4] Borden, N. H. (1964). The Concept of the Marketing Mix, p. 7. Journal of Advertising Research, 2, pp.   7–12.   Retrieved   from   http://www.guillaumenicaise.com/wp-content/uploads/2013/10/Borden-1984_The-concept-of-marketing-mix.pdf

[5] Constantinides, E. (2006). *op. cit.*

[6] Wani, T. (2013). From 4Ps to SAVE: A Theoretical Analysis of Various Marketing Mix Models. Business Sciences International Research Journal, 1(1), pp. 1–9. https://doi.org/10.2139/ssrn.2288578

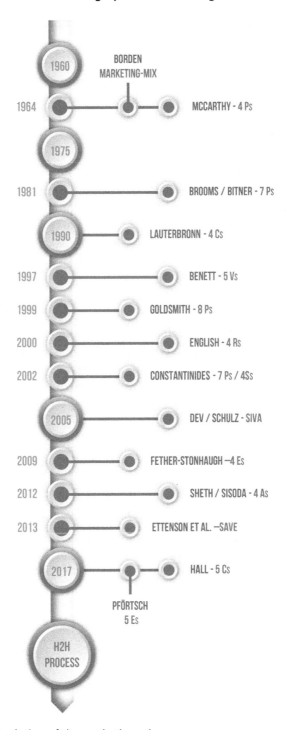

Fig. 5.1   The evolution of the marketing mix

American business linked management science to the art of mass marketing and rocketed to the moon."[7]

The main critique of the marketing mix originates from its focus on the manageable organizational elements (strong production focus) while failing to implement the customer perspective.[8] The missing customer orientation makes the 4Ps unsuitable for todays' more complex business landscape in which the customer and the relationship with her are considered the center of attention.[9]

Apart from the advancements coming from Relationship Marketing, the new perspective brought in by Service Marketing and the Service-Dominant Logic also find no reflection in the marketing mix, as Dev and Schultz point out: "[T]he four Ps are grounded in a manufacturing mindset and need to be adapted to reflect the service economy."[10] With its focus on products and organizational elements, the marketing mix is deeply rooted in the Goods-Dominant Logic of the time of its creation and provides an outbound, inside-out view of managing the enterprise.[11] This is not compatible with the S-DL introduced by Vargo and Lusch.[12]

The discrepancy towards the S-DL becomes especially evident when looking at the changes that communication went through. In marketing attributed to Goods-Dominant Logic, the communication stream flowed mainly in one direction, from the firm towards the customer (*promotion*). The S-DL, however, necessitates dialogue between customer and firm.[13] When Lauterborn was introducing his 4C framework, he formulated: "Forget promotion. The word is communication. All good advertising creates a dialogue".[14]

Ettenson, Conrado, and Knowles[15] further postulate that especially for B2B firms, the application of the 4P framework with its product-oriented

---

[7] Lauterborn, B. (1990). New Marketing Litany: Four P's Passe; C-Words Take Over, p. 26. Advertising Age, 61(41), p. 26. Retrieved from http://www.business.uwm.edu/gdrive/Wentz_E/International%20Marketing%20465%20Fall%202014/Articles/New%20Marketing%20Litany.PDF

[8] Dann, S. (2011, July 5–7). The Marketing Mix Matrix [Conference paper]. Paper presented at the Academy of Marketing Conference 2011, Liverpool, United Kingdom. Retrieved from https://www.researchgate.net/profile/Stephen_Dann/publication/267559484_The_Marketing_Mix_Matrix/links/54b6024b0cf2318f0f9a0743.pdf

[9] Wani, T. (2013). *op. cit.*

[10] Dev, C. S., & Schultz, D. E. (2005). Simply SIVA: Get results with the new marketing mix, p. 38. Marketing Management, 14(2), pp. 36–41. Retrieved from https://www.scopus.com/record/display.uri?eid=2-s2.0-17444418649&origin=inward&txGid=047497a80a4b341498c747b3d30eff31

[11] Dev, C. S., & Schultz, D. E. (2005). *op. cit.*

[12] Vargo, S. L., & Lusch, R. F. (2004). *op. cit.*

[13] Lusch, R. F., & Vargo, S. L. (2006). *op. cit.*, p. 286.

[14] Lauterborn, B. (1990). *op. cit.*, p. 26.

[15] Ettenson, R., Conrado, E., & Knowles, J. (2013). Rethinking the 4 P's. Harvard Business Review, 91(1/2), p. 26. Retrieved from https://hbr.org/2013/01/rethinking-the-4-ps

focus is a hindrance on the way from product to service and solution providers. They summarize the shortcomings of the marketing mix for B2B firms:

> It [the 4P model] leads their marketing and sales teams to stress product technology and quality even though these are no longer differentiators but are simply the cost of entry. It underemphasizes the need to build a robust case for the superior value of their solutions. And it distracts them from leveraging their advantage as a trusted source of diagnostics, advice, and problem solving.[16]

Nevertheless, many industrial companies like Westinghouse, GE, and Caterpillar applied the concept. Various attempts with the goal of eradicating these flaws of the marketing mix have been made, some of which we will now examine in more detail.

The 4C Framework by Lauterborn

The 4C model was a direct answer to the traditional marketing mix, providing a new element for each of its corresponding counterparts. Instead of *product*, focus lays on *consumer wants and needs*; *price* is replaced by the *consumer's cost to satisfy his wants and needs*; instead of *place*, Lauterborn emphasizes *convenience to buy*; and lastly, *promotion* gets thrown overboard for *communication*.[17] With the introduction of this framework, orientation was shifted from products to consumers.[18] The replacement of promotion with the communication aspect of the 4Cs provided a fresh perspective on how to engage with customers—not attempting to lure customers into buying but cooperating with them and embracing the dialogue, rather than the monologue.[19] Immediately, Procter & Gamble, Nestle, and Unilever adopted the 4C concepts. In their book, *The New Marketing Paradigm*, Schultz et al. recapitulate: "Enter a new age of advertising [with the 4Cs]: respectful, not patronizing; dialogue-seeking, not monologic, responsive, not formula-driven. It speaks to the highest point of common interest, not the lowest common denominator".[20]

---

[16] Ettenson, R., Conrado, E., & Knowles, J. (2013). *op. cit.*, p. 26.
[17] Lauterborn, B. (1990). *op. cit.*, p. 26.
[18] Schultz, D. E., Tannenbaum, S. I., & Lauterborn, R. F. (1994). The New Marketing Paradigm: Integrated Marketing Communications. Lincolnwood, IL: NTC Publishing.
[19] Lauterborn, B. (1990). *op. cit.*, p. 26.
[20] Schultz, D. E., Tannenbaum, S. I., & Lauterborn, R. F. (1994). *op. cit.*, p. 13.

The SIVA Mix by Dev and Schultz

The SIVA model, too, gives a more customer-focused response to the product- and organization-oriented 4P Mix. It builds on four principles:

> Develop and manage solutions not just products, offer information instead of simply promoting, create value instead of obsessing with price, and provide access wherever, whenever, and however the customer wants to experience your solution rather than thinking merely where to place your products.[21]

Different from the resource-oriented approach that the marketing mix usually takes, SIVA is looking at the market as a starting point. The first step in the SIVA model is, therefore, the gathering of deep, *valuable insights* about the customers. Starting from the customer perspective, the firm then decides if and how it can set up *value propositions* for the customers making use of its resources.[22] The SIVA Mix therefore presents a counterpart to the marketing mix (firm-/resource-oriented; SIVA and 4Ps as "complementary mechanisms"[23]), helping to "translate the needs of the market into actionable business behaviors".[24] Many specialty stores and service companies like Starbucks applied this principle.

The SAVE Approach by Ettenson, Conrado, and Knowles

Ettenson et al.[25] introduced a solution-focused approach for B2B companies, with the same goal of replacing product and services thinking and its focus on technological differentiation features with a customer-oriented view. And while, initially, its implementation was intended only for B2B companies, it can be seen as a viable successor to the 4Ps also in B2C firms.[26] Similar to the other members of the marketing mix model family introduced here, the SAVE approach tries to shift marketing and management thinking from product-centeredness to customer-centricity, where marketers "[d]efine offerings by the needs they meet, not by their features, functions, or technological superiority".[27] Its only difference to the predecessor model SIVA is the element of *education* as a replacement for *information*, laying emphasis on a

---

[21] Dev, C. S., & Schultz, D. E. (2005). *op. cit.*, p. 38.

[22] Dev, C. S., & Schultz, D. E. (2005). *op. cit.*

[23] Dann, S. (2011, July 5–7). *op. cit.*, para. 1.

[24] Dann, S. (2011, July 5–7). *op. cit.*

[25] Ettenson, R., Conrado, E., & Knowles, J. (2013). *op. cit.*, p. 26.

[26] Wani, T. (2013). *op. cit.*

[27] Ettenson, R., Conrado, E., & Knowles, J. (2013). *op. cit.*, p. 26.

dialogue-based two-way communication and education, which is simply the next logical step towards consistently implementing customer centricity.[28] This way of communicating is in perfect harmony with the S-DL as it treats the customers as operant, rather than as operand resource and follows the principles of inbound marketing, a clear turning away from the 4P "one-size-fits-all" mass marketing. It was developed at Motorola Solutions and has gotten applied at ABB, Siemens, John Deere, its German subsidiary Wirtgen Group, and many other machinery and engineering companies.

The 5Cs by Hall

The most recent addition to B2B Marketing concepts that we will discuss here is the 5C framework proposed by Hall. Introduced in 2017, the framework comes with many parallels to the H2H Process, attempting the effective transition of B2B Marketing into the digital age.[29]

With its 5Cs *communication*, *channel*, cost, *customer solution*, and *community*, the 5C Mix brings up various new tools for B2B marketers to respond to the consequences of digitalization changing the market. It integrates concepts like Content Marketing, deploys innovative tools like social listening to improve solutions offered to customers, and focuses on satisfying increasingly complex customer demands regarding a seamless, consistent experience across all channels.[30]

The 5E Model by Pfoertsch

The latest model presented here is the 5E marketing mix from Pfoertsch (see Fig. 5.2). It is based on the 4P developments of the SIVA model and for B2B SAVE but, in contrast, explicitly integrates the brand into the mix, which in the other models was only captured as sub-item of the product. This is rooted in the fact that nowadays, trust in the brand is an essential component of the customer relationship.[31] Another important characteristic of the 5E Mix is the dynamic character inherent to it, different from the more static understanding of the traditional marketing mix. The 5Es are specifically future-oriented and do not only statically describe the state of operative marketing at a given point in time.[32] Pfoertsch notes: "[With the 5Es] we have a marketing mix

---

[28] Wani, T. (2013). *op. cit.*

[29] Hall, S. (2017). Innovative B2B Marketing: New Models, Processes and Theory. New York, NY: Kogan Page.

[30] Hall, S. (2017). *op. cit.*

[31] Pfoertsch, W. A., & Sponholz, U. (2019). *op. cit.*

[32] Pfoertsch, W. A., & Sponholz, U. (2019). *op. cit.*

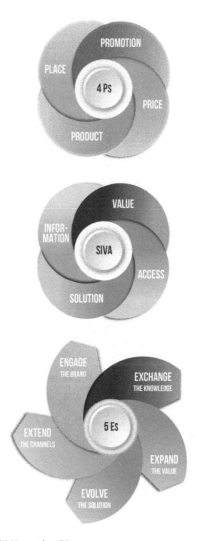

Fig. 5.2 From 4Ps and SIVA to the 5Es

that contains the requirements of digital transformation and inbound marketing, integrates the brand into the mix and is also conceptually conceived as a dynamic model".[33] Advanced service providers like Accenture, EY, IBM, and SAP have applied this new approach. The development of the most important marketing mix models is displayed the Fig. 5.2.

Concluding the review of the different marketing mix alternatives, Table 5.1 provides an overview of the key propositions of the discussed models and what H2H Marketing can adopt for its iterative process. The H2H Process is

---

[33] Pfoertsch, W. A., & Sponholz, U. (2019). *op. cit.*

Table 5.1   Different marketing mix models for H2H marketing

Evolutionary steps	Key propositions	Consequences for H2H marketing
4Ps by McCarthy	• Checklist of manageable elements. • Simple and easy to use. • Applicable to different kinds of products and services and forms of marketing.	• H2H Marketing should also provide a clear checklist without artificially reducing the complexity of reality. • H2H Marketing should be applicable to a wide range of industries and business activities.
4Cs by Lauterborn	• Customer orientation. • Convenience as an important driver for customers.	• H2H Marketing must think customer-oriented when planning and implementing marketing measures. • Convenience should be considered as a motive in the analysis of buying behavior and as a characteristic in the offer on the supplier side.
SAVE by Ettenson, Conrado, and Knowles	• Practical implementation of the S-DL. • Solution-oriented mindset. • Offering solutions to customer problems and needs, no product and technology centricity. • Two-way, bidirectional communication. • Interaction-oriented. • Value as the basis for pricing. • Educating customers as the goal of communication.	• H2H Marketing should also try to implement the principles of the S-DL into a practicable solution approach. • H2H Marketing should always focus on customer problems and needs as a starting point of all considerations. • H2H Marketing has to be relationship- and interaction-oriented. • Pricing in H2H Marketing should follow the quantification of the value that the offer has for the customer in his context ("value-based pricing"). • The provider's information offering should add value to customers and assist them in making proper use of the solutions offered.

(continued)

Table 5.1 (continued)

Evolutionary steps	Key propositions	Consequences for H2H marketing
5Cs by Hall	• Marketing as a process that always starts with the customer. • Developing value propositions is of central importance. • Omnichannel presence. • Content Marketing. • Delivering end-to-end solutions.	• H2H Marketing should be organized as a process. • H2H Marketing should always start with the customer and have her in consideration. • Developing a value proposition is a central task for H2H Marketing; value proposition here is defined as value offer, not value promise. • H2H Marketing should develop value propositions that present end-to-end solutions. • A seamless channel experience (Omnichannel), if desired by the customers, should be ensured by H2H Marketing. • Content Marketing providing relevant and useful content to customers without bothering them should form part of H2H Marketing.
5Es by Pfoertsch	• Integration of the brand into the marketing mix. • Future-oriented, adaptive marketing, not describing the past. • The importance of trust in the context of the brand's function.	• H2H Marketing should integrate the brand into the marketing process and ensure that all measures consistently strengthen the brand. • The brand pursues the goal of building trust, which is central to the relationship with the customer. • H2H Marketing should be applicable to all developmental stages of a firm, from start-ups to large corporations.

built upon working principles of previous approaches but in a new combination adapted to modern market conditions and with a revolutionary iterative process form.

5.1.2   The H2H Process

The H2H Process introduced here follows a structure of five steps:

1. Find an *H2H problem.*
2. Gather *deep insights.*

3. Develop a *value proposition.*
4. Inform, advise, and entertain with *valuable content.*
5. Enable and manage *access* with networks.

In the following, a step-by-step instruction will be provided on how H2H Marketing can be successfully implemented on an operative level using the iterative and flexible H2H Process. However, before entering into the details of the process, it is necessary to make a few remarks on the nature of the H2H Process.

Being iterative, by definition, the process can be initiated at any point depending on the respective setting of tasks. In the case of a start-up company, for example, the entire process can be completed to fill all fields of the H2H Canvas and thus develop a functioning business model. On the other hand, in case a new value proposition is to be developed to solve an already identified H2H problem, it is sufficient to start with the development of the value proposition. There is also the possibility and encouragement to iterate back into past phases, to put newly gained knowledge to the test and to find a new design angle (see Fig. 5.3).

Besides the iterative H2H Process character, all findings from the H2H Marketing Model are incorporated into the H2H Process. The identification of a complex human problem as the starting point for the development of a value proposition and the strategic positioning of a company are new in

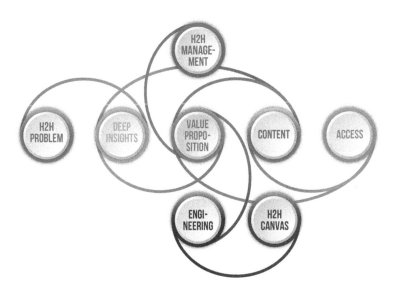

Fig. 5.3 The iterative H2H process

marketing and represent one of the core principles of H2H Marketing. With this, conventional differentiation strategies based on cost leadership and differentiation through performance features do not become completely obsolete, only secondary.

5.1.3   H2H Marketing at the Fuzzy Front End of Innovation

The *human insights* phase ensures that H2H Marketing is both *insight-* and *data-driven* and only develops, communicates, and provides access to service based on these valuable insights. In doing so, H2H Marketing will not only operate at the back end of innovation but explicitly makes an effort to participate at the *fuzzy front end of innovation.*

The term was first brought up by Smith and Reinertsen[34] and refers to the phase at the start of the innovation process between recognizing the emergence of an opportunity and initiating first developmental steps. This phase is characterized by uncertainty and risks, which is part of the reason why managers usually limit themselves to only concentrating on the back end of innovation.[35] In addition, although innovation management provides tools to assess risks and help in decision-making, the fuzziness inherent to the front end of innovation requires executives to be willing to *take risks* and to *experiment*, which goes to show how Design Thinking can play a crucial role in innovation management.[36]

"The *early front-end activities* include the identification of a problem or opportunity and the accompanying screening and evaluation processes. [...] General Motors also called this the 'bubble-up-process', where the strategic decisions for the new product development are made".[37] This is where H2H Marketing can step in and get involved. In the first steps of the process, H2H Marketers have the intent to condense deep customer insights from methods like social listening, netnography, and trend scouting, which provide useful aid to get to know more about the customers' real needs.[38] In contrast to that, traditional approaches to research hardly yield relevant results as "customers

---

[34] Smith, P. G., & Reinertsen, D. G. (1991). Developing products in half the time. New York, NY: Van Nostrand Reinhold.

[35] Gassmann, O., & Schweitzer, F. (2014). *op. cit.*

[36] Gassmann, O., & Schweitzer, F. (2014). *op. cit.*

[37] Gassmann, O., & Schweitzer, F. (2014). *op. cit.*, p. 5.

[38] Gassmann, O., & Schweitzer, F. (2014). *op. cit.*

do not always tell marketers what they really think and do. In fact, they are not always able to articulate what they really think and do, even if they want to".[39]

Design Thinking, both as a mindset and as a set of tools, further helps in developing human-centered, problem-solving ideas and concepts at the front end of innovation.[40] Chen and Venkatesh found that design-driven companies use *end-user profiles*, similar to the persona concept of H2H Marketing, as a form of visualizing a typical customer and to validate *new, disruptive* design, instead of relying mainly on traditional research on end-users, which does not uncover latent needs, being limited to the sphere of the already known.[41] Design Thinking can be integrated holistically into the *early front-end activities* of recognizing an opportunity, as well as the *later front-end activities* of making use of the opportunity, creating and evaluating concepts and ideas, along the whole front end.[42] "*Design Thinking*, can help the fuzzy front end to innovate faster, with rapid prototyping and iterations, for a better market fit and generally create more radical innovations".[43] Not only Design Thinking but also the other components of the H2H Marketing Model provide fertile ground for front-end innovation (see Fig. 5.4[44]).

Digitalization makes it possible to study consumers in social structures of the Internet via netnography, for example, and enables firms to access completely new ideas and trends that can be derived from the online world.[45] Moreover, the S-DL, with the understanding of co-created value emphasizing the importance of the customer's perspective, facilitates the identification of new trends and market needs with strong orientation on the individual customer.[46]

---

[39] Kotler, P., Kartajaya, H., & Setiawan, I. (2017). *op. cit.*, p. 111.

[40] Chen, S., & Venkatesh, A. (2013). An investigation of how design-oriented organisations implement design thinking. Journal of Marketing Management, 29(15/16), pp. 1680–1700. https://doi.org/10.1080/0267257X.2013.800898

[41] Chen, S., & Venkatesh, A. (2013). *op. cit.*

[42] Gassmann, O., & Schweitzer, F. (2014). *op. cit.*

[43] Leifer, L. J., & Steinert, M. (2014). Dancing with Ambiguity: Causality Behavior, Design Thinking, and Triple-Loop-Learning, p. 141. In O. Gassmann, & F. Schweitzer (Eds.), Management of the Fuzzy Front End of Innovation (pp. 141–158). Cham, Switzerland: Springer International Publishing.

[44] Gassmann, O., & Schweitzer, F. (2014). *op. cit.*, p. 7. Design Thinking, Digitization and the H2H Marketing notion were added.

[45] Eser, D., Gaubinger, K., & Rabl, M. (2014). Sprint Radar: Community-Based Trend Identification. In O. Gassmann, & F. Schweitzer (Eds.), Management of the Fuzzy Front End of Innovation (pp. 275–280). Cham, Switzerland: Springer International Publishing.

[46] Payne, A. F., Storbacka, K., & Frow, P. (2008). Managing the co-creation of value. Journal of the Academy of Marketing Science, 36(1), pp. 83–96. https://doi.org/10.1007/s11747-007-0070-0

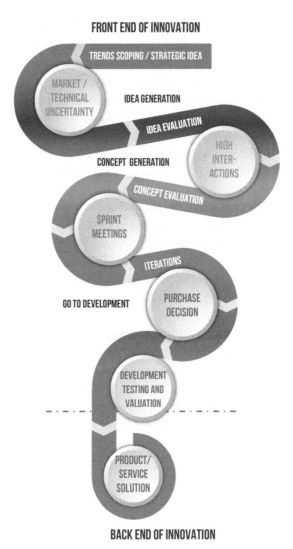

Fig. 5.4 H2H Marketing at the fuzzy front end of innovation

With a high degree of uncertainty and many undefined factors at the beginning of the innovation process, the playing field of possible concepts, trends, and ideas is vast. Through flexible iterations that do not necessarily need to be carried out sequentially, the "scope of action" gets condensed throughout the process.[47] In a similar fashion, Design Thinking tries to *condense* and

---

[47] Gassmann, O., & Schweitzer, F. (2014). *op. cit.*

implement findings gathered in previous *diverging* phases into its process.[48] Innovation Marketing has a variety of strategic tasks, as shown in Fig. 5.5.[49]

It becomes evident that H2H Marketing must have a coordinating function inside the innovation process. Marketers must take on a cross-functional role within the company that skillfully connects the various parties involved from different corporate functions.[50]

The general orientation of the company with regard to innovation also plays a decisive role. Companies' innovation can focus on *exploration* and *exploitation*.[51] Exploration refers to disruptive innovation aiming to create completely new offerings, while exploitation focuses on getting the most out of already existing products, incrementally refining the offerings.[52] These two choices confront many firms and their management with a dilemma, to which

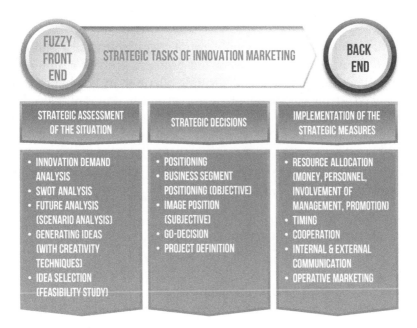

Fig. 5.5 Strategic tasks of innovation marketing

[48] Lindberg, T., Meinel, C., & Wagner, R. (2011). *op. cit.*

[49] Adapted from *Innovations marketing* (second ed., p. 41), by V. Trommsdorff, & F. Steinhoff, 2013, München, Germany: Franz Vahlen. "Fuzzy Front End" and "Back End" added.

[50] Trommsdorff, V., & Steinhoff, F. (2013). *op. cit.*

[51] Martin, R. L. (2009). The Design of Business: Why Design Thinking is the Next Competitive Advantage. Boston, MA: Harvard Business Review Press.

[52] Li, C.-R., Lin, C.-J., & Chu, C.-P. (2008). The nature of market orientation and the ambidexterity of innovations. Management Decision, 46(7), pp. 1002–1026. https://doi.org/10.1108/00251740810890186

they mostly respond by focusing solely on either one or the other. The mental trap executives usually fall into is to believe that both approaches to innovation are somehow mutually exclusive, when in reality a combination of both is needed for an enterprise to be sustainable,[53] the achievement of which Li et al. call "organizational ambidexterity".[54] Two different forms of interpreting market orientation are needed: a proactive market orientation for discontinuous *exploration* and a responsive market orientation for fostering gradual *exploitation*. The authors summarize[55]:

> A proactive market orientation indicates that the managers focus on understanding and satisfying customers' latent needs, defined as the needs of which the customer is unaware. Conversely, a responsive market orientation shows that the managers focus on understanding and satisfying customers' expressed need, defined as the need of which the customer is aware.

H2H Marketing integrates this ambidextrous synergy by taking into account both the latent, undiscovered needs and problems and the customers' pain points and needs regarding already existing offerings. By combining exploration to avoid getting pushed out of the market and becoming obsolete through fierce competition and exploitation to exploit market potentials and finance new exploration efforts, H2H Marketers can strengthen the longevity of their business, implementing both the creative and intuitive, as well as the analytical side.[56] Fujifilm managed to transition from the analogue photo to digital and could expand into related areas.[57]

5.1.4   Elements of Co-creation and Value Proposition

As discussed in previous chapters, the roles of firms and customers in the value creation process are bound to constant change.[58] The ever-increasing importance of value co-creation is also reflected in the H2H Process and specifically in the understanding of the value proposition, which follows the logic of the

---

[53] Martin, R. L. (2009). *op. cit.*

[54] Li, C.-R., Lin, C.-J., & Chu, C.-P. (2008). *op. cit.*, p. 1005.

[55] Li, C.-R., Lin, C.-J., & Chu, C.-P. (2008). *op. cit.*

[56] Martin, R. L. (2009). *op. cit.*

[57] Detail description cold be found in: Kotler, P., Komori, S. (2020). Never Stop – Winning Through Innovation. Canada, Kotler Impact Montreal.

[58] See also Gummesson, E., Kuusela, H., & Närvänen, E. (2014). Reinventing marketing strategy by recasting supplier/customer roles. Journal of Service Management, 25(2), pp. 228–240. https://doi.org/10.1108/JOSM-01-2014-0031

S-DL and other schools of thought. The newer Customer-Dominant Logic says that value is created when making use of the product and service offerings (*value-in-use*) that, by default, inevitably integrates the customer into the value creation.[59]

A value proposition in H2H Marketing is a *value offer* not a *value promise*. Value is not created by the offering firm, but rather "[…] is always uniquely and phenomenological determined by the beneficiary"[60] and therefore is not something that can be subject to a promise. The term value promise in H2H Marketing finds use in the Content Marketing section, in the function of communicating the *possible value* or *potential value*.

Classic *products* and *services* constitute the obvious elements of the value propositions set in H2H Marketing. Based on the findings from S-DL and digitalization, these are complemented by *software* and *hardware, information, brand,* and the customer's experience with the provider across all touchpoints,—*customer experience* and, during use, *user experience*. From the point of view of H2H Marketing, IT hardware and goods in kind (product), as well as IT software and rendering of services, are comparable due to their characteristics of tangibility, storability, etc. Therefore, IT hardware and goods in kind are summarized here under the term *hardware* and IT software and services under the term *software*. The user experience is subsumed under the term customer experience. Regarding the information component of the value proposition, it should be noted that it is only understood as an offer of value if it is itself an object of commercialization. Information with the purpose of communicating the value of the offer, value promise, or assisting the customer in the correct use of the product falls into the category of Content Marketing in H2H Marketing. Service in the sense of the S-DL is added in Fig. 5.6 to make clear that it is the fundamental basis for the exchange of value.

On the part of the provider, the service consists of the application of his competencies via the value proposition. The service of the customer consists in the application of his knowledge and skills, in order to assist in the development of the value proposition and to use the value proposition in his context to create *value in context*. In addition, there is the payment of value proposition as financial feedback, in exchange for the value creation opportunity he granted access to. In the following, these components will be discussed in detail.

[59] Robra-Bissantz, S. (2018). Entwicklung von innovativen Services in der Digitalen Transformation. In M. Bruhn, & K. Hadwich (Eds.), Service Business Development: Strategien – Innovationen – Geschäftsmodelle: Band 1 (pp. 261–288). Wiesbaden, Germany: Springer Gabler.
[60] Vargo, S. L., & Lusch, R. F. (2008). *op. cit.*, p. 7.

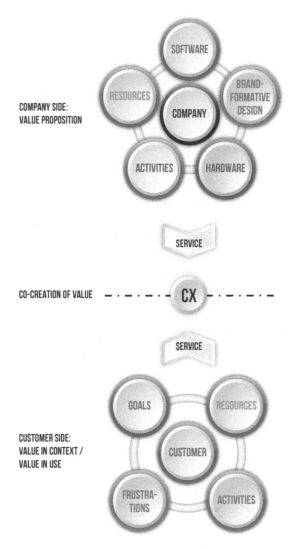

Fig. 5.6 Components of the co-created value proposition in H2H marketing

The five components of the value proposition are to be managed and constantly and iteratively analyzed and adjusted:

- Hardware.
- Software.
- Information.
- Brand.
- Customer experience.

A great example can be found in the fashion industry. The largest textile company Inditex Industria de Diseño Textil, S.A., is a Spanish multinational clothing company, which succeeded in perfecting these principles in their flagship brand Zara and delivers designs copied from the fashion show runway in the shortest time.

5.1.5 Operative Marketing as Iterative Process Through the H2H Canvas

To implement the steps of the process, the H2H Canvas delivers practical guidance for marketers. As a modified version of the traditional business model canvas, it can help to visualize the findings and direction of the H2H Process, regardless of which step of the process was selected as the starting point. The H2H Canvas should be filled separately for each identified H2H problem (see Fig. 5.7).

The major difference to the original business model canvas lies in the attention given to the co-creative aspect of H2H Marketing and in integrating the brand into the initial consideration of innovative solutions. All digital giants like Google, Facebook, Amazon, Apple, Alibaba, etc. are following the iterative process of the 5E Marketing Mix. Each of them developed their own application in outperforming other incumbents.

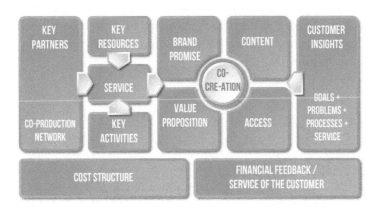

Fig. 5.7 The H2H Canvas

5.2   The H2H Process: A Close-Up View

Every H2H Process starts with a briefing, regardless of whether the process is run through completely or only partially. A good briefing has always been and remains an important prerequisite for the later success of a project. In marketing, briefings are common practice especially when awarding contracts to external service providers, but this should also establish itself *internally* in H2H Marketing. A good briefing should be structured as follows[61]:

- A briefing should be formulated in writing and discussed verbally in person.
- It should be comprehensive and brief at the same time.
- Instructions should be precise and unambiguous (understandable to the recipient) yet deliberately leave space for creativity.
- It should be concrete, e.g., by giving illustrative examples.
- It should motivate.
- It should be adapted if necessary (the iteration principle also applies here).
- The briefing should be drafted by the supervisor but validated by both parties, the supervisor and the employees, for whom the briefing is intended.

The written formulation has the advantage that the briefing fulfils a documentation function and can be used again and again during the process, in order to recall the original requirements that were agreed upon. It is also particularly important to constantly update and revise the briefing document. The overarching goal of a briefing is always to counteract the emergence of misunderstandings as a result of information asymmetries or different perceptions of spoken words.[62] Microsoft is famous for their ever-present briefings and debriefings meeting.

---

[61] Hartleben, R. E., & von Rhein, W. (2014). Kommunikationskonzeption und Briefing: Ein praktischer Leitfaden zum Erstellen zielgruppenspezifischer Konzepte (3rd. ed.), p. 299f. Erlangen, Germany: Publicis. In this book we will use only a condensed version of Hartleben's recommendations. For a more detailed elaboration on how to conduct an effective briefing the reader may refer to pp. 299–307 of the cited book.

[62] Hartleben, R. E., & von Rhein, W. (2014). *op. cit.*

5.2.1 H2H Problem

H2H Marketing always starts with a human problem that is to be solved. As such, the "initial problem" can either be found (*passive problem search*) in which an employee or business partner encounters a problem in his environment that he is not yet aware of or the search for a problem can be initiated by the company itself (*active search for problems*; see Fig. 5.8).

Companies in the sportswear industry like Nike and Adidas are applying this approach continuously. Marketers in today's highly connected world have many ways of searching, finding, and analyzing customer problems. In the following, three methods for active problem identification will be introduced; however, this overview is not to be understood as a comprehensive, but rather as an outline of the most interesting and promising techniques for H2H Marketing.

Netnography

With growing connectivity, new ways of studying customers and product users have emerged, one of them being netnography, which combines ethnographic research with the online world, its communities, and tribal structures. Developed by Robert Kozinets, netnography motivates interested market

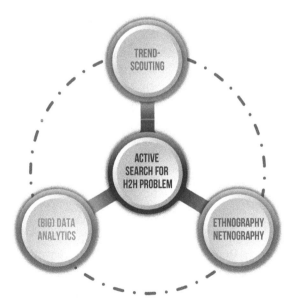

Fig. 5.8 Active search for problems in H2H marketing

researchers to immerse themselves deeply in the socio-cultural environment of people in their online communities in order to understand their behavior better.[63] For marketers, it offers an effective way of studying and getting deep insights about communities revolving around their product or brand.[64] With abundant and easily accessible data, netnography is a potent tool to identify problems and offers inspiration for product and service innovation.[65] It can further help to understand the mechanism behind the creation of brand meaning, which is strongly influenced by the socio-cultural environment, co-created under use of the customer's resources and individually determined.[66] In sum, netnography offers an effective and intuitive way of understanding customers in their natural environment from which authentic findings untainted by maybe otherwise biased traditional market research can be derived.[67] Google is the master of the universe in this kind of applications, but Spotify is also applying these principles very successfully.

Trend Scouting

Trend scouting aims at detecting trends in an early developmental stage and includes focusing on both megatrends, that are easy to track, and smaller trends, that are harder to identify but can have strong relevance for firms.[68] In comparison to other methods of innovation research, trend scouting is not as straightforward and can feel counterintuitive to the researcher, as it is not based on insights from the past, but rather tries to detect a direction for the present and future:[69]

> The aim of trend scouting *today* is to know what's in fashion *tomorrow*: Consumer habits and taste tendencies are to be detected at an early stage and recognized

---

[63] Kozinets, R. V. (2015). *op. cit.*

[64] Özbölük, T., & Dursun, Y. (2017). Online brand communities as heterogeneous gatherings: a netnographic exploration of Apple users. Journal of Product & Brand Management, 26(4), pp. 375–385. https://doi.org/10.1108/JPBM-10-2015-1018

[65] Heinonen, K., & Medberg, G. (2018). Netnography as a tool for understanding customers: implications for service research and practice. Journal of Services Marketing, 32(6), pp. 657–679. https://doi.org/10.1108/JSM-08-2017-0294

[66] Drengner, J., Jahn, S., & Gaus, H. (2013). *op. cit.*

[67] Kozinets, R. V. (2015). *op. cit.*

[68] Rohrbeck, R. (2014). Trend Scanning, Scouting and Foresight Techniques. In O. Gassmann, & F. Schweitzer (Eds.), Management of the Fuzzy Front End of Innovation (pp. 59–73). Cham, Switzerland: Springer International Publishing.

[69] Judt, E., & Klausegger, C. (2010). Bankmanagement-Glossar: Was ist Trendscouting? bank und markt, 3, p. 46. Retrieved from https://www.kreditwesen.de/bank-markt/ergaenzende-informationen/archiv-daten/trendscouting-id12805.html

before they spread. [...] Trend scouting tells companies whether and in which direction the existing range of services needs to be changed, to meet the needs of tomorrow's customers.[70]

While it may be hard for marketers to get accustomed to trend scouting in the beginning, the developments in connectivity have provided them with a pool of rich data treasures to track down trends waiting to be used and discovered.[71] IDEO, the design and consultancy company, is helping many of their clients to identify new developments in the market. Companies like Lego and Panera Bread benefit from this concept to update and expand their offerings.

With the detection of H2H problems in mind, companies can explore major trends possibly affecting humanity in future. A proper method to filter out relevant trends represents a question: Which of these trends might have a negative impact on the fulfilment of human needs?

Big Data Analytics

Big Data, if used correctly, can be a treasure trove for marketers. A particularly interesting way to utilize Big Data Analytics is presented in social listening, also referred to as social media monitoring:

> The aim of Social Listening is to capture what is being reported about the company, its brands and products on social media. For this purpose, unstructured data from various social media and possibly other Internet sources (Twitter, Facebook, blogs, forums, news pages, etc.) are [...] systematically collected and processed.[72]

For firms, it is a way of obtaining authentic, unfiltered market research information that with traditional market research methods can be hard to capture. "Customers are more comfortable and open to tell their fellow customers what they think and do. The natural conversations in the customers' own environments help them articulate their deepest anxieties and desires".[73]

It can further help to identify which communities are worthwhile studying through netnography or social listening, the difference between the two being the level of engagement and participation. While netnographers take a deep

---

[70] Judt, E., & Klausegger, C. (2010). *op. cit.*

[71] Rohrbeck, R. (2014). *op. cit.*

[72] Rumler, A., & Ullrich, S. (2016). Social-Media-Monitoring und -Kontrolle, p. 100. PraxisWISSEN Marketing, 1, pp. 94–112. https://doi.org/10.15459/95451.7. Translation from German to English.

[73] Kotler, P., Kartajaya, H., & Setiawan, I. (2017). *op. cit.*, p. 111.

dive into the customer's environment and effectively becomes a part of it, social listeners take a more passive role in mainly monitoring and tracking in the role of an external observer.[74] Facebook and the changes in their data algorithm demonstrated the effectiveness in many cases.

5.2.2 Human Insights

In this step of the iterative process, empathic, ethno- and netnographic, as well as quantitative methods are used to provide deep insights into the emotional and cognitive structure of people. Beside the task to understand (potential) customers, marketing still has the task to understand the marketplace and has to deliver key figures like market potential, market volume, market shares, and market growth rates among others. Here, we focus on the qualitative task to generate human insights. These insights should help to examine whether the identified H2H problem really is a problem that prevents people from achieving their personal objectives. In this phase, both approaches are up for discussion and are important, exploring a problem on the basis of already existing goods and services and exploring it independently from existing goods and services.

The human insight phase should include the following steps to achieve the above objectives:

- Achieve a *shared understanding of the task* in the team and together with the supervisor through a briefing.
- Explore the problem together and achieve a *shared understanding of the problem.*
- *Gain deep insights* from people who may share the problem, using qualitative and quantitative methods.
- *Condense the collected findings and realizations* to groups of persons and specific problem aspects, for which solutions are to be found later.

Understanding the H2H Task and Exploring the Problem Space

In this step, it is essential that the team members develop a shared understanding of the problem. The fact that the team in the previous step explores the problems together is that they, due to their great diversity, have a lot of methodological knowledge for problem analysis but also opinions and points

---

[74] Kozinets, R. V. (2015). *op. cit.*

of view that make a multifaceted problem analysis possible in the first place. In this step, the team members develop into so-called immediate experts[75] by acquiring as much knowledge as possible about the background of the problem and the user group.

To effectively enable an empathic immersion in the customer, it can be useful to map the customer journey along all touchpoints to visualize the experience and, if necessary, to fall back on it. In addition, at this point, all previous findings should be documented in writing and communicated with the other team members to be on the same page, going into the next research phase. Together, the team looks for answers to the following questions to structure the problem space and the further course of the process:

- Do we all understand the problem in the same way? Are there differing perspectives on the problem? Are there various facets?
- Who has the problem and what are their needs, expectations, and feelings when they think about the problem? Are there different user groups that can be differentiated? Are there so-called extreme users, and if so, what are their needs, expectations, and feelings?
- Who are the involved stakeholders and what are their needs, expectations, and feelings when they think about the problem?
- What are the possible causes and effects of the problem?
- What is the context of the problem, what is the framework: political, economic, social, technical, environmental, and legal?

It is important to put always the customer perspective first. This means, of course, listening to the customers, understanding and solving their problems, representing their interests, and using their special skills to create value. In H2H Marketing, the customer can be any other important stakeholder. In any case, they are all human beings!

Ethnography/Netnography

In this partial phase, the team, usually in groups of two, is busy collecting and analyzing data over a determined period of time in order to obtain surprising insights, needs, and expectations. The results are presented and explained to the other members in between so that the other teams can build on the findings and criticize them. It is important that the process participants inside

---

[75] Grots, A., & Pratschke, M. (2009). *op. cit.*

their team exchange roles (observer and recorder) and rotate between the user groups that are to be researched and the associated methods that are to be applied. This increases multi-perspectivity and reduces the problem of distortion of personal perceptions. The problem should be illuminated variably from all sides, including unorthodox ways. The most important methods for the knowledge acquisition phase are the ethnographic methods of observation and interview, netnographic studies to understand customers in their online environments, and empathic methods such as apprenticing, as well as the structuring methods of customer journey and blueprinting.

Big Data

At the same time, the evaluation of data can be generated by means of data mining and data analytics to obtain in-depth insights into people and their user behavior. The data can be analyzed from available market research studies, own or external databases with user data from the Internet, or with data from smart products/goods for identifying possible patterns, which also serve to generate possible problems, needs, and expectations and surprising findings.[76]

An important recommendation is to ask the right questions and then evaluate the data. This sounds unconventional, but many companies first collect data, store it, process it, and convert it so that they can subsequently utilize it further. "[…] organizations should start in what might seem like the middle of the process, implementing analytics by first defining the insights and questions needed to meet the big business objective and then identifying those pieces of data needed for answers".[77] H2H Marketing agrees but suggests an addition to that. First, possible insights from qualitative field research and quantitative market research should be determined and then checked with Big Data Analytics to determine whether these hypothetical findings are reflected in the data.

---

[76] Stone, M. L. (2014). Big Data for Media [Report]. Retrieved from Reuters Institute for the Study of Journalism   website: https://reutersinstitute.politics.ox.ac.uk/sites/default/files/2017-04/Big%20 Data%20For%20Media_0.pdf
[77] LaValle, S., Lesser, E., Shockley, R., Hopkins, M. S., & Kruschwitz, N. (2011). *op. cit.*, p. 25f.

Structuring and Condensing Findings

The collected findings are then presented and analyzed by the entire team. The aim of this phase is to condense the information so that different user groups can be identified and prioritized. The prioritized target group then is to be described empathically (see Fig. 5.9). To obtain accurate insights and to create a consensus in the team, an empathy map can facilitate purposive, customer-centric thinking. By using these techniques, the team can find starting points for further developing and adapting the range of products and services for customers, to tackle the initial H2H problem based on customer experience.

In the following step, H2H Marketing combines traditional market segmentation and the persona concept to eliminate blind spots inherent in each of them and to get a comprehensive picture of the market, the solution, and its user, the customer. The two concepts each have their own strengths and weaknesses. The market segment comprises a larger group of users and their demographic details and can provide information on the size of a market

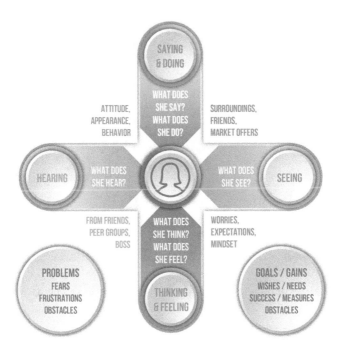

Fig. 5.9 Exemplary empathy map

segment and the monetary value that the segment could generate (see Fig. 5.10).[78]

In her book *Designing for the Digital Age*, Kim Goodwin sums up the benefits of traditional market research, while pointing out the shortcomings when it comes to taking the user into account[79]:

A good segmentation model will also include an estimate of the number of potential customers represented by that segment and the amount of money they can be expected to spend. However, [...] market research (and therefore market segmentation) tends to focus on what messages will sell a product rather than on how people will use a product over time.[80]

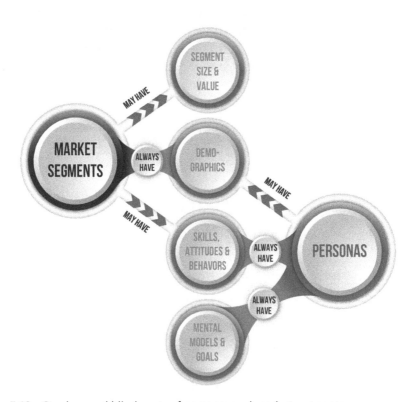

Fig. 5.10 Overlaps and blind spots of personas and market segments

[78] Goodwin, K. (2009). Designing for the Digital Age: How to Create Human-Centered Products and Services. Indianapolis, IN: Wiley.

[79] Adapted from Goodwin, K. (2009), p. 237.

[80] Goodwin, K. (2009). *op. cit.*

By bringing the persona concept into the equation, the outcome changes. This combination of Design Thinking with marketing methods and skills makes it possible to match the desirability for potential users of a solution with the economic and technological feasibility, following the logic of the trifecta of innovation discussed earlier (see Sect. 2.1). When the desirability is ensured, the segmentation and subsequent quantification of the market, defined by the problem to be solved, can be launched in order to make sure that the solution is economically viable. When a customer group has been selected and described empathically as a persona, the problem is formulated in such a way that it becomes an abductive question in the form of a "how might we?", which contains the search direction itself.

(Pre-)Develop a Value Proposition

The next logical step is creating a value proposition for the identified users of a possible solution. The value proposition is the core part of the H2H Process and follows the co-creation postulate of the S-DL, actively integrating the customer into the development of the value proposition.[81] For Vargo and Lusch, "marketing is a continuous series of social and economic processes that is largely focused on operant resources with which the firm is constantly striving to make better value propositions than its competitors".[82] This is consistent with the H2H Marketing approach, which sees the development of a differentiating value proposition as a central task.

It should have become clear from the discussion of the S-DL in earlier chapters (see Sect. 2.2) that value can only be generated with the value proposition by the customer herself in her context. Therefore, the focus shifts from the offering to the value creation process with the customer, in which the customer perspective on a recognized problem is incorporated via the exchange of knowledge and skills into a tailored value proposition, the use of which in turn leads to the solution of the problem.

As such, H2H Marketing agrees with the notion of the S-DL that companies can only offer a value proposition, not a value promise, and that in the end, the customer individually determines the value, not the firm. Of course, it is also one of the tasks of H2H Marketing to find an easy to understand and convincing argument that explains to the customer why he should use the value proposition, i.e., a *value promise* as communication of the value

---

[81] Vargo, S. L., & Lusch, R. F. (2008). *op. cit.*
[82] Vargo, S. L., & Lusch, R. F. (2004). *op. cit.*, p. 5.

proposition. However, H2H Marketing sees this as the task of Content Marketing, which is why it is not part of the value proposition but of the *content field* in the H2H Canvas and the H2H Process.

The basis for the value proposition is the Value Proposition Canvas,[83] which is further developed by H2H Marketing and complemented with the co-creation principle of the S-DL. H2H Marketing follows the principle that the competencies of a company and the customer are determined by its key resources and activities. However, hardware, software, and services function are vessels for the transportation of skills and knowledge for the benefit of the customer and are, thus, part of the service offered to the customer.[84] The customer can but does not have to be involved in the development of the value proposition. In the following, the components of the value proposition will be discussed in detail.

5.2.3   Leveraging Network Knowledge and Skills

Manufacturing products, services, and traditional distribution channels will remain relevant in the future, but that it is no longer sufficient to increase simply the variety of products with innovation efforts as a competitive edge.[85] The customers want to create an experience with the value proposition for themselves from which they derive their value in their context when using it.[86] In addition, traditional sales channels are no longer sufficient to make the products and services accessible to the customer. For this purpose, companies and customers increasingly have to use network structures to make co-created, individual experiences and new innovative solutions possible[87]:

> An experience environment can be thought of as a robust networked combination of company capabilities including technical and social capabilities, and consumer interaction channels including devices and employees, flexible enough to accommodate a wide range of individual context-and-time-specific needs and

---

[83] Osterwalder, A., Pigneur, Y., Smith, A., Bernarda, G., & Papadakos, P. (2014). Value Proposition Design. Hoboken, NJ: Wiley.

[84] See e.g. Vargo, S. L., & Lusch, R. F. (2016). *op. cit.*

[85] Prahalad, C. K., & Ramaswamy, V. (2003). *op. cit.*

[86] Lusch, R. F., & Vargo, S. L. (2014). *op. cit.*

[87] Prahalad, C. K., & Ramaswamy, V. (2003). *op. cit.*

preferences. Because a customer's desired experiences cannot be determined a priority, experience environments must actively involve consumers—as individuals and as communities—to accommodate a range of possible customer-company interactions and thereby a variety of potential co-creation experiences.[88]

This concept of experience environments follows the premises of the S-DL[89] and builds the foundation of network understanding for H2H Marketing. In H2H Marketing, the knowledge and skills of providers and customers form the basis for the development of value propositions. Competence requirements are becoming ever higher because of increasing digitalization and disappearance of certain industries and country barriers.[90] For this reason, the search for the missing competencies for the customer should not end within the company's own boundaries but also rely on leveraging the competencies from others inside the experience network. The competence to integrate itself into networks that are important for the development of tailor-made value propositions is therefore also gaining in importance.

5.2.4 Products and Services as Service for the Customer

In H2H Marketing, products and services are subsumed under *service* to the customer, following the premises of the S-DL, stating that both products and services are the results of the application of knowledge and skills (operant resources) and therefore service to the beneficiary.[91] The focus is on how the competencies that the customer demands from the company or the experience network[92] can be manifested in the form of products and services.

Human Experience Design

Customer experience was already discussed in Sect. 4.2. In this section, the customer experience is now discussed as a component under the aspect of the design of the value proposition, differentiating the terms *user experience* (UX) and *customer experience* (CX). The transition towards an *experience*

---

[88] Prahalad, C. K., & Ramaswamy, V. (2003). *op. cit.*

[89] At least implicitly, as the S-DL and its premises were introduced one year later (see Vargo and Lusch 2004. *op. cit.*).

[90] Prahalad, C. K., & Ramaswamy, V. (2003). *op. cit.*

[91] Vargo, S. L., & Lusch, R. F. (2008). *op. cit.*

[92] Prahalad, C. K., & Ramaswamy, V. (2003). *op. cit.*

society was already recognized as early as 1992 by German sociologist Gerhard Schulze[93] and found its way into the business world.[94] However, it left open many questions, and executives did not fully grasp it.[95] What was understood was that CX is the most important determining factor for competitive advantages to maintain and expand a position in the market.[96] H2H Marketing integrates the customer experience into the value proposition and understands that UX is a part of the CX, like *usability* is subsumed under UX, and refers to experiences with an interactive product.[97] The CX, though, involves the entire customer journey and is a holistic unification of the entirety of experiences and emotions that a customer has with a brand and its stakeholders, along all touchpoints, across all channels.[98]

Customer Experience Management (CXM) should be understood in a broader sense and should involve not only its primary target group,[99] the customer, but also the other members of the value creation network, namely, employees and partners, with which H2H Marketing explicitly agrees. "Loyal and satisfied customers are the result of loyal and satisfied employees. You can't have one without the other"[100]—a view prevalent among other authors as well.[101,102]

Similar to the creation of value in the S-DL, an experience with a brand is also perceived individually in the personal context of the customer and evaluated accordingly.[103] By shifting the focus towards providing individual, exceptional experiences, firms leave G-DL thinking of transactional and product

---

[93] Schulze, G. (1992). Die Erlebnisgesellschaft: Kultursoziologie der Gegenwart. Frankfurt, Germany: Campus. The original German title of his book is *Die Erlebnis-Gesellschaft*, which in English means "Experience Society".

[94] E.g. Prahalad, C. K., & Ramaswamy, V. (2003). *op. cit.*

[95] Hassenzahl, M. (2011). User Experience and Experience Design. In M. Soegaard, & R. F. Dam (Eds.), Encyclopedia of Human-Computer Interaction. Aarhus, Denmark: The Interaction Design Foundation.

[96] Rusnjak, A., & Schallmo, D. R. A. (2018). Gestaltung und Digitalisierung von Kundenerlebnissen im Zeitalter des Kunden Vorgehensmodell zur Digitalen Transformation von Business Models im Kontext der Customer Experience. In A. Rusnjak, & D. R. A. Schallmo (Eds.), Customer Experience im Zeitalter des Kunden: Best Practices, Lessons Learned und Forschungsergebnisse (pp. 1–40). Wiesbaden, Germany: Springer Gabler.

[97] Robier, J. (2016). UX Redefined: Winning and Keeping Customers with Enhanced Usability and User Experience. Cham, Switzerland: Springer International Publishing.

[98] Rusnjak, A., & Schallmo, D. R. A. (2018). *op. cit.*

[99] Goldhausen, K. (2018). Customer Experience Management – Der Weg ist das Ziel. In A. Rusnjak, & D. R. A. Schallmo (Eds.), Customer Experience im Zeitalter des Kunden: Best Practices, Lessons Learned und Forschungsergebnisse (pp. 41–94). Wiesbaden, Germany: Springer Gabler.

[100] Goldhausen, K. (2018). *op. cit.*

[101] Kotler, P., Kartajaya, H., & Setiawan, I. (2017). *op. cit.*

[102] Sisodia, R. S., Sheth, J. N., & Wolfe, D. (2014). *op. cit.*

[103] Kreutzer, R. T. (2018a). Customer Experience Management – wie man Kunden begeistern kann. In A. Rusnjak, & D. R. A. Schallmo (Eds.), Customer Experience im Zeitalter des Kunden: Best Practices, Lessons Learned und Forschungsergebnisse (pp. 95–119). Wiesbaden, Germany: Springer Gabler.

orientation behind and follow the path of transition towards real customer and human orientation. In this way, the CXM in H2H Marketing can help to place the human being at the center of all considerations. CXM should aim to create positive experiences that inspire the customer and ultimately bind them to the company, creating loyalty.[104] "[J]ust one moment of unexpected delight from a brand is all it takes to transform a customer into the brand's loyal advocate".[105] With the customer as the starting point, the entire customer journey should be aligned and designed to enable a seamless experience across channel and platform boundaries.[106]

For implementing experience design, a simple conceptual model is needed. It consists of three layers: Why, What and How. While "[t]he *What* addresses the things people can do through an interactive product".[107] *How* refers to "the typical realm of the interaction designer—to make given functionality accessible in an aesthetically pleasing way".[108] The *Why* then reflects the customer's underlying motivation to use a certain device. The author lays out that traditionally, many companies tend to start with the *What* instead of putting the customer's needs and desires first (*Why*). This is similar to the golden circle of Simon Sinek discussed in Chap. 2.

In Fig. 5.11, a typical example of listening to music (the *What*) is shown. There is a multitude of ways to make sure customers can listen to music (the *How*).[109]

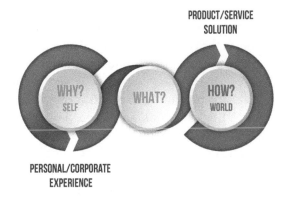

Fig. 5.11 From Why to How in experience design

---

[104] Kreutzer, R. T. (2018a). *op. cit.*

[105] Kotler, P., Kartajaya, H., & Setiawan, I. (2017). *op. cit.*, p. 59.

[106] Rusnjak, A., & Schallmo, D. R. A. (2018). *op. cit.*

[107] Hassenzahl, M. (2011). *op. cit.*, Why, What and How section, para. 2.

[108] Hassenzahl, M. (2011). *op. cit.*, Why, What and How section, para. 3.

[109] Hassenzahl, M. (2011). *op. cit.*, Why, What and How section, para. 6.

Firms will typically focus on the product side of the experience Design Thinking. What they forget in this process is to ask why the customer wants, for example, to listen to music. Maybe she wants to relax with some classical music after a long workday, or maybe she looks for motivational impulses while she is doing an intense workout. Whatever his motivation is, the investigation should start with the *Why* as the first step.[110] This is also the foundational premise of H2H Marketing, where human desirability, empathy, and contextual understanding of the human come first and feasibility and cost considerations second.

Summarizing, it should be pointed out again that H2H Marketing's main task in developing the value proposition is to explore why people want to use a value proposition and that the customer-oriented design of the multidimensional customer experience forms an integral part of the value proposition itself.

Price as Quantification of the Value for the Customer

Although having far-reaching consequences for an enterprise's profitability, the price of goods and services is not a popular topic among executives and business scholars. In his article *Towards value-based priceing*, Hinterhuber identifies various misconceptions about the nature of prices and their effects on customers and market share. The first trap executives seem to have fallen into is the belief that customers view price as crucially important, while, as he argues, research points in the contrary direction "that customers are frequently unaware of prices paid and that price is one of the least important purchase criteria for them".[111] Another misconception he sees is in the presumed incompatibility of charging premium prices and at the same time have a large market share. For her, "[h]igh market share and high prices can be achieved if prices truly reflect high customer value".[112] This is in line with how price is defined, setting the basic price formula as "price = value".[113]

For her, "[t]he price a customer is willing to pay, and therefore, the price a company can achieve, is always a *reflection of the perceived value* [emphasis

---

[110] Hassenzahl, M. (2011). *op. cit.*

[111] Hinterhuber, A. (2004). Towards value-based pricing—An integrative framework for decision making, p. 765. Industrial Marketing Management, 33(8), pp. 765–778. https://doi.org/10.1016/j.indmarman.2003.10.006

[112] Hinterhuber, A. (2004). *op. cit.*

[113] Simon, H. (2015). Confessions of the Pricing Man: How Price Affects Everything, p. 13. Cham, Switzerland: Springer International Publishing.

added] of the product or service in the customer's eyes".[114] This connection of the price to the individually perceived value, although not expressed explicitly, contains the results of rethinking pricing in the light of the S-DL. It is the individually perceived value-in-use that serves as a measure of value for customers and suggests that the price should be part of a firm's value proposition.[115]

For example, price becomes part of the concept of value proposition, because value propositions are exchanged and value-in-use expands the time horizon for a supplier firm to remain involved with the customers' use and experience of goods sold. [...] Hence, the offering may have a price set or negotiated as part of the value proposition, but this price is not confirmed as value until it is assessed or experienced by the customer in use.[116] If the price is to represent the value in the customer's individual context, then the price can no longer be calculated using traditional methods such as markup calculation. However, how should a price be determined that reflects the actual value of the proposition? This question can only be answered if it is possible to determine the value of the service provided to the customer. The value of the offer must, therefore, be quantified in monetary terms. The approach proposed here and implemented into H2H Marketing was introduced as a model for value-based pricing.[117] On some points, H2H Marketing sees room for additions or disagrees with the value-based pricing model, as not everything proposed by the author is in line with the H2H philosophy.

A four-step process is proposed[118]:

1. Define pricing objectives.
2. Analyze the key elements of pricing decisions.
3. Select profitable price ranges.
4. Implement price changes.

Note that this pricing model is conceptualized as a continuous process, meaning constantly adapting to changes in the market, in customer behavior, or other factors. Further, the objectives must take into account the relationships to all other marketing decisions, meaning that, for example, price positioning should not be considered separately from brand positioning.[119]

---

[114] Simon, H. (2015). *op. cit.*
[115] Kowalkowski, C. (2010). *op. cit.*
[116] Kowalkowski, C. (2010). *op. cit.*
[117] Hinterhuber, A. (2004). *op. cit.*
[118] Hinterhuber, A. (2004). *op. cit.*
[119] See also Simon, H. (2015). *op. cit.*

The second step is to analyze the strategic triangle[120] consisting of the customer (MBV), the company (RBV), and the competition (MBV). This analysis forms the foundation for following pricing decisions. The following steps to analyze the three parties involved are presented[121]:

- To understand the customer base: "[E]conomic value analysis: the understanding of the sources of economic value of a product to different clusters of customers".[122] From the point of view of H2H Marketing, the analysis should be conducted for each customer segment (persona) and not be limited to only economic values.

The cost-volume-profit (CVP) analysis of company: "CVP analysis: the understanding of the implications of price and volume changes on company profitability". In H2H Marketing, the target costing method is used in addition.

- "Competitive analysis: the understanding of trends in competitive pricing, product offerings, and strategies."

The value analysis, as well as the CVP analysis and target costing, will be discussed in more detail, while for more detailed information on the competitive analysis, the reader is referred to the relevant literature.[123]

Analysis from the Customer Perspective

Value analysis from the client's perspective aims to identify the different sources of value and to quantify them in monetary terms. Instead of determining the customer's willingness to pay for a product, the price of the next best alternative that is available to the customer on the market is ascertained and taken as reference. On top of this reference price, the value difference to the reference service is then added. The analysis follows these steps, whereby H2H Marketing swapped the positions of the first two steps, while everything else has been left untouched[124]:

1. "Segment the market."

---

[120] Ohmae, K. (1982). The strategic triangle: A new perspective on business unit strategy. European Management Journal, 1(1), pp. 38–48. https://doi.org/10.1016/S0263-2373(82)80016-9

[121] Hinterhuber, A. (2004). *op. cit.*, p. 768.

[122] Hinterhuber, A. (2004). *op. cit.*

[123] E.g. Hering, E. (2014). Wettbewerbsanalyse für Ingenieure. Wiesbaden, Germany: Springer Vieweg.

[124] For the following direct quotation of the analysis steps see Hinterhuber, A. (2004). *op. cit.*

2. "Identify the cost of the competitive product and process that consumer views as best alternative."
3. "Identify all factors that differentiate the product from the competitive product and process."
4. "Determine the value to the customer of these differentiating factors." As a way of assessing the value, conjoint analysis or procedures such as focus groups, benchmarking, or customer workshops could be applied.
5. "Sum the reference value and the differentiation value to determine the total economic value." Since values will differ from segment to segment, a *value pool* is formed that includes the different values each customer group derives from a given product or service.
6. "Use the value pool to estimate future sales at specific price points."

An important note to conclude, the customer perspective is that in H2H Marketing, this process is not only carried out for customer segments but for all partners in the value creation network, because service is exchanged with them as well.

Value Analysis from the Provider's Perspective

The analysis is included in H2H Marketing here for use in the context of price adjustments, but not in the process of newly developed offerings, where there is no reference value to fall back on. For this purpose, H2H Marketing uses target costing in an effort to integrate market and customer orientation into cost management.[125] However, target costing is only briefly presented here. For further research, the reader is referred to the relevant literature on the subject.[126]

Target costing in itself is the logical counterpart to the cost-plus method[127] and is market and customer-oriented (MBV, outside-in view) based on what a product is allowed to cost, unlike the cost-plus method that is resource and company-oriented (RBV, inside-out view), focusing on what a product will cost, determined on the basis of the company's cost to produce it.[128]

In the previous section, the price was determined by analyzing the value from the customer's point of view. The result of this analysis is used here as *target sales price* from which then the *target profit* that the firm defines is

---

[125] Dirnberger, D. (2013). Target Costing und die Rolle des Controllings im Zielkostenmanagement. München, Germany: GRIN.

[126] See e.g. Dollmayer, A. (2003). Target Costing: Modernes Zielkostenmanagement in Theorie und Praxis. Marburg, Germany: Tectum.

[127] Dirnberger, D. (2013). *op. cit.*

[128] Horsch, J. (2015). Kostenrechnung: Klassische und neue Methoden in der Unternehmenspraxis (2nd. ed.). Wiesbaden, Germany: Springer Gabler.

deducted in order to arrive at the *target costs*. These are then used as the starting point for further considerations. The target costs are then compared with the estimated prime costs. If the estimated costs are higher than the target costs, the costs must be reduced to the level of the target costs in order to achieve the desired profit. Concluding, "Target costing is not a mere calculation tool, [...] but rather an instrument of behavioral control and a tool for target-oriented communication between development, production and marketing and can contribute to the reduction of the often existing language barriers".[129]

5.2.5 Inform, Advise, and Entertain with Valuable Content

The paragraphs below will discuss communication as a modern operative task of H2H Marketing influenced by the three factors of the H2H Marketing Model.

Content Marketing: Help, Don't Sell!

Content Marketing seems to be on everyone's lips these days and finds versatile uses in both B2B and B2C companies. Moreover, while the concept of convincing customers with helpful content is not new, digitalization developments manifesting in constant connectivity, new information behavior, and the rise of social media and other new channels have fueled its popularity. With classic outbound marketing not yielding the positive results it once did,[130] firms must find other ways of reaching their customers, relying more and more on useful content in order to convince them.

Content Marketing consists in producing and distributing useful content that informs, gives tips and recommendations, entertains, or gives new creative ideas, whereby the company positions itself as an expert in a certain subject area. The aim is to acquire new customers and increase customer loyalty by building a trust-based relationship with them. With the catchy phrase "communicating without selling" describes the "art and science of regularly sharing valuable information with your target audience that aligns with and reinforces your brand."[131]

---

[129] Horsch, J. (2015). *op. cit.*

[130] Godin, S. (2007). *op. cit.*

[131] Harad, K. C. (2013). Content Marketing Strategies to Educate and Entertain, p. 18. Journal of Financial Planning, 26(3), pp. 18–20. Retrieved from https://www.onefpa.org/journal/Pages/Content%20Marketing%20Strategies%20to%20Educate%20and%20Entertain.aspx

The special thing about Content Marketing is the change of perspective, away from the focus on your own products and services towards a focus on the needs and interests of your customers; it constitutes a "cultural change from 'selling' to 'helping'".[132] By offering helpful or entertaining content in order to be found by interested customers instead of concentrating on the promotion of the products themselves, Content Marketing bridges the transition from outbound to inbound marketing (see Table 5.2[133]).

Content Marketing combines the characteristics of inbound marketing presented in Table 5.2 and leaves out intrusive Interruption Marketing, practically applying the communication changes that the S-DL propagates.[134] Customers are operant resources,[135] and communication with them should follow a dialogical not monologue form. They note that value traditionally is "[p]romised by *selling* the benefits",[136] but in a dialogical approach, should be "[e]mergent in *learning* together: co-created and integrated",[137] which precisely reflects the nature of Content Marketing. Content Marketing by nature follows the inbound principles but can for maximization of the effects be combined with outbound measures.[138]

Table 5.2 Comparison of outbound and inbound marketing

Inbound marketing	Outbound marketing
Earning interest and attention through relevance	Enforce interest and attention through communication pressure
Communication in two directions	Communication in one direction
Customers come via search engines and social media	Customers come via paid advertisements
Marketers convince through added value	Marketers persuade with sales phrases
Marketers want to sell indirectly	Marketers want to sell directly

---

[132] Holliman, G., & Rowley, J. (2014). Business to business digital content marketing: marketers' perceptions of best practice, p. 269. Journal of Research in Interactive Marketing, 8(4), pp. 269–293. https://doi.org/10.1108/JRIM-02-2014-0013

[133] This table has been translated from German to English. Adapted from Lean Content Marketing: Groß denken, schlank starten. Praxisleitfaden für das B2B-Marketing (2nd ed., p. 4), by S. T. von Hirschfeld, & T. Josche, 2018, Heidelberg, Germany: O'Reilly.

[134] Godin, S. (2007). *op. cit.*

[135] Vargo, S. L., & Lusch, R. F. (2008). *op. cit.*

[136] Ballantyne, D., & Aitken, R. (2007). *op. cit.*, p. 367.

[137] Ballantyne, D., & Aitken, R. (2007). *op. cit.*

[138] von Hirschfeld, S. T., & Josche, T. (2018). *op. cit.*

H2H Content Marketing

Content Marketing forms an integral part in the operational H2H Marketing, however, with certain adjustments. The basic idea of enriching the lives of customers with helpful content that is relevant to them instead of suffocating them with oppressive advertising is fully in line with the human philosophy and way of viewing customers of H2H Marketing. However, H2H Marketing broadens the concept of content in two respects. H2H Content Marketing should do justice to the idea of *edutainment* by always providing educating/advising (education function) and/or entertaining (entertainment function) content.[139] Traditional Content Marketing mainly focuses on the digital world, while H2H Content Marketing embraces both the digital *and* the analog, encouraging to break down known boundaries and to think Content Marketing beyond the digital world. In-person analog Content Marketing can be done, for example, with events, like a conference or fair.[140]

Furthermore, content in H2H Marketing is not only used to acquire new customers but also to help existing customers to better understand the value proposition and to use it correctly. This is intended to support the customer in the co-creation of value by using the value proposition to achieve the highest possible value-in-use. Thanks to digitalization, personalized, tailor-made content can be made available. The basis for content development in H2H Marketing should again be the concept of persona.[141]

For practical implementation of Content Marketing, the *Lean Content Marketing* approach (see Fig. 5.12[142]) is used, whose creators follow the same philosophy on which H2H Marketing is based:

> The decisive factor for a fruitful dialogue is that it is conducted from human to human. Automated e-mails or tweets, as well as sales follow-up calls, are not suitable for winning the trust of potential customers. In order to credibly invite [customers to] a dialogue, a personal touch, authenticity, and appreciation are required.[143]

---

[139] Harad, K. C. (2013). *op. cit.*

[140] Wang, W. L., Malthouse, E. C., Calder, B., & Uzunoglu, E. (in press). B2B content marketing for professional services: In-person versus digital contacts. Industrial Marketing Management. https://doi.org/10.1016/j.indmarman.2017.11.006

[141] von Hirschfeld, S. T., & Josche, T. (2018). *op. cit.*

[142] von Hirschfeld, S. T., & Josche, T. (2018). *op. cit.*

[143] von Hirschfeld, S. T., & Josche, T. (2018). *op. cit.*

Fig. 5.12 The lean content marketing cycle

Lean Content Marketing builds on the idea of the *lean start-up*[144] and follows the principle of "Build, Measure, Learn".[145] At first, a company starts with small content units and waits for user feedback, which it then analyzes. In a constantly repeating loop, new content is then created and adapted, always based on the findings of the market feedback. The goal is to create efficient content, not cheap, as is often mistakenly assumed under the term lean. It provides valuable assistance to the target group and helps the firm to engage and learn more about them. It offers a way to quickly implement a Content Marketing strategy and learn more about customers' step by step which may seem counterintuitive to marketers in the beginning.

Following the idea of the minimum viable product of the lean start-up method, a *Minimum Viable Content* (MVC) is generated, which is then tested on the customer according to the aforementioned principle, in order to learn from it and improve the content iteratively. The following sequence of steps to implement Lean Content Marketing[146] is suggested:

1. Create organizational and technical preconditions for Content Marketing.

---

[144] Ries, E. (2011). The Lean Startup: How today's entrepreneurs use continuous innovation to create radically successful businesses (1st ed.) . New York, NY: Crown Business.

[145] von Hirschfeld, S. T., & Josche, T. (2018). *op. cit.*, p. 12. Heidelberg, Germany: O'Reilly.

[146] von Hirschfeld, S. T., & Josche, T. (2018). *op. cit.*, p. 47.

2. Collect and evaluate the existing content in a content audit.
3. Start with a minimal functional content version (MVC).
4. Continuously check and analyze the content, formats, and channels used.
5. Continuously improve the MVC.
6. Have the courage to leave the chosen path and start again with the MVC.

In the following section, a simplified version based on the same principles, but only including the principal pillars, of the cycle will be presented.

H2H Content Marketing in Practice

In the following we will examine the following key points of the Lean H2H Content Marketing cycle.[147]

5.2.6   Setting Goals, Audience Mapping, and Planning

In a first step, marketers should think about what they want to achieve with their content. Content Marketing goals are derived from the overarching goals of the corporation and the marketing department[148] and usually fall into one of two categories: building and strengthening the brand or increasing sales.[149] It is recommended for formulating the goals using the SMART framework: *S*pecific, *M*easurable, *A*chievable, *R*easonable, and *T*ime-Bound.

Having defined the goals, marketers then should pinpoint the audience to which they direct the content. For this, a target group should first be identified which is then described in more detail with the persona concept,[150] following the combination of market segmentation and persona modeling presented earlier. This should be as precise as possible to be able to create personalized content of high relevance. Without knowing about the customer's problems and pain points, as well as their hopes and dreams, providing useful content that makes people come back for more is not possible.[151]

Furthermore, in this phase it should be planned which content is to be distributed by whom, with which format, via which channels, and at which

---

[147] Note: These steps are a combination of what Kotler et al. (2017) and von Hirschfeld and Josche (2018) propose.
[148] von Hirschfeld, S. T., & Josche, T. (2018). *op. cit.*
[149] Kotler, P., Kartajaya, H., & Setiawan, I. (2017). *op. cit.*
[150] von Hirschfeld, S. T., & Josche, T. (2018). *op. cit.*
[151] Kotler, P., Kartajaya, H., & Setiawan, I. (2017). *op. cit.*

point in time. These planned parameters must be in alignment with the customers' needs and their phase in the customer journey.[152]

Content Audit, Ideation, and Creation of the MVC

After setting up the goals, the phase revolving the content starts. In a first step, the Content Marketing team should perform an inventory of already existing content and check which part of the content meets the requirements to be used in the next steps.[153]

Then, based on what was defined during the target audience, analysis marketers should generate a *Minimum Viable Content* using already existing content from the audit and/or newly created material, to start the feedback loop. For this purpose, the team must draw on the previous findings (*human insights*) to contrast the interests, goals, and frustrations of the audience with its own expertise. The content should, therefore, be derived from the comparison of the MBV and the RBV. Their overlapping area is referred to as the *sweet spot* (see Fig. 5.13), in which meaning and significance for the recipient as well as trust in the content provider can arise.[154]

Depending on the needs and wishes of the audience, different content formats can be used. On a blog, companies can discuss industry-specific topics in articles. Whitepapers inform readers, for example, about new developments in their market, and webinars can be used to impart in-depth knowledge about the industry. Other popular forms include videos, podcasts, and webcasts.[155]

Also, in the Content Marketing area of H2H Marketing, the co-creation principle is integral. When looking for authentic content that connects with

Fig. 5.13 Content marketing as sweet spot between the customer and the firm

---

[152] von Hirschfeld, S. T., & Josche, T. (2018). *op. cit.*

[153] von Hirschfeld, S. T., & Josche, T. (2018). *op. cit.*

[154] von Hirschfeld, S. T., & Josche, T. (2018). *op. cit.*

[155] Halligan, B., & Shah, D. (2018). *op. cit.*

the audience, marketers should not forget about the customers themselves as a source for content. User-generated content (UGC) can deliver impressive results above all through its authenticity, as content created by actual users of the firm's offerings often can generate more trust in the audience than firm-produced content.[156] H2H Marketing supports the idea of using the new digital platforms to actively encourage the customer base to form part of content creation, involving them in a more direct manner and giving a voice to brand advocates.

To get started with the MVC, marketers should follow the *sweet spot* principle (Fig. 5.13[157]), looking to align the company's expertise with what helps the target groups in achieving their goals or solving their problems. The recipients should be encouraged to engage in dialogue with the firm in order to get as much and useful feedback as possible.[158]

Companies should not shy away from providing *truly valuable* information, although it may seem counterintuitive in the beginning, as the more positive effects are achieved the more remarkable the content is.[159] "If content is not high quality, original, and rich, a content-marketing campaign becomes a waste of time and sometimes backfires".[160] So, Content Marketing is a somewhat double-edged sword. It involves a lot of effort creating remarkable content, and if not done correctly, it can cause a backlash.[161] On the other hand, it enables "marketing beyond the budget," where creativity and not the size of the marketing budget is crucial for marketing success, an uplifting message especially for smaller companies.[162] The content published in the next step does not necessarily have to be created by the company itself, if the team lacks the necessary skills, but can also be given to external content producers to ensure that the quality requirements are met.[163]

Content Distribution

When it comes to distributing the content, marketers must make two decisions, one of more general nature, digital or analog distribution, and the

[156] Bernazzani, S. (2017, June 13). The 10 Best User-Generated Content Campaigns on Instagram [Blog post]. Retrieved from https://blog.hubspot.com/marketing/best-user-generated-content-campaigns

[157] Adapted from von Hirschfeld, S. T., & Josche, T. (2018). *op. cit.*, p. 26.

[158] von Hirschfeld, S. T., & Josche, T. (2018). *op. cit.*

[159] Halligan, B., & Shah, D. (2018). *op. cit.*

[160] Kotler, P., Kartajaya, H., & Setiawan, I. (2017). *op. cit.*, p. 129.

[161] Kotler, P., Kartajaya, H., & Setiawan, I. (2017). *op. cit.*

[162] Halligan, B., & Shah, D. (2018). *op. cit.*, p. 53.

[163] von Hirschfeld, S. T., & Josche, T. (2018). *op. cit.*

second more specific, which category of media channel? Although Content Marketing today focuses mainly on digital content and distribution channels, H2H Marketing explicitly also includes analogue variants of it to add a more human note to it, which follows: "In-person events allow the more meaningful human-to-human interactions that digital content marketing lacks".[164]

Today's connectivity makes it much easier for companies to distribute their content in a highly targeted way. When selecting the channel category (see Fig. 5.14[165]), some important aspects play a driving role, such as the customer journey of the audience or the goals that shall be achieved with the content.

Owned media (website, blogs, own communities, own social media) are practical because they are always available and can be freely published on them. However, its sphere of influence is limited, as it mainly delivers content to an already established base of prospective customers.[166] Thus, owned media, like, for example, a company newsletter, is more suitable to build and maintain a relationship and to qualify leads.[167]

On *paid media* channels, the company places content for the distribution of which payment is required (banner ads, Facebook ad). "Paid media are typically used to reach and acquire new prospective audiences in an effort to build brand awareness and drive traffic to owned media channels".[168] Access

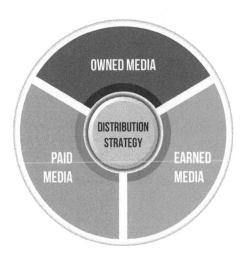

Fig. 5.14 Media channels for content marketing

[164] Kotler, P., Kartajaya, H., & Setiawan, I. (2017). *op. cit.*, p. 130.

[165] Adapted from von Hirschfeld, S. T., & Josche, T. (2018). *op. cit.*, p. 40.

[166] Kotler, P., Kartajaya, H., & Setiawan, I. (2017). *op. cit.*

[167] von Hirschfeld, S. T., & Josche, T. (2018). *op. cit.*

[168] Kotler, P., Kartajaya, H., & Setiawan, I. (2017). *op. cit.*, p. 131.

to *earned media* channels, on the other hand, is not simply attainable through payment but must be earned over a longer period of time. A company will dispose over earned media channels if its content spreads via word-of-mouth due to the remarkable quality or high expenditure to promote the content.[169]

Besides the goal that the distribution of the content is based on, practical considerations should also be taken into account. For example, publishing content on social networks offers the opportunity to interact with the target group and get to know more about them. This is of course very helpful to build a relationship with the audience, but it also involves more resources than just uploading and distributing content, like a video or podcast on the firm-owned website. In addition, the choice of channel and platform should be adapted to the preferences and behavior of customers considering where they usually get their information.

Content Marketing Evaluation and Improvement Loop

In the first step of the Lean Content Marketing process presented here, clear strategic goals, whether sales or brand-oriented, were set. The success of pursuing these goals should be measured to have a clear view of the results and, if necessary, make the right adjustments. Furthermore, the H2H Content Marketing should be measured across the five steps of the customer path introduced earlier.[170] An overview of metrics for Content Marketing along the customer path is given in Fig. 5.15. After having reviewed the effectiveness and results of the content, the MVC iteration cycle can then start again.

5.2.7 Access: Making the Value Proposition Available to Customers

Direct contact with the customer is of immense strategic importance today, because without it, it is not possible for companies to compete against larger dealers and platforms.[171] To make the value proposition available to customers, companies must demonstrate flexibility and design the channel architecture according to the customer's wishes. The customer decides when and

---

[169] Kotler, P., Kartajaya, H., & Setiawan, I. (2017). *op. cit.*

[170] Kotler, P., Kartajaya, H., & Setiawan, I. (2017). *op. cit.*

[171] Kegelberg, J. (2018). Auslaufmodell Omnichannel – Die Plattformökonomie integriert den Handel. In I. Böckenholt, A. Mehn, & A. Westermann (Eds.), Konzepte und Strategien für Omnichannel-Exzellenz: Innovatives Retail-Marketing mit mehrdimensionalen Vertriebs- und Kommunikationskanälen (pp. 373–383). Wiesbaden, Germany: Springer Gabler.

Fig. 5.15 Metrics for content marketing along the 5A customer path

where he wants to buy something, not the company. Electronic platforms are becoming increasingly important in this context.[172]

Omnichannel Integration

As connectivity speeds up the world, customers in what is termed the *Now Economy* demand fast delivery of products and immediate satisfaction of their needs and desires, wherever and whenever they want. And while some prominent B2C companies like Airbnb, Uber, and Amazon Prime have already recognized this trend and have aligned themselves to customer wishes, there is still a lot of catching up to do, especially in the B2B area.[173]

[172] Kreutzer, R. T. (2018b). Holistische Markenführung im digitalen Zeitalter – Voraussetzung zur Erreichung einer Omnichannel-Exzellenz. In I. Böckenholt, A. Mehn, & A. Westermann (Eds.), Konzepte und Strategien für Omnichannel-Exzellenz: Innovatives Retail-Marketing mit mehrdimensionalen Vertriebs- und Kommunikationskanälen (pp. 111–147). Wiesbaden, Germany: Springer Gabler.

[173] Spanier, G. (2017). The Now Economy: 'Uber's children'. Business Transformation, pp. 12–13. Retrieved from https://www.raconteur.net/business-transformation-2017

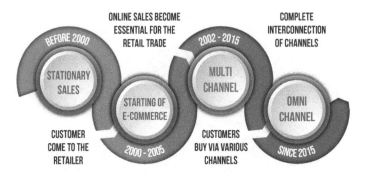

Fig. 5.16   From stationary sales to Omnichannel integration

In addition to the immediate gratification that customers expect, we have seen the rise of new channel structures and moving patterns along them as a result of combining once separated channels, leading many firms to turn to Omnichannel Marketing. This aims to align and integrate online and offline channels for a seamless customer experience across all touchpoints,[174] as shown in Fig. 5.16.[175]

Two of these new moving patterns along the channel architecture are *Web Rooming* and *Showrooming*, both showcasing parts of the challenges that firms are facing in retail today. Showrooming customers (store-to-online path) first visit offline retail stores to do research on the product and experience it close-up. The actual purchase then happens online, where, after deciding offline on what to buy, customers look online for the best price or other favorable extras. A Web Rooming customer, on the other hand, will first look up the products he is interested in online to and then buy it in an offline store, a practice especially popular among millennials. Businesses which make their products available only via one type of channel are experiencing difficulties in reaching these customer groups.[176]

To respond to these new buying patterns, firms, in recent years, are relying on Multichannel and Omnichannel approaches. H2H Marketing follows the definition of Omnichannel Management as follows:

Omnichannel Management uses and interconnects all available communication and sales channels to enable simultaneous use of multiple channels on both the

[174] Mehn, A., & Wirtz, V. (2018). Stand der Forschung – Entwicklung von Omnichannel-Strategien als Antwort auf neues Konsumentenverhalten. In I. Böckenholt, A. Mehn, & A. Westermann (Eds.), Konzepte und Strategien für Omnichannel-Exzellenz: Innovatives Retail-Marketing mit mehrdimensionalen Vertriebs- und Kommunikationskanälen (pp. 3–35). Wiesbaden, Germany: Springer Gabler.

[175] Adapted from Mehn, A., & Wirtz, V. (2018). *op. cit.*, p. 7.

[176] Kang, J.-Y. M. (2018). Showrooming, Web rooming, and User-Generated Content Creation in the Omnichannel Era. Journal of Internet Commerce, 17(2), pp. 145–169. https://doi.org/10.108 0/15332861.2018.1433907

customer and vendor sides. *The customer is at the heart of the strategy* [emphasis added], can actively manage the purchasing process and has complete control over transparency and data integration.[177]

This definition also shows the difference between Multichannel and Omnichannel models. Multichannel retailing means that a customer has the opportunity to purchase products on different sales channels, stationary and online. However, there is no integration of the channels, and the communication and the transactions that take place via the channels are dictated by the company, following an inside-out mindset and the RBV. The Omnichannel, on the other hand, places the human being in the center, recognizes her as a competent individual empowered to determine the rules of the game, by deciding when and where to pass through which steps of the customer path, and therefore takes the MBV following the outside-in philosophy.

In order to achieve a workable integration in the sense of the Omnichannel, holistic brand management that consistently unites the online and offline world is a key prerequisite. Thinking should no longer follow a dualistic mindset that distinguishes between online and offline, but instead, *no-line* thinking, i.e., without differentiation, should be embraced,[178] in the same way as customers are already doing today.[179]

When implementing an Omnichannel strategy, the complete customer path must be evaluated, especially the three moments of truth (see Fig. 5.17[180]). The Zero Moment of Truth (ZMOT) describes first impressions of a brand of anticipatory nature based on reports, recommendations, or videos. The First Moment of Truth (FMOT), on the other hand, describes the first direct contact with a product or service offering in which previously established brand expectations, for example, through advertising are reconciled with reality and validated. The last step in the validation process by the customer is the actual use, called the Second Moment of Truth, where the value promise made by the brand is tested for its worth.[181]

The ZMOT is of particular importance in this context as it is only influenced indirectly by the companies. Companies should try to achieve a positive outcome by introducing Review and Rating Management (RRM). The influence that expressed experiences, recommendations, and opinions of the

---

[177] Mehn, A., & Wirtz, V. (2018). *op. cit.*, p. 12.

[178] Kreutzer, R. T. (2018b). *op. cit.*

[179] Heinemann, G., & Gaiser, C. W. (2016). *op. cit.*

[180] Adapted from Kreutzer, R. T. (2018a). *op. cit.*, p. 109.

[181] Kreutzer, R. T. (2018b). *op. cit.*

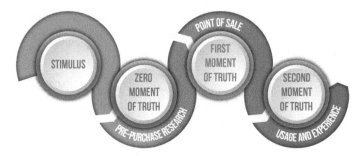

Fig. 5.17 Moments of truth along the customer path

social environment have on today's individual buyer is a factor that a large number of companies are still neglecting. RRM should aim to generate as many positive social signals as possible—likes, reviews, shares, and comments—and build brand trust. Content Marketing also plays a decisive role in this.[182]

It can be concluded that H2H Marketing promotes the integration of touchpoints and channels to enable a seamless customer experience. The foundation for this is the customer path, which should be analyzed and visualized along all touchpoints across all channels (*no-line*). The most important touchpoints and the most popular customer paths should be identified and integrated without any disconnect.[183] With such an integrated Omnichannel solution, channel hopping, meaning the constant switching between different information and distribution channels, then should be possible.[184] Omnichannel integration should follow the guiding principle of H2H Marketing, putting the human being into the focus and aligning the channels and touchpoints in complete accordance with his needs and wishes.

The Rise of Social Commerce

As a logical consequence of the establishment of social networks and the increase in the importance of the social environment in purchasing decisions, a growing convergence of e-commerce and social media is taking place, a phenomenon known as *Social Commerce*. This development follows an

[182] Kreutzer, R. T. (2018b). *op. cit.*

[183] Kotler, P., Kartajaya, H., & Setiawan, I. (2017). *op. cit.*

[184] Heinemann, G., & Gaiser, C. W. (2016). *op. cit.*

evolutionary trajectory, starting with ratings and reviews (first level of Social Commerce), followed by recommendations and referrals (second level), and culminating in social shopping (third level), where customers shop via social media in interaction with their social environment.[185] The effects of Social Commerce manifest themselves in three different forms, which will be briefly explained.[186]

5.2.8 Socialization of e-Commerce

This is the term used to describe social media elements such as ratings, recommendations, and shared ideas being woven into e-commerce. A classic example is Facebook Connect, which allows users to conveniently log in to a variety of shopping or community sites without having to register separately. Typically, websites also integrate other social plug-ins such as the like button or the comment function of Facebook.[187] Kotler et al. in this regard note that "brick-and-mortar shopping is all about social lifestyle and status; [...] it is also about the *human-to-human connections* [emphasis added] that usually happen in offline channels".[188] The socialization process also adds a more human note to e-commerce that is usually lacking.[189]

Commercialization of Social Media

There is a trend towards the opening of social media for the direct sale of products, which makes it a sales channel for retailers in addition to its traditional function as a communication channel. In most cases, however, the transactions take place offsite on the websites of the retailers, which are accessed via a link on the social media platforms. Also, in this case, Facebook is a prime example, but other platforms such as Twitter and YouTube are gradually opening up to the trend.[190]

---

[185] Heinemann, G., & Gaiser, C. W. (2016). *op. cit.*
[186] Heinemann, G., & Gaiser, C. W. (2016). *op. cit.*
[187] Heinemann, G., & Gaiser, C. W. (2016). *op. cit.*
[188] Kotler, P., Kartajaya, H., & Setiawan, I. (2017). *op. cit.*, p. 143.
[189] Heinemann, G., & Gaiser, C. W. (2016). *op. cit.*
[190] Heinemann, G., & Gaiser, C. W. (2016). *op. cit.*

Social Commerce in Its Pure Form

Real Social Commerce occurs when the entire transaction takes place on-site via a self-sufficient shop set up on the social media platform. Overall, the development of Social Commerce is still in its infancy, especially its pure form is rare so far. It is also possible that consumers will ultimately refuse to use social media as a shopping channel.[191] The cryptocurrency Libra announced by Facebook for 2020[192] could, however, set new impulses in this context.

For H2H Marketers, it is important to understand that the lines between social media and e-commerce are blurring, even if it is not yet clear whether Social Commerce will prevail. An emerging company in this area is OMIKRON, with a data quality suite for CRM and ERP and the e-commerce search optimization Fact-Finder. Fact-Finder is an AI-driven on-site search and merchandising for Social Commerce.

5.3 The H2H Process as Operative Process of H2H Marketing

New marketing activities, in a world of outbound and inbound marketing, need to have a process character and must react instantly to fast-changing environments. Marketing for start-ups differs significantly from marketing for incumbent companies, not only because of different financial situations but also because of different priorities. The full value of the flexible, iterative H2H Process appears obvious in this context. Firstly, a start-up will focus on the search and the comprehensive understanding of an H2H problem. Second, it will focus on the development of a proper value proposition to solve this problem together with collaboration partners and the customers. There won't be a lot of time for content marketing or branding. In contrast, an incumbent company might focus on digital content marketing because the company concludes that there is a major issue in content marketing. Good news here: Any company in any situation can use the H2H Process and iterate forward and backward easily. The whole process is lean and experimental by nature. Any idea, no matter what phase (customer insights, value proposition design, content, branding, etc.), can be tested, and the learning process of the

---

[191] Heinemann, G., & Gaiser, C. W. (2016). *op. cit.*

[192] Richert, M. (2019, July 3). Tschüss Bargeld, Hallo Libra! Facebooks schwingt sich zum weltgrößten Finanzdienstleister auf. FOCUS Online. Retrieved from https://www.focus.de/finanzen/boerse/gastkolumne-tschues-bargeld-willkommen-libra_id_10892195.html

lean concept will allow all kind of companies in all kind of situations a fast improvement of their marketing. We have to stress again that the successful application of the H2H Process will depend on the corporate mindset of the companies who try to apply it. Reality shows that only a few companies are prepared to forget about existing heavily formalized structures and procedures to apply the lean principle of H2H Marketing.

Digitalization provides all the means for instant, real-time reactions. User interfaces can be designed for all target audiences and can be multidirectional. Channels open up from multi- to Omnipresence. Unthinkable ways of delivery will emerge from 3D printing to augmented reality or holograms. We are just at the beginning, but with the iterative H2H Process, this kind of alterations could be integrated in any marketing activity. Design Thinking gives this approach numerous opportunities for advanced innovations at the back and front end of the innovation process. Marketing will be insight-driven and will be much closer to the customer than ever.

The Service-Dominant Logic emphasizes a co-creation of value and brand, builds on the importance of trust, and enables the new marketing process to be in the middle of any business decision (see Fig. 5.18).

Fig. 5.18 The H2H process inside the H2H marketing model

The integration of Design Thinking, Service-Dominant Logic, and digitalization within the framework of the H2H Marketing Model enables marketing decisions not only at the functional corporate level but also on the corporate governance level and makes it meaningful for everybody in the company. The new marketing mindset with new methods and processes enables the new H2H Marketing and creates a flexible-iterative procedure that brings up new possibilities in the hyper-competitive world.

Storyline

Finally, we have got to know the H2H Process as the last "brave action" in our story of H2H Marketing. We started with the evolution of the marketing mix and comprehend that the H2H Process is a logical evolutionary stage of the mix. The other concepts still contribute with some characteristics to the H2H Process. The process can be used from the "fuzzy front end" until the "back end" of innovation. The elements of co-creation and the approval that you only can propose value are key for the comprehension. The process itself is operational, iterative, and adaptable to all kind of business.

We learned about the single stages in the process. We always should start with a good briefing into an H2H Process challenge. The relation to a human problem is imperative in the process. We have not to start the process always with the detection of a human problem, but we should always keep the problem in mind when we start with a later phase. To understand the human problem fully, you must generate insights about the humans who (might) have this problem. Only if you do so, you can design a proper value proposition that covers several components including the essential customer experience. Value-based pricing is one of the difficult tasks the team has to conduct. We understood that H2H Content Marketing is not only used to promise value to the customer but to increase the probability to get the value by using it properly in the individual context of the customer. We learned that H2H Content Marketing broadens the concept of content marketing and that it uses the principles of the lean start-up method to make it more experiential and more agile. We then displayed the evolutionary process from stationary sales to the Omnichannel concept in order to make information and the value propositions accessible to the customers. Social Commerce represents the latest channel development. Finally, we summarized the impact of Design Thinking, Service-Dominate Logic, and digitalization on the practice of H2H Marketing as operational process. In the next chapter, we will step into the final stage of our story by finding meaning in our troubled business world today.

Questions

1. What is new with the H2H Process and how?
2. Does H2H Marketing help to handle "organizational ambidexterity"?
3. Why is the design of a value proposition the core task in the H2H Process and how does this differ from the traditional marketing practice?
4. Why is the customer experience (CX) an integral part of the value proposition in H2H Marketing? How can you design it? Which questions have to be answered? Why should you start with the "why"?
5. How does H2H Content Marketing broaden the concept of content marketing?
6. Why does H2H Marketing talk about "access" and not "distribution" anymore?
7. Explain the impact of Design Thinking, S-DL, and digitalization on the H2H Process.

References

Ballantyne, D., & Aitken, R. (2007). Branding in B2B markets: Insights from the service-dominant logic of marketing. *Journal of Business & Industrial Marketing, 22*(6), 363–371. https://doi.org/10.1108/08858620710780127.

Bernazzani, S. (2017, June 13). *The 10 best user-generated content campaigns on Instagram* [Blog post]. Retrieved from https://blog.hubspot.com/marketing/best-user-generated-content-campaigns

Borden, N. H. (1964). The concept of the marketing mix. *Journal of Advertising Research, 2*, 7–12. Retrieved from http://www.guillaumenicaise.com/wp-content/uploads/2013/10/Borden-1984_The-concept-of-marketing-mix.pdf

Chen, S., & Venkatesh, A. (2013). An investigation of how design-oriented organisations implement design thinking. *Journal of Marketing Management, 29*(15/16), 1680–1700. https://doi.org/10.1080/0267257X.2013.800898.

Constantinides, E. (2006). The marketing mix revisited: Towards the 21st century marketing. *Journal of Marketing Management, 22*(3/4), 407–438. https://doi.org/10.1362/026725706776861190.

Dann, S. (2011, July 5–7). *The marketing mix matrix* [Conference paper]. Paper presented at the Academy of Marketing Conference 2011, Liverpool, United Kingdom. Retrieved from https://www.researchgate.net/profile/Stephen_Dann/publication/267559484_The_Marketing_Mix_Matrix/links/54b6024b0cf2318f0f9a0743.pdf

Dev, C. S., & Schultz, D. E. (2005). Simply SIVA: Get results with the new marketing mix. *Marketing Management, 14*(2), 36–41. Retrieved from https://www.scopus.com/record/display.uri?eid=2-s2.0-17444418649&origin=inward&txGid=0 47497a80a4b341498c747b3d30eff31

Dirnberger, D. (2013). *Target costing und die Rolle des Controllings im Zielkostenmanagement.* München: GRIN.

Dollmayer, A. (2003). *Target costing: Modernes Zielkostenmanagement in Theorie und Praxis*. Marburg: Tectum.

Drengner, J., Jahn, S., & Gaus, H. (2013). Der Beitrag der Service-Dominant Logic zur Weiterentwicklung der Markenführung. *Die Betriebswirtschaft, 73*(2), 143–160. Retrieved from https://www.academia.edu/12178909/Der_Beitrag_der_Service-Dominant_Logic_zur_Weiterentwicklung_der_Markenf%C3%BChrung

Eser, D., Gaubinger, K., & Rabl, M. (2014). Sprint Radar: Community-based trend identification. In O. Gassmann & F. Schweitzer (Eds.), *Management of the fuzzy front end of innovation* (pp. 275–280). Cham: Springer.

Ettenson, R., Conrado, E., & Knowles, J. (2013). Rethinking the 4 P's. *Harvard Business Review, 91*(1/2), 26. Retrieved from https://hbr.org/2013/01/rethinking-the-4-ps

Gassmann, O., & Schweitzer, F. (2014). Managing the unmanageable: The fuzzy front end of innovation. In O. Gassmann & F. Schweitzer (Eds.), *Management of the fuzzy front end of innovation* (pp. 3–14). Cham: Springer.

Godin, S. (2007). *Permission marketing*. London: Simon & Schuster.

Goldhausen, K. (2018). Customer experience management – Der Weg ist das Ziel. In A. Rusnjak & D. R. A. Schallmo (Eds.), *Customer experience im Zeitalter des Kunden: Best Practices, Lessons Learned und Forschungsergebnisse* (pp. 41–94). Wiesbaden: Springer Gabler.

Goodwin, K. (2009). *Designing for the digital age: How to create human-centered products and services*. Indianapolis, IN: Wiley.

Grots, A., & Pratschke, M. (2009). Design thinking – Kreativität als Methode. *Marketing Review St. Gallen, 26*(2), 18–23. https://doi.org/10.1007/s11621-009-0027-4.

Gummesson, E., Kuusela, H., & Närvänen, E. (2014). Reinventing marketing strategy by recasting supplier/customer roles. *Journal of Service Management, 25*(2), 228–240. https://doi.org/10.1108/JOSM-01-2014-0031.

Hall, S. (2017). *Innovative B2B marketing: New models, processes and theory*. New York, NY: Kogan Page.

Halligan, B., & Shah, D. (2018). *Inbound-Marketing: Wie Sie Kunden online anziehen, abholen und begeistern* (D. Runne, Trans.). Weinheim: Wiley-VCH.

Harad, K. C. (2013). Content marketing strategies to educate and entertain. *Journal of Financial Planning, 26*(3), 18–20. Retrieved from https://www.onefpa.org/journal/Pages/Content%20Marketing%20Strategies%20to%20Educate%20and%20Entertain.aspx

Hartleben, R. E., & von Rhein, W. (2014). *Kommunikationskonzeption und Briefing: Ein praktischer Leitfaden zum Erstellen zielgruppenspezifischer Konzepte* (3rd ed.). Erlangen: Publicis.

Hassenzahl, M. (2011). User experience and experience design. In M. Soegaard & R. F. Dam (Eds.), *Encyclopedia of human-computer interaction*. The Interaction Design Foundation: Aarhus, Denmark.

Heinemann, G., & Gaiser, C. W. (2016). *SoLoMo – Always-on im Handel: Die soziale, lokale und mobile Zukunft des Omnichannel-Shopping* (3rd ed.). Wiesbaden: Springer Gabler.

Heinonen, K., & Medberg, G. (2018). Netnography as a tool for understanding customers: Implications for service research and practice. *Journal of Services Marketing, 32*(6), 657–679. https://doi.org/10.1108/JSM-08-2017-0294.

Hering, E. (2014). *Wettbewerbsanalyse für Ingenieure.* Wiesbaden: Springer.

Hinterhuber, A. (2004). Towards value-based pricing—An integrative framework for decision making. *Industrial Marketing Management, 33*(8), 765–778. https://doi.org/10.1016/j.indmarman.2003.10.006.

Holliman, G., & Rowley, J. (2014). Business to business digital content marketing: Marketers' perceptions of best practice. *Journal of Research in Interactive Marketing, 8*(4), 269–293. https://doi.org/10.1108/JRIM-02-2014-0013.

Horsch, J. (2015). *Kostenrechnung: Klassische und neue Methoden in der Unternehmenspraxis* (2nd ed.). Wiesbaden: Springer Gabler.

Judt, E., & Klausegger, C. (2010). Bankmanagement-Glossar: Was ist Trendscouting? *bank und markt, 3*, 46. Retrieved from https://www.kreditwesen.de/bank-markt/ergaenzende-informationen/archivdaten/trendscouting-id12805.html

Kang, J.-Y. M. (2018). Showrooming, webrooming, and user-generated content creation in the omnichannel era. *Journal of Internet Commerce, 17*(2), 145–169. https://doi.org/10.1080/15332861.2018.1433907.

Kegelberg, J. (2018). Auslaufmodell Omnichannel – Die Plattformökonomie integriert den Handel. In I. Böckenholt, A. Mehn, & A. Westermann (Eds.), *Konzepte und Strategien für Omnichannel-Exzellenz: Innovatives Retail-Marketing mit mehrdimensionalen Vertriebs- und Kommunikationskanälen* (pp. 373–383). Wiesbaden: Springer Gabler.

Kotler, P., Kartajaya, H., & Setiawan, I. (2017). *Marketing 4.0: Moving from traditional to digital.* Hoboken, NJ: Wiley.

Kotler, P., & Komori, S. (2020). *Never stop – Winning through innovation.* Canada, Kotler Impact Montreal.

Kowalkowski, C. (2010). What does a service-dominant logic really mean for manufacturing firms? *CIRP Journal of Manufacturing Science and Technology, 3*(4), 285–292. https://doi.org/10.1016/j.cirpj.2011.01.003.

Kozinets, R. V. (2015). *Netnography: Redefined.* Los Angeles, CA: Sage.

Kreutzer, R. T. (2018a). Customer experience management – wie man Kunden begeistern kann. In A. Rusnjak & D. R. A. Schallmo (Eds.), *Customer Experience im Zeitalter des Kunden: Best practices, lessons learned und Forschungsergebnisse* (pp. 95–119). Wiesbaden: Springer Gabler.

Kreutzer, R. T. (2018b). Holistische Markenführung im digitalen Zeitalter – Voraussetzung zur Erreichung einer Omnichannel-Exzellenz. In I. Böckenholt, A. Mehn, & A. Westermann (Eds.), *Konzepte und Strategien für Omnichannel-Exzellenz: Innovatives Retail-Marketing mit mehrdimensionalen Vertriebs- und Kommunikationskanälen* (pp. 111–147). Wiesbaden: Springer Gabler.

Lauterborn, B. (1990). New marketing litany: Four P's Passe; C-words take over. *Advertising Age, 61*(41), 26. Retrieved from http://www.business.uwm.edu/gdrive/Wentz_E/International%20Marketing%20465%20Fall%202014/Articles/New%20Marketing%20Litany.PDF

LaValle, S., Lesser, E., Shockley, R., Hopkins, M. S., & Kruschwitz, N. (2011). Big data, analytics and the path from insights to value. *MIT Sloan Management Review, 52*(2), 21–32. Retrieved from https://sloanreview.mit.edu/article/big-data-analytics-and-the-path-from-insights-to-value/

Leifer, L. J., & Steinert, M. (2014). Dancing with ambiguity: Causality behavior, design thinking, and triple-loop-learning. In O. Gassmann & F. Schweitzer (Eds.), *Management of the fuzzy front end of innovation* (pp. 141–158). Cham: Springer.

Li, C.-R., Lin, C.-J., & Chu, C.-P. (2008). The nature of market orientation and the ambidexterity of innovations. *Management Decision, 46*(7), 1002–1026. https://doi.org/10.1108/00251740810890186.

Lindberg, T., Meinel, C., & Wagner, R. (2011). Design thinking: A fruitful concept for IT development? In H. Plattner, C. Meinel, & L. Leifer (Eds.), *Design thinking: Understand – improve – apply* (pp. 3–18). Berlin: Springer.

Lusch, R. F., & Vargo, S. L. (2006). Service-dominant logic: Reactions, reflections and refinements. *Marketing Theory, 6*(3), 281–288. https://doi.org/10.1177/1470593106066781.

Lusch, R. F., & Vargo, S. L. (2014). *Service-dominant logic: Premises, perspectives, possibilities.* Cambridge: Cambridge University Press.

Martin, R. L. (2009). *The design of business: Why design thinking is the next competitive advantage.* Boston, MA: Harvard Business Review Press.

Mehn, A., & Wirtz, V. (2018). Stand der Forschung – Entwicklung von Omnichannel-Strategien als Antwort auf neues Konsumentenverhalten. In I. Böckenholt, A. Mehn, & A. Westermann (Eds.), *Konzepte und Strategien für Omnichannel-Exzellenz: Innovatives retail-marketing mit mehrdimensionalen Vertriebs- und Kommunikationskanälen* (pp. 3–35). Wiesbaden: Springer Gabler.

Ohmae, K. (1982). The strategic triangle: A new perspective on business unit strategy. *European Management Journal, 1*(1), 38–48. https://doi.org/10.1016/S0263-2373(82)80016-9.

Osterwalder, A., Pigneur, Y., Smith, A., Bernarda, G., & Papadakos, P. (2014). *Value proposition design.* Hoboken, NJ: Wiley.

Özbölük, T., & Dursun, Y. (2017). Online brand communities as heterogeneous gatherings: A netnographic exploration of Apple users. *Journal of Product & Brand Management, 26*(4), 375–385. https://doi.org/10.1108/JPBM-10-2015-1018.

Payne, A. F., Storbacka, K., & Frow, P. (2008). Managing the co-creation of value. *Journal of the Academy of Marketing Science, 36*(1), 83–96. https://doi.org/10.1007/s11747-007-0070-0.

Pfoertsch, W. A., & Sponholz, U. (2019). *Das neue marketing-mindset: Management, Methoden und Prozesse für ein Marketing von Mensch zu Mensch.* Wiesbaden: Springer Gabler.

Prahalad, C. K., & Ramaswamy, V. (2003). The new frontier of experience innovation. *MIT Sloan Management Review, 44*(4), 12–18. Retrieved from https://sloanreview.mit.edu/article/the-new-frontier-of-experience-innovation/

Richert, M. (2019, July 3). *Tschüss Bargeld, Hallo Libra! Facebooks schwingt sich zum weltgrößten Finanzdienstleister auf.* FOCUS Online. Retrieved from https://www.focus.de/finanzen/boerse/gastkolumne-tschues-bargeld-willkommen-libra_id_10892195.html

Ries, E. (2011). *The lean startup: How today's entrepreneurs use continuous innovation to create radically successful businesses* (1st ed.). New York, NY: Crown Business.

Robier, J. (2016). *UX redefined: Winning and keeping customers with enhanced usability and user experience.* Cham: Springer.

Robra-Bissantz, S. (2018). Entwicklung von innovativen Services in der Digitalen Transformation. In M. Bruhn & K. Hadwich (Eds.), *Service business development: Strategien – Innovationen – Geschäftsmodelle: Band 1* (pp. 261–288). Wiesbaden: Springer Gabler.

Rohrbeck, R. (2014). Trend scanning, scouting and foresight techniques. In O. Gassmann & F. Schweitzer (Eds.), *Management of the fuzzy front end of innovation* (pp. 59–73). Cham: Springer.

Rumler, A., & Ullrich, S. (2016). Social-Media-Monitoring und -Kontrolle. *PraxisWISSEN Marketing, 1*, 94–112. https://doi.org/10.15459/95451.7.

Rusnjak, A., & Schallmo, D. R. A. (2018). Gestaltung und Digitalisierung von Kundenerlebnissen im Zeitalter des Kunden Vorgehensmodell zur Digitalen Transformation von Business Models im Kontext der Customer Experience. In A. Rusnjak & D. R. A. Schallmo (Eds.), *Customer Experience im Zeitalter des Kunden: Best Practices, Lessons Learned und Forschungsergebnisse* (pp. 1–40). Wiesbaden: Springer Gabler.

Schultz, D. E., Tannenbaum, S. I., & Lauterborn, R. F. (1994). *The New marketing paradigm: Integrated marketing communications.* Lincolnwood, IL: NTC Publishing.

Schulze, G. (1992). *Die Erlebnisgesellschaft: Kultursoziologie der Gegenwart.* Frankfurt: Campus.

Simon, H. (2015). *Confessions of the pricing Man: How price affects everything.* Cham: Springer.

Sisodia, R. S., Sheth, J. N., & Wolfe, D. (2014). *Firms of endearment: How world-class companies profit from passion and purpose* (2nd ed.). Upper Saddle River, NJ: Pearson Education.

Smith, P. G., & Reinertsen, D. G. (1991). *Developing products in half the time.* New York, NY: Van Nostrand Reinhold.

Spanier, G. (2017). The now economy: 'Uber's children'. *Business Transformation,* 12–13. Retrieved from https://www.raconteur.net/business-transformation-2017

Stone, M. L. (2014). *Big data for media* [Report]. Retrieved from Reuters Institute for the Study of Journalism website https://reutersinstitute.politics.ox.ac.uk/sites/default/files/2017-04/Big%20Data%20For%20Media_0.pdf

Trommsdorff, V., & Steinhoff, F. (2013). *Innovationsmarketing* (2nd ed.). München: Franz Vahlen.

Vargo, S. L., & Lusch, R. F. (2004). Evolving to a new dominant logic for marketing. *Journal of Marketing, 68*(1), 1–17. https://doi.org/10.1509/jmkg.68.1.1.24036.

Vargo, S. L., & Lusch, R. F. (2008). Service-dominant logic: Continuing the evolution. *Journal of the Academy of Marketing Science, 36*(1), 1–10. https://doi.org/10.1007/s11747-007-0069-6.

Vargo, S. L., & Lusch, R. F. (2016). Institutions and axioms: An extension and update of service-dominant logic. *Journal of the Academy of Marketing Science, 44*(1), 5–23. https://doi.org/10.1007/s11747-015-0456-3.

von Hirschfeld, S. T., & Josche, T. (2018). *Lean content marketing: Groß denken, schlank starten. Praxisleitfaden für das B2B-Marketing* (2nd ed.). Heidelberg: O'Reilly.

Wani, T. (2013). From 4Ps to SAVE: A theoretical analysis of various marketing mix models. *Business Sciences International Research Journal, 1*(1), 1–9. https://doi.org/10.2139/ssrn.2288578.

6

Finding Meaning in a Troubled World

Companies that commit themselves to the H2H Marketing philosophy can make a positive contribution to solving social problems by becoming proactive change agents. The philosophy is in line with the Davos Manifesto 2020, which states that the Universal Purpose of a Company in the Fourth Industrial Revolution "Is to engage all its stakeholders in shared and sustained value creation. In creating such value, a company serves not only its shareholders, but all its stakeholders—employees, customers, suppliers, local communities and society at large. The best way to understand and harmonize the diverse interests of all stakeholders is through a shared commitment to policies and decisions that strengthen the long-term prosperity of a company."[1]

The Davos Manifesto speaks with the language of the H2H Marketing approach, which champions companies to have a stronger position of trust. This is not only beneficial for them but also entails great responsibility to all stakeholders, as society increasingly turns to companies to help with societal problems, and the practice of brand activism becomes an indispensable imperative.[2] The Davos Manifesto sees a "company being more than an economic unit generating wealth."

Charles Schwab demands that companies fulfil a "human and societal aspirations as part of the broader social system. Performance must be measured not only on the return to shareholders, but also on how it achieves its

---

[1] See Klaus Schwab (2019), Founder and Executive Chairman, World Economic Forum in his article *Davos Manifesto 2020: The Universal Purpose of a Company in the Fourth Industrial Revolution*. Retrieved from https://www.weforum.org/agenda/2019/12/davos-manifesto-2020-the-universal-purpose-of-a-company-in-the-fourth-industrial-revolution/

[2] Sarkar, C., & Kotler, P. (2018). *op. cit.*

© The Author(s), under exclusive license to Springer Nature Switzerland AG 2021
P. Kotler et al., *H2H Marketing*, https://doi.org/10.1007/978-3-030-59531-9_6

environmental, social and good governance objectives. Executive remuneration should reflect stakeholder responsibility."[3]

This means that a company has a multidimensional scope of activities, not only to serve all those stakeholders who are directly engaged but to act itself as a stakeholder—together with governments and civil society—of our global future. Corporate global citizenship requires a company to harness its core competencies and its entrepreneurship, skills, and relevant resources in collaborative efforts with other companies and stakeholders to improve the state of the world. All this is in line with our understanding of Human-to-Human Marketing. The near future in particular, which offers a great deal of conflict potential, poses difficult questions for companies.

The economist Dr. Markus Krall calculated before the coronavirus crisis that the financial system will come under severe pressure and will start to waver in the next 1 to 2 years.[4] His prediction was based on the twofold effect of the European central bank's zero interest rate policy. First, the low interest rate has worked as an indirect subsidy for European firms, which would have not been able to finance their capital costs. In Germany, the average long-term failure rate of companies lies between 1.5% and 2%. In the years after the last financial crisis, this value dropped consistently towards 0.5%. This means that firms that should have gone bankrupt were kept alive artificially, estimates range from 170,000 to 300,000 outstanding firm bankruptcies in Germany (bankruptcies that got only postponed, not prevented). These companies represent an enormous risk for banks and other companies with which they do business, as they are only kept alive by constant refinancing through new borrowing and in the event of an increase in interest rates will default as debtors. After the corona pandemic, the situation got worse.

The second consequence of the zero-interest policy is the erosion of earnings for the banks that experience shrinking margin, which causes more and more of them to slip into the red and, as a consequence, melts down their equity capital basis. As a result of the shortage of banks' equity capital, the volume of credit they are allowed to grant will decline and consequently so will the amount of money circulating in the financial system. This could set a vicious circle in motion that will first hit the previously mentioned "zombie firms," whose failure could then drag the remaining actors down with them as well. The low interest rate thus works in two opposite directions: It cannot rise, as the unprofitable companies will go bankrupt, but it cannot remain low

[3] Sarkar, C., & Kotler, P. (2018). *op. cit.*
[4] Speaker's Corner. (2019, March 3). "Es ist eine verdammte Lüge" – Dr. Markus Krall (Roland Baader-Treffen 2019) [Video file]. Retrieved from https://www.youtube.com/watch?v=AWCyL3gcOzw

indefinitely without reducing the banks' equity capital to such an extent that they can no longer provide sufficient credit.[5]

Economist Max Otte further illustrated that the zero-interest policy is negatively impacting societal well-being by increasing inequality. As a consequence of low interest rates, asset price inflation took place during the last years, benefitting the wealthy who hold assets like stocks and real estate and penalize the lower part of society who miss out on these positive developments while additionally having to pay higher rents. This is one of the mechanisms that transfer wealth from the bottom to the top part of society.[6] The USA is also showing signs of tension: Trump announced a credit need of 1.1 trillion USD for 2019, and for the next years, even higher deficits are forecasted. The record levels reached by US junk bonds and leveraged loans further aggravate the situation.[7] For the corona crisis, the USA initiated a stimulus package of 2 trillion which will enlarge the overall depth burden.

We think polarization in society and politics, and a generally low level of trust, are dividing society.[8] In such times, people have started to rely on companies to bring about positive societal change and problem resolution. As a response, companies should try to set a good example and take the role of a trust anchor for the communities in which they are operating. Let us turn to digitalization and its impact on society, with a prime example where companies can become actively involved. In his most recent work, the German philosopher Precht examines the effects of digitalization on society and concludes that the concept of traditional work must be completely rethought.[9] Thus, new technology is changing not only the private lives of consumers but also their working lives. Automation will eliminate a large proportion of today's jobs, which will fundamentally change entire industries, e.g., insurance, banking, public transport, and public administration. Inevitably, a large proportion of people will lose their jobs in the long run. Precht argues that the highly qualified jobs created by digitalization are not suitable to stop this trend in any way, because for the first time in an industrial revolution, not as many new jobs will be created as will be lost, as was the case before. Moreover, for

---

[5] Speaker's Corner. (2019, March 3). *op. cit.*

[6] Otte, M. (2019). Weltsystemcrash: Krisen, Unruhen und die Geburt einer neuen Weltordnung. München, Germany: FinanzBuch.

[7] Homm, F., & Hessel, M. (2019). Der Crash ist da: Was Sie jetzt tun müssen! Anlagen, Immobilien, Ersprarnisse, Arbeit. München, Germany: FinanzBuch.

[8] Sarkar, C., & Kotler, P. (2018). *op. cit.*

[9] Precht, R. D. (2018). *op. cit.*

the new jobs that are created, qualifications are needed that a recently laid-off bus driver or insurance employee does not possess.[10]

This development has various drastic consequences. If a big part of society is not earning money, how can they make ends meet? And to whom will companies market their products, if a large share of the consumer base experiences substantial losses in its purchasing power? These questions are igniting the discussions about Universal Basic Income (UBI), which also is an integral part of Precht's utopia for the digital age. A reasonably high UBI could counteract the problem of job loss and associated social decline while providing a more stable level of demand and services to businesses. For the philosopher, the interesting question is not if it will be introduced at a large scale but, rather, when. Different forms of financing a UBI of up to 1500 Euros are being discussed, ranging from a productivity tax on the work done by machines and robots to a more realistic approach like a European financial transaction tax.[11]

For Precht, digitalization can bring about two different outcomes. The first alternative is a two-class society, which is created by the fact that a part of the people still have a regular job and mainly do well-paid and highly qualified work, while the second part of society without a job descends socially and lags behind in society. This dystopia can be mitigated by the second alternative of UBI. In a society in which everyone receives a guaranteed basic income, no one is forced to work only for money and to occupy monotonous, non-fulfilling jobs. People will have greater freedom to pursue their interests and creativity when monotonous jobs no longer fill their day. Activities that contribute to the further development of society with the newly gained time and freedom, such as artistic activities, starting a business, and taking care of the young and elderly, could gain much more momentum. Of course, there will also be members of society who will spend their time without positively contributing to society, but this should be the exception.[12]

Digitalization is also criticized for undermining democracy and civil rights. Asking a group of young people the provocative question if they would rather give up their cell phone or their voting right, the answer would prove this point. Constant surveillance and tracking, e.g., through smartphones, represent an immense intrusion into the private lives of citizens and are a reality which many prefer to push out of their mind. The revelations brought to light by Edward Snowden and Julian Assange made a broader part of the population aware of the extent to which they are being monitored.

---

[10] Precht, R. D. (2018). *op. cit.*

[11] Precht, R. D. (2018). *op. cit.*

[12] Precht, R. D. (2018). *op. cit.*

In addition, the gradual elimination of cash ("war on cash") through digitalization of payment transactions, albeit practical, further restricts civil liberties. A system without cash makes the citizen completely transparent and creates the basic conditions for a totalitarian system, similar to the idea of the Chinese Social Scoring System, in which the citizen is defenseless against the control and influence of state, big corporations, and financial institutions.[13] German journalist Norbert Häring describes in detail how major actors in politics, Wall Street, and the Silicon Valley, the *Better Than Cash Alliance*, the *Alliance for Financial Inclusion*, the *Consultative Group*, the *Financial Action Task Force*, and many others, take organized action against cash, undermining democratic structures and bypassing social consensus to make profit out of digitalizing payment transactions.[14]

The effects of digitalization show only one facet of worrisome developments. In *Confronting Capitalism*,[14] major shortcomings of the current capitalist system are described. Among the long list of shortcomings are persistent poverty, income inequality, capitalism's short-term orientation, and environment exploitation.[15] This indicates the broad range in which companies can take an active leadership role to improve the current situation. In *Advancing the Common Good*, tools are named that businesses can use to increase social action[16]:

1. Education and ethics
2. Dialogue and debate
3. Social cause marketing
4. Social media marketing
5. Lobbying
6. Legal action
7. Protest actions

The topic of sustainability has enormous impact on the way we bring or have to bring change to businesses, partners, and consumers. We showed methods, strategies, and mindset principles for business leaders of corporations to solve the game changing challenges that our generation has to face.

---

[13] Otte, M. (2019). *op. cit.*

[14] Häring, N. (2018). Schönes neues Geld: PayPal, WeChat, Amazon Go: Uns droht eine totalitäre Weltwährung. Frankfurt, Germany: Campus.

[15] Kotler, P. (2015). Confronting Capitalism: Real Solutions for a Troubled Economic System. New York, NY: AMACOM.

[16] For the following see Kotler, P. (2019). Advancing the Common Good: Strategies for Businesses, Governments, and Nonprofits, p. 96. Santa Barbara, CA: Praeger.

The goal is to lead a business that matches profitability but, even more crucially and primarily, sustainment and beneficial growth. During the last decades, business success was connected to high turnover of high-margined products on the market. Societies asked for more product and service variety, which companies used to exhaust their market potential to the fullest—with each product launch they strived for the next competitive advantage. Did they look for a higher purpose?

6.1   And the World Wakes Up

Former prime minister of the UK, David Cameron, stated: "Every economic and political theory or action must set about providing each inhabitant of the planet with the minimum wherewithal to live in dignity and freedom, with the possibility of supporting a family, education children, praising god and developing one's own human potential. This is the main thing, in the absence of such a vision, all economic activity is meaningless."[17] External challenges relevant to every human on this planet are becoming more transparent, and as a result, people are asking for changes. Impacts on human health and nature band the millennial generation who are demanding that their voices be heard by the status quo generation who currently hold the power in politics and business. In this context, the relevance of every business person's actions needs to be questioned. Businesses have to be evaluated from different angles on how to bring changes to their specific operations while preserving top-line growth. The Human-to-Human Marketing approach incorporates sustainability concerns for every single human, no matter which organization they operate for. All actions effect users, customers, employees, media, governments, NGOs, communities, investors, and suppliers. They are the sustainability stakeholders for whom marketing activities have direct impact, indirect impact, or enabler impact.

By applying the Human-to-Human approach to the Sustainability Edge base model (see Fig. 6.1),[18] communicating sustainability is a fundamental and ethical challenge that needs to raise awareness by and for people, and not for P&L statements. Sustainability is a topic that every human being can somehow relate to. Depending on the way communication is conducted, it can have various impacts. Sending sincere and honest messages and joining forces for a mutual goal is more important than ever when it comes to

---

[17] Minister David Cameron, cited in Apte, S. & Sheth, J. (2016), *op. cit.*, p. 6.
[18] Adapted from Apte & Sheth (2016), *op. cit.*, p. 33.

Fig. 6.1 Integrating "the Sustainability Edge" into the H2H approach

promoting more sustainable ways to do business. The core of communication is not the product itself anymore but methods, lifestyles, and superior beliefs; things we as humans share or, if not yet, can relate to.

A great example is Lamoral Coatings, the world most durable coating. The company's mission is to reduce drastically the replacement of materials and opening new markets through a unique technology and key collaborations with diverse industries. They provide solutions for many people's main concern in the middle of their bullseye. Lamoral Coatings claim is taming time.

The bullseye chart by Apte and Sheth (see Fig. 6.2[19]) shows about every person's most concerned perspective. This needs to be addressed in appropriate sustainability communication—it's not about the community or nation but about the human itself in the center of concerns. Consequently, one could assume that the Human-to-Human approach increases in effectiveness and relevance to the respective stakeholder groups from the outside-in.

Comparing the last decades of economic growth, not too many companies have identified their role to educate consumers. But in a morally and ethically acceptable manner, which is what the H2H approach promotes, this is the future of marketing—honest marketing with an intended purpose. Modern organizations and companies have the responsibility not only to promote sustainability but to make this world a better place, from the inside

_____
[19] Adapted from Apte & Sheth (2016), *op. cit.*, p. 39.

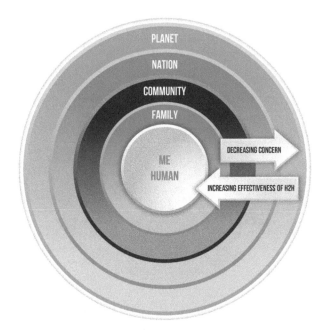

PLANET

NATION

COMMUNITY

FAMILY

ME
HUMAN

DECREASING CONCERN

INCREASING EFFECTIVENESS OF H2H

Fig. 6.2 The bullseye principle matched with the assumed effectiveness of H2H Marketing

and outside. Examples from AT&T, IKEA, or Unilever show how huge corporations can leverage their market power to change their impact towards more sustainability and, because of that, grow in efficiency, profitability, and market share.

In order for this change towards a society of meaning to actually work, a rethinking must take place, which is certainly possible as the past examples show. Nowadays, social status and recognition are closely linked to work, while unemployment is strongly stigmatized. If, however, in the near future a large proportion of people will no longer be pursuing work in the traditional sense, the image of a non-working person must be socially revalued. This may seem impossible today, but the image that only someone who works for money is worth something only emerged in the course of the last two centuries and is not irreversible. Therefore, a transformation must take place away from an extrinsically motivated performance society towards a society of meaning that follows intrinsic motivation:

A human utopia is based on what makes people happy in general and gives meaning to their lives. All modern technology is to be seen and evaluated in this context. It should not try to adapt the human being to the technology but should orient itself to his needs.[20]

H2H Marketing starts exactly at the point where technological and other developments begin with their relevance for the human being. Since politics seem paralyzed and unable to act, companies are being demanded to become involved as decisive agents in the fight for a humane society and to represent an anti-pole to the partially prevailing digitalization mania. The aim is to counteract the dehumanized society in which "autonomy has been exchanged for convenience, freedom for comfort and luck for calculation".[21] Fujifilm is a great case study for this kind of transformation. Many companies can paralyze about the fear of business disruption—but this can also be a motivator. In 2012, Kodak went bankrupt because it could not respond to the rise of digital photography and to smartphone cameras. The rival company Fujifilm started a bold transformation journey, based on well-executed diversification and cooperation with all their stakeholders.

Sisodia et al. described in their book *Firms of Endearment* that a transitioning process to a society of meaning is already taking place. "Indeed, looking at the magnitude of change in the business world, it is not overreaching to suggest that a historic *social transformation of capitalism* is underway".[22] This transitioning phase, as previously mentioned, is named the "Age of Transcendence," in which consumer needs, aspirations, and dreams are changing fundamentally, oriented towards purpose, passion, and experiences transcending materialistic needs, with people also craving for an economic system that is built for the many, not the few. They explain: "The Age of Transcendence signifies a cultural watershed in which the physical (materialistic) influences that dominated culture in the twentieth century ebb while metaphysical (experiential) influences become stronger".[23]

A main driver for this development is found in the demographic change, taking place worldwide. With an aging society, passion- and purpose-related issues gain much more momentum, with topics that dominate societal discourse and change in thinking. In addition, with people living longer, their values, mentalities, and spiritual ideals are passed onto the next generation.[24]

---

[20] Precht, R. D. (2018). *op. cit.*, p. 172.

[21] Precht, R. D. (2018). *op. cit.*, p. 69.

[22] Sisodia, R. S., Sheth, J. N., & Wolfe, D. (2014). *op. cit.*, p. XXII.

[23] Sisodia, R. S., Sheth, J. N., & Wolfe, D. (2014). *op. cit.*, p. XXIX.

[24] Sisodia, R. S., Sheth, J. N., & Wolfe, D. (2014). *op. cit.*

A transformation of capitalism is needed, as various authors express their views on its achievements, as well as the numerous pitfalls[25,26] Robert Reich, in his book *Saving Capitalism*, explains in detail how the rules of the game have been swayed slowly and subtly in favor of big corporations and wealthy individuals. This comes at the cost of ordinary people who pay the price for it. Political clout accompanied rising wealth, merging economic with political power in an unholy alliance. Reich remarks aptly: "Money and power are inextricably linked. And with power has come influence over the market mechanism. The invisible hand of the marketplace is connected to a wealthy and muscular arm".[27]

He also shows that the repetitive discussion about free market versus government intervention is misleading and an impediment to a fruitful debate, because it conceals the fact that there is no market without rules set by the governments defining how to handle property, monopoly, contracts, bankruptcy, and enforcement of the rules. By setting the rules, the government effectively creates the market. When capitalism is discussed, however, all too often, the dispute of free market versus government intervention prevails, with the majority of politicians promoting deregulation and rules in favor of the rich. Much more important, is the consideration of who should benefit from the rules and in whose favor they are formulated—the many or the few. In the long run, a population that feels that the system is rigged will not tolerate it. Already, ordinary citizens (especially in the USA) feel that they are cut off from progress. The middle class has shrunk steadily, and wage development has lagged far behind economic development. The mixture of political and economic power that is not working for the middle class is contributing to an enormous loss of trust. As history shows, without healthy trust, a modern society cannot flourish and offer its citizens stability.[28]

In the "Age of Transcendence," as described by Sisodia,[29] business as usual is no longer sufficient to be successful in the long run. Porter and Kramer[30] provide the same prognosis and note that traditional competitive factors such as price and quality are often no longer sufficient to generate a sustainable

---

[25] Kotler, P. (2015). *op. cit.*

[26] Mackey, J., & Sisodia, R. (2013). Conscious Capitalism: Liberating the Heroic Spirit of Business. Boston, MA: Harvard Business Press.

[27] Reich, R. (2017). Saving Capitalism: For the Many, Not the Few, p. 11. London, United Kingdom: Icon Books.

[28] Reich, R. (2017). *op. cit.*

[29] Sisodia, R. S., Sheth, J. N., & Wolfe, D. (2014). *op. cit.*

[30] Porter, M. E., & Kramer, M. R. (2011). Creating Shared Value – How to reinvent capitalism – and unleash a wave of innovation and growth. Harvard Business Review, 89(1/2), pp. 62–77. Retrieved from https://hbr.org/2011/01/the-big-idea-creating-shared-value

competitive advantage. Instead, leading firms focus more and more on societal issues, which distinguished them from their competitors. The goal of this is to create *Shared Value*, which the two authors define as "policies and operating practices that enhance the competitiveness of a company while simultaneously advancing the economic and social conditions in the communities in which it operates"[31] According to the authors, shared value opportunities can be generated with three main approaches.[32]

Reconceiving Products and Markets

The needs and wishes of society are manifold, and to a large extent, they are not taken into account. These can include health-related issues, especially with the population getting older or making a positive contribution to the environment combatting global warming. Opportunities are vast and represent a tremendous potential for growth and innovations, which go hand in hand with societal progress and benefits. Important is that the initial consideration originates from the needs of society and answers how these could be satisfied with the company's products.[33]

However, care should be taken to really act in the interest of society and not to take advantage of it, as all too often happens under the code name of *financial inclusion*, another word for the abolishment of cash and the digitalization of payment processes.[34] There are numerous prominent examples of how financial inclusion with the publicly propagated goal of helping the poor, empowering them and lifting them out of poverty, results in the exact opposite, pushing customers or users further into poverty, while big corporations and banks profit from it.[35]

One example is the microcredit business inspired by Nobel Peace Prize winner Muhammad Yunus. The endeavor sadly turned negative, with banks taking advantage of poor clients without financial education. Clients were charged horrendous interest rates and pushed into financial ruin with the

---

[31] Porter, M. E., & Kramer, M. R. (2011). *op. cit.*, p. 66.

[32] For the three following points see Porter, M. E., & Kramer, M. R. (2011). *op. cit.*

[33] Porter, M. E., & Kramer, M. R. (2011). *op. cit.*

[34] Häring, N. (2018). *op. cit.*

[35] For a comprehensive examination of the efforts that are made to eliminate cash and digitize payment processes please refer to the book *Schönes neues Geld* by Norbert Häring (see reference list). He describes in detail how major actors in politics, Wall street and the Silicon Valley (above all the *Better Than Cash Alliance*, the *Alliance for Financial Inclusion*, the *Consultative Group*, the *Financial Action Task Force* and many others) take organized action against cash, undermine democratic structures and bypass social consensus to make profit out of digitizing payment transactions and pursuing power interests.

constant danger that they will default on money lent to them. This set in motion similar mechanisms as during the subprime crisis.[36]

Redefining Productivity in the Value Chain

Focusing on societal issues is strongly linked to productivity. An employee that is healthy thanks to good working conditions will be more productive and will have fewer days spent on sick leave. So, for example, offering fitness/wellness courses to employees results in firms contributing to both societal well-being *and* their business.[37] Moreover, it does not stop there. Granting higher wages and benefits to employees can reduce personnel turnover with its associated costs, as well as positively affect the CX.[38] In their analysis on *Firms of Endearment* (FoEs), Sisodia et al. make the connection between elevated wages and business profitability, which, from a narrow perspective of viewing the enterprise, may seem mutually exclusively. They remark:

> All this may seem counterintuitive, but in case after case, FoEs with higher labor costs actually have lower labor costs per dollar of income as well as lower marketing costs. [...] The line-by-line way of looking at costs, treating each line item as an independent variable, inescapably obscures crucial connections between compensation and productivity, income and profits.[39]

Seeing the link between societal focus and productivity, it is of no surprise that the *Firms of Endearment* that Sisodia et al. have investigated are highly profitable and outperform their competitors that do not follow a stakeholder focus or the shared value principles. Paradoxically, in that way, it is possible to create supreme shareholder value by following a strict stakeholder orientation.[40]

Apart from the aforementioned employee health and worker safety, there are numerous other levers that companies can use, including energy and water use, employee skills, and environmental impact, to boost company productivity and create shared value.[41]

---

[36] Häring, N. (2018). *op. cit.*

[37] Porter, M. E., & Kramer, M. R. (2011). *op. cit.*

[38] Sisodia, R. S., Sheth, J. N., & Wolfe, D. (2014). *op. cit.*

[39] Sisodia, R. S., Sheth, J. N., & Wolfe, D. (2014). *op. cit.*, p. 96.

[40] Sisodia, R. S., Sheth, J. N., & Wolfe, D. (2014). *op. cit.*

[41] Porter, M. E., & Kramer, M. R. (2011). *op. cit.*

Enabling Local Cluster Development

Shared value and the activities of the FoEs on that matter are not just another CSR charade that assumes that there is a fixed "economic pie" that needs to be distributed differently, e.g., giving money to charity instead of investing it into the company or giving back to shareholders. Instead, it aims for a bigger pie that benefits all the parties involved. Porter points out the example of the fair trade practice of paying farmers a premium for better living conditions, a traditional CSR example redistributing wealth from one party to another.[42] Porter and Kramer show that this revenue redistribution only results in a slight increase in the farmers' wages, typically between 10% and 20%. They instead recommend a different approach:

> A shared value perspective [...] focuses on improving growing techniques and strengthening the local cluster of supporting suppliers and other institutions in order to increase farmers' efficiency, yields, product quality, and sustainability. This leads to a bigger pie of revenue and profits that benefits both farmers and the companies that buy from them.[43]

Successful companies, therefore, do not follow a narrow, one-dimensional view but an integrated, holistic vision. Their leaders recognize the interdependence and interconnectedness of all the involved stakeholder groups and consequently try to balance the needs of all of them,[44] what Gummesson calls *balanced centricity*.[45] The goal is to create a bigger pie, more value, so that the stakeholders can benefit from it, and not in a zero-sum game manner creating benefit for one group at the expense of another, but from productivity and value gains out of the symbiosis of entrepreneurial activity and the good of society.[46,47]

The current situation is a clear call to action for firms to get active as positive agents of change for society beyond CSR efforts. Companies, business leaders, politicians, and ordinary people—they are all called upon to give business a more human touch, characterized by empathy, creativity, and affection. A social transformation of capitalism and zeitgeist can succeed if

---

[42] Porter, M. E. (2011, January 5). Rethinking Capitalism [Video file]. Retrieved from https://hbr.org/2011/01/rethinking-capitalism

[43] Porter, M. E., & Kramer, M. R. (2011). *op. cit.*, p. 65.

[44] Sisodia, R. S., Sheth, J. N., & Wolfe, D. (2014). *op. cit.*

[45] Gummesson, E. (2008). Extending the service-dominant logic: From customer centricity to balanced centricity. Journal of the Academy of Marketing Science, 36(1), pp. 15–17. https://doi.org/10.1007/s11747-007-0065-x

[46] Porter, M. E., & Kramer, M. R. (2011). *op. cit.*

[47] Sisodia, R. S., Sheth, J. N., & Wolfe, D. (2014). *op. cit.*

corporations and government alike do their share in society,[48] fondly in collaboration with all cooperation partners. Together, the future can be changed: first, on a small scale at the level of business and marketing but subsequently, on a bigger scale helping society and the economic system,[49] for a caring cooperation today and a future worth living tomorrow!

6.2   The Future in Resonance

In 2005, when sociologist Hartmut Rosa published his much-cited book *Acceleration: The Change in Time Structures in Modernity*, "deceleration" and "mindfulness" were not yet societal trends. Today, more than a decade later, mindfulness is increasingly becoming mainstream. In this context, Rosa has now taken up his thoughts on acceleration again. In his book *Resonance: A Sociology of Our Relationship to the World*, he puts the absurdity of current business into a social framework and promises nothing less than the solution to our acceleration problem. However, this is not achieved by decelerating loudly but through resonance.

According to Rosa, modern societies are characterized by the fact that they can only stabilize themselves dynamically. They are constantly dependent on growth, acceleration, and compression of innovation in order to be able to maintain their structure or the status quo. This pressure to increase has consequences for the way of life, life orientation, and life experience of each individual for herself and his environment.

Rosa doesn't see acceleration as a bad thing per se: "Nobody wants slow internet or a slow fire brigade." Slow movements are less about slowness per se than the "transformation of the world." In this state, people don't try to control things and handle them quickly and efficiently. It is much more inspired by encounters, by places, by music, and by nature—the basis of every creative process and, ultimately, a successful and meaningful life.

Central to the idea of a successful life is the term resonance. The acoustic-physical term resonance (Latin: "reverberate") describes a specific relationship between two vibrating bodies. This specific relationship of resonance only arises when the vibration of one body stimulates the natural frequency of the other. This leads to two key properties:

- It is a strictly relational term
- Resonance is genuinely process-oriented

---

[48] Reich, R. (2017). *op. cit.*
[49] Sisodia, R. S., Sheth, J. N., & Wolfe, D. (2014). *op. cit.*

Such a relationship always requires a medium capable of resonance. Resonance thus concretely denotes a mode of how subject and world relate to each other. How is the world experienced? When is it perceived as oncoming and when is it dismissive?

A look at the world of work illustrates Rosa's thoughts. Contrary to many views, most people enjoy working but only as long as they receive confirmation (praise, recognition, appreciation, satisfaction, contacts) in their work. But whether it's bakers, nursing staff, cleaning staff, or knowledge workers, as soon as general conditions deteriorate and people are restricted in performing their tasks and can no longer perform them optimally due to personnel savings, time pressure, etc., not only the subject/work relationship suffers; the subject/world relationship changes to the negative. The world is perceived as dismissive and life as unjust.

This means that resonance goes beyond the ideas of mindfulness and deceleration. It is more than just the motto: "If you are in the right mood, the world is in order." From this perspective, conditions and their design do not play major roles; only "event oases" are created in the same framework. However, life can only succeed if we perceive our environment and we are ready to enter into resonance relationships and thus forego part of our autonomy. To make resonance relationships a matter of course, we need a change in society (see Fig. 6.3[50]). We need a culture in which gaps in a résumé give rise

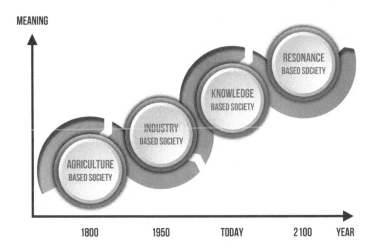

Fig. 6.3 Development to resonance-based society

---

[50] Adapted from Schuett, P. (2013). *Der Einstieg in die Resonanzgesellschaft* [Presentation]. Retrieved from https://de.slideshare.net/pschu/knowtech2013-peter-schuettibmresonanzgesellschaft?from_action=save

to a creative exchange and not to exclusion. We need a culture that works for schools as resonance rooms, because only in those areas where subjects are really touched and gripped by something, where they risk themselves and are ready for self-transformation, can true innovative and outstanding achievements and ideas arise. Just overcoming everyday alienation creates resonances and leads to being connected to the world.

6.3   Ending the Story

Now, we want to finish our story about the new H2H Marketing. We started with the "Call to Adventure" and introduced the *Current State of Marketing* and asked ourselves where marketing was heading and what it meant for marketers and consumer. The challenges are multifold. Companies can apply unethical marketing, by considering their own benefits over consumer benefit, but they also can do it the other way around with inane marketing. We favor an equal benefit distribution and guide you to a balanced H2H Marketing approach. The options are promising and show the opportunity for creating a better world. We then showed you how to apply the new concepts of H2H Marketing. These can lead to a fundamental new understanding of our profession by integrating sustainability considerations. We offer you the H2H Marketing compass to give you a tool to calibrate your decisions.

After this "Call for Adventure," we continued the "Great Journey" with the development of the *New Marketing Paradigm* and the presentation of the *H2H Marketing Model*. With the development of the H2H Marketing Model and the evolution to the H2H Marketing concept, a new way of marketing management is possible. Integrating Design Thinking, Service-Dominant Logic, and digitalization into marketing redirects the focus of marketing to a stakeholder-oriented concept, which is in line with the Davos Manifesto 2020 and which shifts the focus back to a valuable contribution of marketing in the field of meaningful innovations (Fig. 6.4).

The story continued with the "brave action" by introducing the *Elements of H2H Marketing*. The foundation was the H2H Mindset, which looks at human problems and its desirability and feasibility for a viable business. A better understanding of the intangible and individual requirements and the possibilities of co-creation are encouraged. Of vital importance, trust is, and will be, the only currency for any business transaction, and companies need to take it seriously in their brand management to develop the new H2H

THE NEW MARKETING PARADIGM
H2H MARKETING

ELEMENTS OF
H2H MARKETING

GREAT JOURNEY

BRAVE ACTION

DIGITALIZATION

SERVICE DOMINANT LOGIC

DESIGN THINKING

THE EVOLUTION TO
H2H MARKETING

SUSTAINABLE
MANAGEMENT CHALLENGE

FIRMS OF ENDEARMENT

CURRENT STATE OF MARKETING

H2H
MARKETING

H2H MINDSET

H2H MANAGEMENT

H2H PROCESS

WORLD WAKES UP

FUTURE IN RESONANCE

FINDING MEANING

CALL FOR ADVENTURE

SOLUTION AND RETURN

THE CURRENT STATE
OF MARKETING

FINDING MEANING IN
A TROUBLED WORLD

Fig. 6.4 H2H Marketing as a complete story

Marketing. In detail, we give you profound insights into the map for the unknown terrain, and we give you the opportunity exploring your own great journey. Many CMOs have followed this approach, and with more to follow, the world will become a better place for it.

The "solution and return" of the story was told through the introduction of the *H2H Process Operative Marketing*. We introduced an iterative process, based on new technological capabilities provided through the digitalization and Design Thinking. Many challenges have to be overcome to put everything into play for the new mindset of H2H Marketing.

At the end of the story, we offered new solutions and attempt to help you find meaning in the troubled world we live in. We hope that our thoughts and suggestions can provide a path for the future for many companies with our hero of the story—the new H2H Marketing. *We hope that you enjoyed the journey as much as we did!*

Questions

1. Why is the Davos manifest in line with H2H Marketing?
2. How do recent developments in politics, economics, society, and digitaliza-tion increase the need for H2H Marketing as mindset, management approach, and operational process in companies?
3. What are the big problems facing humanity, which companies can play a key role in understanding and solving and can thus position and distinguish themselves among the key stakeholders?
4. How are brand management and reputation management in H2H marketing connected to the mentioned socio-cultural changes?
5. How can companies using H2H Marketing generate shared value?
6. How do you explain that Firms of Endearment are more profitable than other companies despite the fact that they invest much more money into the well-being of their employees?
7. What do you mean by the term "resonance" and how does it fit into H2H Marketing?

References

Apte, S., & Sheth, J. (2016). *The sustainability edge: How to drive top-line growth with triple-bottom-line thinking.* Rotman-UTP Publishing.

Gummesson, E. (2008). Extending the service-dominant logic: From customer cen-tricity to balanced centricity. *Journal of the Academy of Marketing Science, 36*(1), 15–17. https://doi.org/10.1007/s11747-007-0065-x.

Häring, N. (2018). *Schönes neues Geld: PayPal, WeChat, Amazon Go: Uns droht eine totalitäre Weltwährung.* Frankfurt: Campus.

Homm, F., & Hessel, M. (2019). *Der Crash ist da: Was Sie jetzt tun müssen! Anlagen, Immobilien, Ersprarnisse, Arbeit.* München: FinanzBuch.

Kotler, P. (2015). *Confronting capitalism: Real solutions for a troubled economic system.* New York, NY: AMACOM.

Kotler, P. (2019). *Advancing the common good: Strategies for businesses, governments, and nonprofits.* Santa Barbara, CA: Praeger.

Mackey, J., & Sisodia, R. (2013). *Conscious capitalism: Liberating the heroic spirit of business.* Boston, MA: Harvard Business Press.

Otte, M. (2019). *Weltsystemcrash: Krisen, Unruhen und die Geburt einer neuen Weltordnung.* München: FinanzBuch.

Porter, M. E. (2011, January 5). *Rethinking capitalism* [Video file]. Retrieved from https://hbr.org/2011/01/rethinking-capitalism

Porter, M. E., & Kramer, M. R. (2011). Creating Shared Value – How to reinvent capitalism – and unleash a wave of innovation and growth. *Harvard Business Review, 89*(1/2), 62–77. Retrieved from https://hbr.org/2011/01/the-big-idea-creating-shared-value.

Precht, R. D. (2018). *Jäger, Hirten, Kritiker: Eine Utopie für die digitale Gesellschaft* (6th ed.). München: Goldmann.

Reich, R. (2017). *Saving capitalism: For the many, not the few*. London: Icon Books.

Sarkar, C., & Kotler, P. (2018). *Brand activism: From purpose to action* (Kindle edition). n.p.: IDEA Bite Press. Retrieved from www.amazon.com

Schuett, P. (2013). *Der Einstieg in die Resonanzgesellschaft* [Presentation]. Retrieved from https://de.slideshare.net/pschu/knowtech2013-peter-schuettibmresonanzge sellschaft?from_action=save

Schwab, K. (2019). Davos Manifesto 2020: The Universal purpose of a company in the fourth industrial revolution. *World Economic Forum.*https://www.weforum. org/agenda/2019/12/davos-manifesto-2020-the-universal-purpose-of-a-company-in-the-fourth-industrial-revolution/

Sisodia, R. S., Sheth, J. N., & Wolfe, D. (2014). *Firms of endearment: How world-class companies profit from passion and purpose* (2nd ed.). Upper Saddle River, NJ: Pearson Education.

Speaker's Corner. (2019, March 3). *"Es ist eine verdammte Lüge" – Dr. Markus Krall (Roland Baader-Treffen 2019)* [Video file]. Retrieved from https://www.youtube. com/watch?v=AWCyL3gcOzw

References

Achrol, R. S., & Kotler, P. (1999). Marketing in the network economy. *Journal of Marketing, 63*, 146–163. https://doi.org/10.2307/1252108.

Adlin, T., & Pruitt, J. (2009). Putting personas to work: Using data-driven personas to focus product planning, design, and development. In A. Sears & J. A. Jacko (Eds.), *Human-computer interaction: Development process* (1st ed., pp. 95–120). Boca Raton, FL: CRC Press.

Ahrendts, A. (2013). Burberry's CEO on turning an aging British Icon into a Global Luxury Brand. *Harvard Business Review*. Retrieved from https://hbr.org/2013/01/burberrys-ceo-on-turning-an-aging-british-icon-into-a-global-luxury-brand

Apte, S., & Sheth, J. (2016). *The sustainability edge: How to drive top-line growth with triple-bottom-line thinking*. Rotman-UTP Publishing.

Backhaus, K., & Paulsen, T. (2018). Vom Homo Oeconomicus zum Homo Digitalis – Die Veränderung der Informationsasymmetrien durch die Digitalisierung. In M. Bruhn & M. Kirchgeorg (Eds.), *Marketing Weiterdenken: Zukunftspfade für eine marktorientierte Unternehmensführung* (pp. 105–122). Wiesbaden: Springer Gabler.

Ballantyne, D., & Aitken, R. (2007). Branding in B2B markets: Insights from the service-dominant logic of marketing. *Journal of Business & Industrial Marketing, 22*(6), 363–371. https://doi.org/10.1108/08858620710780127.

Bardhi, F., & Eckhardt, G. M. (2012). Access-based consumption: The case of car sharing. *Journal of Consumer Research, 39*(4), 881–898. https://doi.org/10.1086/666376.

Bathen, D., & Jelden, J. (2014). *Marketingorganisation der Zukunft* [Report]. Retrieved from https://www.marketingverband.de/marketingkompetenz/studien/marketingorganisation-der-zukunft/

© The Author(s), under exclusive license to Springer Nature Switzerland AG 2021
P. Kotler et al., *H2H Marketing*, https://doi.org/10.1007/978-3-030-59531-9

Benkenstein, M. (2018). Hat sich das Marketing als Leitkonzept der Unternehmensführung wirklich überlebt? – Eine kritische Stellungnahme. In M. Bruhn & M. Kirchgeorg (Eds.), *Marketing Weiterdenken: Zukunftspfade für eine marktorientierte Unternehmensführung* (pp. 49–64). Wiesbaden: Springer Gabler.

Bernazzani, S. (2017, June 13). *The 10 best user-generated content campaigns on Instagram* [Blog post]. Retrieved from https://blog.hubspot.com/marketing/best-user-generated-content-campaigns

Blatt, M., & Sauvonnet, E. (Eds.). (2017). *Wo ist das Problem?: Mit Design Thinking Innovationen entwickeln und umsetzen* (2nd ed.). München: Franz Vahlen.

Bopp, A., & Burkhard, M. (n.d.). *Die inhärenten Erfolgsfaktoren von Design Thinking* [Report on an internal university project].

Borden, N. H. (1964). The concept of the marketing mix. *Journal of Advertising Research, 2*, 7–12. Retrieved from http://www.guillaumenicaise.com/wp-content/uploads/2013/10/Borden-1984_The-concept-of-marketing-mix.pdf

Brooks, R., & Goldstein, S. (2008). The mindset of teachers capable of fostering resilience in students. *Canadian Journal of School Psychology, 23*(1), 114–126. https://doi.org/10.1177/0829573508316597.

Brown, T. (2008). Design thinking. *Harvard Business Review, 86*(6), 84–92. Retrieved from https://hbr.org/2008/06/design-thinking

Bruhn, M. (2018). Marketing Weiterdenken in der marktorientierten Unternehmensführung – Entwicklungen und Zukunftsthemen der Marketingdisziplin. In M. Bruhn & M. Kirchgeorg (Eds.), *Marketing Weiterdenken: Zukunftspfade für eine marktorientierte Unternehmensführung* (pp. 25–48). Wiesbaden: Springer Gabler.

Bruhn, M., & Kirchgeorg, M. (Eds.). (2018). *Marketing Weiterdenken: Zukunftspfade für eine marktorientierte Unternehmensführung.* Wiesbaden: Springer Gabler.

Buchanan, R. (1992). Wicked problems in design thinking. *Design Issues, 8*(2), 96–100.

Burmann, C., Halaszovich, T., Schade, M., & Hemmann, F. (2015). *Identitätsbasierte Markenführung: Grundlagen – Strategie – Umsetzung – Controlling* (2nd ed.). Wiesbaden: Springer Gabler.

Carlgren, L., Rauth, I., & Elmquist, M. (2016). Framing design thinking: The concept in idea and enactment. *Creativity and Innovation Management, 25*(1), 38–57. https://doi.org/10.1111/caim.12153.

Chen, Y. (2009). Possession and access: Consumer desires and value perceptions regarding contemporary art collection and exhibit visits. *Journal of Consumer Research, 35*(6), 925–940. https://doi.org/10.1086/593699.

Chen, S., & Venkatesh, A. (2013). An investigation of how design-oriented organisations implement design thinking. *Journal of Marketing Management, 29*(15/16), 1680–1700. https://doi.org/10.1080/0267257X.2013.800898.

Claßen, M. (2016). *Marktorientierung in Business-to-Business-Märkten: Eine empirische Untersuchung von mehrstufigen Marketingstrategien.* Wiesbaden: Springer Gabler.

Cone Communications. (2017). *2017 Cone Gen Z CSR study: How to Speak Z* [Report]. Retrieved from http://www.conecomm.com/research-blog/2017-genz-csr-study

Constantin, J. A., & Lusch, R. F. (1994). *Understanding resource management.* Oxford, OH: Planning Forum.

Constantinides, E. (2006). The marketing mix revisited: Towards the 21st century marketing. *Journal of Marketing Management, 22*(3/4), 407–438. https://doi.org/10.1362/026725706776861190.

Costa, P. T., & McCrae, R. R. (2008). *The revised NEO personality inventory (NEO-PI-R).* London: Sage.

Court, D., Elzinga, D., Mulder, S., & Vetvik, O. J. (2009). The consumer decision journey. *McKinsey Quarterly, 3*, 1–11. Retrieved from https://www.mckinsey.com/business-functions/marketing-and-sales/our-insights/the-consumer-decision-journey

Dann, S. (2011, July 5–7). *The marketing mix matrix* [Conference paper]. Paper presented at the Academy of Marketing Conference 2011, Liverpool, United Kingdom. Retrieved from https://www.researchgate.net/profile/Stephen_Dann/publication/267559484_The_Marketing_Mix_Matrix/links/54b6024b0cf2318f0f9a0743.pdf

Daye, D. (2010, October 17). *The advertising wisdom of Leo Burnett* [Blog post]. Retrieved from https://www.brandingstrategyinsider.com/2010/10/the-advertising-wisdom-of-leo-burnett.html#.XU30uOgzaUk

Deloitte. (2015). *Industry 4.0: Challenges and solutions for the digital transformation and use of exponential technologies* [Report]. Retrieved from https://www2.deloitte.com/tw/en/pages/manufacturing/articles/industry4-0.html

Dev, C. S., & Schultz, D. E. (2005). Simply SIVA: Get results with the new marketing mix. *Marketing Management, 14*(2), 36–41. Retrieved from https://www.scopus.com/record/display.uri?eid=2-s2.0-17444418649&origin=inward&txGid=047497a80a4b341498c747b3d30eff31

Dirnberger, D. (2013). *Target costing und die Rolle des Controllings im Zielkostenmanagement.* München: GRIN.

Dollmayer, A. (2003). *Target costing: Modernes Zielkostenmanagement in Theorie und Praxis.* Marburg: Tectum.

Doyle, C. C., Mieder, W., & Shapiro, F. R. (2012). *The dictionary of modern proverbs.* New Haven, CT: Yale University Press.

Drengner, J., Jahn, S., & Gaus, H. (2013). Der Beitrag der Service-Dominant Logic zur Weiterentwicklung der Markenführung. *Die Betriebswirtschaft, 73*(2), 143–160. Retrieved from https://www.academia.edu/12178909/Der_Beitrag_der_Service-Dominant_Logic_zur_Weiterentwicklung_der_Markenf%C3%BChrung

Dweck, C. S. (2006). *Mindset: The new psychology of success*. New York, NY: Random House.

Dweck, C. S. (2016, January 13). What having a "growth mindset" actually means. *Harvard Business Review*. Retrieved from https://hbr.org/2016/01/what-having-a-growth-mindset-actually-means

Edelman. (2011). *2011 Edelman trust barometer: Global report* [Report]. Retrieved from https://www.slideshare.net/EdelmanInsights/2011-edelman-trust-barometer

Edelman. (2018). *2018 Edelman trust barometer: Global report* [Report]. Retrieved from https://www.edelman.com/sites/g/files/aatuss191/files/2018-10/2018_Edelman_Trust_Barometer_Global_Report_FEB.pdf

Edelman. (2019a). *2019 Edelman trust barometer: Global report* [Report]. Retrieved from https://www.edelman.com/sites/g/files/aatuss191/files/2019-03/2019_Edelman_Trust_Barometer_Global_Report.pdf?utm_source=website&utm_medium=global_report&utm_campaign=downloads

Edelman. (2019b). *2019 Edelman trust barometer special report: In brands we trust?* [Report]. Retrieved from https://www.edelman.com/sites/g/files/aatuss191/files/2019-06/2019_edelman_trust_barometer_special_report_in_brands_we_trust.pdf

Elsbach, K. D., & Stigliani, I. (2018). Design thinking and organizational culture: A review and framework for future research. *Journal of Management, 44*(6), 2274–2306. https://doi.org/10.1177/0149206317744252.

Ernst & Young. (2011). *The digitisation of everything: How organisations must adapt to changing consumer behaviour* [Report]. Retrieved from https://www.ey.com/Publication/vwLUAssets/The_digitisation_of_everything_-_How_organisations_must_adapt_to_changing_consumer_behaviour/%24file/EY_Digitisation_of_everything.pdf

Eser, D., Gaubinger, K., & Rabl, M. (2014). Sprint Radar: Community-based trend identification. In O. Gassmann & F. Schweitzer (Eds.), *Management of the fuzzy front end of innovation* (pp. 275–280). Cham: Springer.

Ettenson, R., Conrado, E., & Knowles, J. (2013). Rethinking the 4 P's. *Harvard Business Review, 91*(1/2), 26. Retrieved from https://hbr.org/2013/01/rethinking-the-4-ps

Fang, Y.-H. (2019). An app a day keeps a customer connected: Explicating loyalty to brands and branded applications through the lens of affordance and service-dominant logic. *Information & Management, 56*(3), 377–391. https://doi.org/10.1016/j.im.2018.07.011.

First Round Review. (2019). How design thinking transformed Airbnb from a failing startup to a billion dollar business. *First Round Review*. Retrieved from https://firstround.com/review/How-design-thinking-transformed-Airbnb-from-failing-startup-to-billion-dollar-business/

Fombrun, C. J., & Van Riel, C. B. M. (2004). *Fame & fortune: How successful companies build winning reputations*. Upper Saddle River, NJ: Pearson Education.

Frey, A., Trenz, M., & Veit, D. (2017). *The role of technology for service innovation in sharing economy organizations – A service-dominant logic perspective.* In Proceedings of the 25th European Conference on Information Systems (ECIS), Guimarães, Portugal, June 5–10, 2017, pp. 1885–1901. Retrieved from https://aisel.aisnet. org/cgi/viewcontent.cgi?article=1120&context=ecis2017_rp

Gaiser, B., Linxweiler, R., & Brucker, V. (Eds.). (2005). *Praxisorientierte Markenführung – Neue Strategien, innovative Instrumente und aktuelle Fallstudien.* Wiesbaden: Gabler.

Gassmann, O., Frankenberger, K., & Csik, M. (2017). *Geschäftsmodelle entwickeln: 55 innovative Konzepte mit dem St. Galler Business Model Navigator* (2nd ed.). München: Carl Hanser.

Gassmann, O., & Schweitzer, F. (2014). Managing the unmanageable: The fuzzy front end of innovation. In O. Gassmann & F. Schweitzer (Eds.), *Management of the fuzzy front end of innovation* (pp. 3–14). Cham: Springer.

Gehrckens, M., & Boersma, T. (2013). Zukunftsvision Retail – Hat der Handel eine Daseinsberechtigung? In G. Heinemann, K. Haug, M. Gehrckens, & dgroup (Eds.), *Digitalisierung des Handels mit ePace: Innovative E-commerce-Geschäftsmodelle unter Timing-Aspekten* (pp. 51–76). Springer Gabler: Wiesbaden.

Gobble, M. M. (2014). Design thinking. *Research Technology Management, 57*(3), 59–61. https://doi.org/10.5437/08956308X5703005.

Godin, S. (2007). *Permission marketing.* London: Simon & Schuster.

Gohar, N., Mehmood, B., & Sair, S. A. (2015, October 29–31). *A brand is no longer what we tell the customer it is – It is what customers tell each other it is: Validation from Lahore, Pakistan* [Conference paper]. Paper presented at the 5th International. Multidisciplinary Conference at ICBS, Lahore, Pakistan. Retrieved from http:// www.sci-int.com/pdf/15135791101%201%20a%2090%202757-2762%20 Nayab%20Gohar-ECO-%20BILAL-11.pdf

Goldhausen, K. (2018). Customer experience management – Der Weg ist das Ziel. In A. Rusnjak & D. R. A. Schallmo (Eds.), *Customer experience im Zeitalter des Kunden: Best Practices, Lessons Learned und Forschungsergebnisse* (pp. 41–94). Wiesbaden: Springer Gabler.

Goodwin, K. (2009). *Designing for the digital age: How to create human-centered products and services.* Indianapolis, IN: Wiley.

Grots, A., & Pratschke, M. (2009). Design thinking – Kreativität als Methode. *Marketing Review St. Gallen, 26*(2), 18–23. https://doi.org/10.1007/ s11621-009-0027-4.

Gummesson, E. (1995). Relationship marketing: Its role in the service economy. In W. J. Glynn & J. G. Barnes (Eds.), *Understanding services management* (pp. 244–268). New York, NY: Wiley.

Gummesson, E. (2008). Extending the service-dominant logic: From customer centricity to balanced centricity. *Journal of the Academy of Marketing Science, 36*(1), 15–17. https://doi.org/10.1007/s11747-007-0065-x.

Gummesson, E. (2011). 2B or not 2B: That is the question. *Industrial Marketing Management, 40*(2), 190–192. https://doi.org/10.1016/j.indmarman.2010.06.028.

Gummesson, E., Kuusela, H., & Närvänen, E. (2014). Reinventing marketing strategy by recasting supplier/customer roles. *Journal of Service Management, 25*(2), 228–240. https://doi.org/10.1108/JOSM-01-2014-0031.

Haderlein, A. (2012). *Die digitale Zukunft des stationären Handels: Auf allen Kanälen zum Kunden.* München: mi-Wirtschaftsbuch.

Haeckel, S. H. (1999). *Adaptive enterprise: Creating and leading sense-and-respond organizations.* Boston, MA: Harvard Business Press.

Hall, S. (2017). *Innovative B2B marketing: New models, processes and theory.* New York, NY: Kogan Page.

Halligan, B., & Shah, D. (2018). *Inbound-Marketing: Wie Sie Kunden online anziehen, abholen und begeistern* (D. Runne, Trans.). Weinheim: Wiley-VCH.

Hansen, N. L. (2018, January 25). *Dear CxO… Just focus on the customer journey!* [Blog post]. Retrieved from https://www.linkedin.com/pulse/dear-cxo-just-focus-customer-journey-nicolaj-l%C3%B8ve-hansen/

Harad, K. C. (2013). Content marketing strategies to educate and entertain. *Journal of Financial Planning, 26*(3), 18–20. Retrieved from https://www.onefpa.org/journal/Pages/Content%20Marketing%20Strategies%20to%20Educate%20and%20Entertain.aspx

Häring, N. (2018). *Schönes neues Geld: PayPal, WeChat, Amazon Go: Uns droht eine totalitäre Weltwährung.* Frankfurt: Campus.

Hartleben, R. E., & von Rhein, W. (2014). *Kommunikationskonzeption und Briefing: Ein praktischer Leitfaden zum Erstellen zielgruppenspezifischer Konzepte* (3rd ed.). Erlangen: Publicis.

Hassenzahl, M. (2011). User experience and experience design. In M. Soegaard & R. F. Dam (Eds.), *Encyclopedia of human-computer interaction.* The Interaction Design Foundation: Aarhus, Denmark.

Hasso Plattner Institute of Design. (2019). *An introduction to design thinking: Process guide.* Retrieved from https://dschool-old.stanford.edu/sandbox/groups/designresources/wiki/36873/attachments/74b3d/ModeGuideBOOTCAMP2010L.pdf

Hasso-Plattner-Institut. (2019a). *Die design thinking-Regeln.* Retrieved from https://hpi.de/school-of-design-thinking/design-thinking/hintergrund/design-thinking-prinzipien.html

Hasso-Plattner-Institut. (2019b). *What is design thinking?* Retrieved from https://hpi-academy.de/en/design-thinking/what-is-design-thinking.html

Häusling, A. (2016). Serie agile tools. *Personalmagazin, 10*, 36–37. Retrieved from https://www.haufe.de/download/personalmagazin-102016-personalmagazin-381028.pdf

Heath, T., & McKechnie, S. (2019). Sustainability in marketing. In K. Amaeshi, J. N. Muthuri, & C. Ogbechie (Eds.), *Incorporating sustainability in management education: An interdisciplinary approach* (pp. 105–131). Cham: Springer. https://doi.org/10.1007/978-3-319-98125-3_6.

Heinemann, G. (2014). *SoLoMo – Always-on im Handel: Die soziale, lokale und mobile Zukunft des Shopping*. Wiesbaden: Springer Gabler.

Heinemann, G., & Gaiser, C. W. (2016). *SoLoMo – Always-on im Handel: Die soziale, lokale und mobile Zukunft des Omnichannel-Shopping* (3rd ed.). Wiesbaden: Springer Gabler.

Heinonen, K., & Medberg, G. (2018). Netnography as a tool for understanding customers: Implications for service research and practice. *Journal of Services Marketing, 32*(6), 657–679. https://doi.org/10.1108/JSM-08-2017-0294.

Henderson, R. (2020). *Reimagining capitalism in a world on fire*. New York: PublicAffairs.

Hering, E. (2014). *Wettbewerbsanalyse für Ingenieure*. Wiesbaden: Springer.

Hinterhuber, A. (2004). Towards value-based pricing—An integrative framework for decision making. *Industrial Marketing Management, 33*(8), 765–778. https://doi.org/10.1016/j.indmarman.2003.10.006.

Hofert, S. (2018). *Das agile Mindset: Mitarbeiter entwickeln, Zukunft der Arbeit gestalten*. Wiesbaden: Springer Gabler.

Holliman, G., & Rowley, J. (2014). Business to business digital content marketing: Marketers' perceptions of best practice. *Journal of Research in Interactive Marketing, 8*(4), 269–293. https://doi.org/10.1108/JRIM-02-2014-0013.

Homburg, C., Vomberg, A., Enke, M., & Grimm, P. H. (2015). The loss of the marketing department's influence: Is it really happening? And why worry? *Journal of the Academy of Marketing Science, 43*(1), 1–13. https://doi.org/10.1007/s11747-014-0416-3.

Homm, F., & Hessel, M. (2019). *Der Crash ist da: Was Sie jetzt tun müssen! Anlagen, Immobilien, Ersparnisse, Arbeit*. München: FinanzBuch.

Horsch, J. (2015). *Kostenrechnung: Klassische und neue Methoden in der Unternehmenspraxis* (2nd ed.). Wiesbaden: Springer Gabler.

How Companies Can Profit from a "Growth Mindset". (2014). *Harvard Business Review*. Retrieved from https://hbr.org/2014/11/how-companies-can-profit-from-a-growth-mindset

IDEO. (2019). *How to prototype a new business* [Blog post]. Retrieved from https://www.ideou.com/blogs/inspiration/how-to-prototype-a-new-business

Johansson-Sköldberg, U., Woodilla, J., & Çetinkaya, M. (2013). Design thinking: Past, present and possible futures. *Creativity and Innovation Management, 22*(2), 121–146. https://doi.org/10.1111/caim.12023.

Jones, P., Clarke-Hill, C., Comfort, D., & Hillier, D. (2008). Marketing and sustainability. *Marketing Intelligence & Planning, 26*(2), 123–130. https://doi.org/10.1108/02634500810860584.

Judt, E., & Klausegger, C. (2010). Bankmanagement-Glossar: Was ist Trendscouting? *bank und markt, 3*, 46. Retrieved from https://www.kreditwesen.de/bank-markt/ergaenzende-informationen/archivdaten/trendscouting-id12805.html

Kagermann, H., Wahlster, W., & Helbig, J. (2013). *Deutschlands Zukunft als Produktionsstandort sichern: Umsetzungsempfehlungen für das Zukunftsprojekt*

Industrie 4.0 [Report]. Retrieved from https://www.bmbf.de/files/
Umsetzungsempfehlungen_Industrie4_0.pdf

Kahneman, D., & Deaton, A. (2010). High income improves evaluation of life but
not emotional well-being. *Proceedings of the National Academy of Sciences, 107*(38),
16489–16493. https://doi.org/10.1073/pnas.1011492107.

Kang, J.-Y. M. (2018). Showrooming, webrooming, and user-generated content creation in the omnichannel era. *Journal of Internet Commerce, 17*(2), 145–169.
https://doi.org/10.1080/15332861.2018.1433907.

Kegelberg, J. (2018). Auslaufmodell Omnichannel – Die Plattformökonomie integriert den Handel. In I. Böckenholt, A. Mehn, & A. Westermann (Eds.), *Konzepte
und Strategien für Omnichannel-Exzellenz: Innovatives Retail-Marketing mit mehrdimensionalen Vertriebs- und Kommunikationskanälen* (pp. 373–383). Wiesbaden:
Springer Gabler.

Kemming, J. D., & Humborg, C. (2010). Democracy and nation brand(ing):
Friends or foes? *Place Branding and Public Diplomacy, 6*(3), 183–197. Retrieved
from https://www.researchgate.net/publication/47378882_Democracy_and_
nation_branding_Friends_or_foes

Kemper, J., Hall, C., & Ballantine, P. (2019). Marketing and sustainability: Business
as usual or changing worldviews? *Sustainability, 11*(3), 780. https://doi.
org/10.3390/su11030780.

King, K. A. (2015). *The complete guide to B2B marketing: New tactics, tools, and techniques to compete in the digital economy.* Upper Saddle River, NJ: Pearson Education.

Koch, T. (2018, March 3). Marketing braucht Haltung! *WirtschaftsWoche Online.*
Retrieved from https://www.wiwo.de/unternehmen/handel/werbesprech-market-
ing-braucht-haltung/21036730.html

Kotler, P. (2015). *Confronting capitalism: Real solutions for a troubled economic system.*
New York, NY: AMACOM.

Kotler, P. (2017). Criticisms and contributions of marketing. Retrieved from https://
www.marketingjournal.org/criticisms-and-contributions-of-marketing-an-
excerpt-from-philip-kotlers-autobiography-philip-kotler/

Kotler, P. (2019). *Advancing the common good: Strategies for businesses, governments,
and nonprofits.* Santa Barbara, CA: Praeger.

Kotler, P., & Armstrong, G. (2010). *Principles of marketing* (13th ed.). Upper Saddle
River, NJ: Pearson.

Kotler, P., Hessekiel, D., & Lee, N. R. (2013). *GOOD WORKS!: Wie Sie mit dem
richtigen Marketing die Welt – und Ihre Bilanzen – verbessern* (N. Bertheau, Trans.).
Offenbach: GABAL.

Kotler, P., Kartajaya, H., & Setiawan, I. (2010). *Die neue Dimension des Marketings:
Vom Kunden zum Menschen* (P. Pyka, Trans.). Frankfurt: Campus.

Kotler, P., Kartajaya, H., & Setiawan, I. (2017). *Marketing 4.0: Moving from traditional to digital.* Hoboken, NJ: Wiley.

Kotler, P., & Komori, S. (2020). *Never stop – Winning through innovation.* Canada,
Kotler Impact Montreal.

Kotler, P., & Pfoertsch, W. A. (2006). *B2B brand management*. Berlin: Springer.

Kotler, P., & Pfoertsch, W. A. (2010). *Ingredient branding: Making the invisible visible* (408 p). Heidelberg: Springer.

Kotler, P., & Rath, G. A. (1984). Design: A powerful but neglected strategic tool. *Journal of Business Strategy, 5*(2), 16–21. https://doi.org/10.1108/eb039054.

Kowalkowski, C. (2010). What does a service-dominant logic really mean for manufacturing firms? *CIRP Journal of Manufacturing Science and Technology, 3*(4), 285–292. https://doi.org/10.1016/j.cirpj.2011.01.003.

Kowalkowski, C. (2011). Dynamics of value propositions: Insights from service-dominant logic. *European Journal of Marketing, 45*(1/2), 277–294. https://doi.org/10.1108/03090561111095702.

Kozinets, R. V. (2015). *Netnography: Redefined*. Los Angeles, CA: Sage.

Kreutzer, R. T. (2018a). Customer experience management – wie man Kunden begeistern kann. In A. Rusnjak & D. R. A. Schallmo (Eds.), *Customer Experience im Zeitalter des Kunden: Best practices, lessons learned und Forschungsergebnisse* (pp. 95–119). Wiesbaden: Springer Gabler.

Kreutzer, R. T. (2018b). Holistische Markenführung im digitalen Zeitalter – Voraussetzung zur Erreichung einer Omnichannel-Exzellenz. In I. Böckenholt, A. Mehn, & A. Westermann (Eds.), *Konzepte und Strategien für Omnichannel-Exzellenz: Innovatives Retail-Marketing mit mehrdimensionalen Vertriebs- und Kommunikationskanälen* (pp. 111–147). Wiesbaden: Springer Gabler.

Kreutzer, R. T., & Land, K.-H. (2016). *Digitaler Darwinismus: Der stille Angriff auf Ihr Geschäftsmodell und Ihre Marke* (2nd ed.). Wiesbaden: Springer Gabler.

Krippendorf, K. (2006). *The semantic turn – A new foundation for design*. Boca Raton, FL: CRC Press.

Kumar, V. (2015). Evolution of marketing as a discipline: What has happened and what to look out for. *Journal of Marketing, 79*(1), 1–9. https://doi.org/10.1509/jm.79.1.1.

Kumar, V., Jones, E., Venkatesan, R., & Leone, R. P. (2011). Is market orientation a source of sustainable competitive advantage or simply the cost of competing? *Journal of Marketing, 75*(1), 16–30. Retrieved from https://www.researchgate.net

Kwasniewski, N., Maxwill, P., Seibt, P., & Siemens, A. (2018, February 1). *Manipulation in der Marktforschung: Wie Umfragen gefälscht und Kunden betrogen werden*. Spiegel online. Retrieved from https://www.spiegel.de/wirtschaft/unternehmen/manipulation-in-der-marktforschung-wie-umfragen-gefaelscht-werden-a-1190711.html#.

Land, K.-H. (2018). Dematerialisierung: Die Neuverteilung der Welt in Zeiten der Digitalen Transformation und die Folgen für die Arbeitswelt. In C. Brüssel & V. Kronenberg (Eds.), *Von der sozialen zur ökosozialen Marktwirtschaft* (pp. 153–166). Wiesbaden: Springer.

Lauterborn, B. (1990). New marketing litany: Four P's Passe; C-words take over. *Advertising Age, 61*(41), 26. Retrieved from http://www.business.uwm.edu/gdrive/Wentz_E/International%20Marketing%20465%20Fall%202014/Articles/New%20Marketing%20Litany.PDF

LaValle, S., Lesser, E., Shockley, R., Hopkins, M. S., & Kruschwitz, N. (2011). Big data, analytics and the path from insights to value. *MIT Sloan Management Review, 52*(2), 21–32. Retrieved from https://sloanreview.mit.edu/article/big-data-analytics-and-the-path-from-insights-to-value/

Leifer, L. J., & Steinert, M. (2014). Dancing with ambiguity: Causality behavior, design thinking, and triple-loop-learning. In O. Gassmann & F. Schweitzer (Eds.), *Management of the fuzzy front end of innovation* (pp. 141–158). Cham: Springer.

Li, C.-R., Lin, C.-J., & Chu, C.-P. (2008). The nature of market orientation and the ambidexterity of innovations. *Management Decision, 46*(7), 1002–1026. https://doi.org/10.1108/00251740810890186.

Liedtka, J. (2018). Why design thinking works. *Harvard Business Review, 96*(5), 72–79. Retrieved from https://hbr.org/2018/09/why-design-thinking-works

Lies, J. (2017). *Die Digitalisierung der Kommunikation im Mittelstand: Auswirkungen von Marketing 4.0.* Wiesbaden: Springer Gabler.

Lindberg, T., Meinel, C., & Wagner, R. (2011). Design thinking: A fruitful concept for IT development? In H. Plattner, C. Meinel, & L. Leifer (Eds.), *Design thinking: Understand – improve – apply* (pp. 3–18). Berlin: Springer.

Linden, E., & Wittmer, A. (2018). *Zukunft Mobilität: Gigatrend Digitalisierung* [Monograph]. Retrieved from https://www.alexandria.unisg.ch/253291/

Lippold, D. (2017). *Marktorientierte Unternehmensführung und Digitalisierung: Management im digitalen Wandel.* Berlin: De Gruyter.

Lusch, R. F., & Vargo, S. L. (2006). Service-dominant logic: Reactions, reflections and refinements. *Marketing Theory, 6*(3), 281–288. https://doi.org/10.1177/1470593106066781.

Lusch, R. F., & Vargo, S. L. (2014). *Service-dominant logic: Premises, perspectives, possibilities.* Cambridge: Cambridge University Press.

Lyke-Ho-Gland, H. (2018). Practical points on design thinking: It's not just empathic design. *American Management Association Quarterly*, 9–12. Retrieved from https://issuu.com/americanmanagementassociation/docs/amaquarterly-summer-18

Mackey, J., & Sisodia, R. (2013). *Conscious capitalism: Liberating the heroic spirit of business.* Boston, MA: Harvard Business Press.

Martin, R. L. (2009). *The design of business: Why design thinking is the next competitive advantage.* Boston, MA: Harvard Business Review Press.

Marx, P. (2011, January 23). The Borrowers: Why buy when you can rent? *The New Yorker.* Retrieved from https://www.newyorker.com/magazine/2011/01/31/the-borrowers

Matzler, K., Stahl, H. K., & Hinterhuber, H. H. (2009). Die customer-based view der Unternehmung. In H. H. Hinterhuber & K. Matzler (Eds.), *Kundenorientierte Unternehmensführung: Kundenorientierung – Kundenzufriedenheit – Kundenbindung* (6th ed., pp. 4–31). Wiesbaden: Gabler.

Mayer-Vorfelder, M. (2012). *Basler Schriften zum Marketing: Vol. 29. Kundenerfahrungen im Dienstleistungsprozess: Eine theoretische und empirische Analyse.* Wiesbaden: Gabler.

McDonagh, P., & Prothero, A. (2014). Sustainability marketing research: Past, present and future. *Journal of Marketing Management, 30*(11–12), 1186–1219. https://doi.org/10.1080/0267257X.2014.943263.

McKinsey & Company. (2018). *Microsoft's next act* [Podcast]. Retrieved from https://www.mckinsey.com/industries/technology-media-and-telecommunications/our-insights/microsofts-next-act

Meffert, H., & Burmann, C. (1996). Identitätsorientierte Markenführung. In H. Meffert, H. Wagner, & K. Backhaus (Eds.), *Arbeitspapier Nr. 100 der Wissenschaftlichen Gesellschaft für Marketing und Unternehmensführung e.V.* Münster: Wissenschaftliche Gesellschaft für Marketing und Unternehmensführung.

Meffert, H., Burmann, C., Kirchgeorg, M., & Eisenbeiß, M. (2019). *Marketing: Grundlagen marktorientierter Unternehmensführung Konzepte – Instrumente – Praxisbeispiele* (13th ed.). Wiesbaden: Springer Gabler.

Mehn, A., & Wirtz, V. (2018). Stand der Forschung – Entwicklung von Omnichannel-Strategien als Antwort auf neues Konsumentenverhalten. In I. Böckenholt, A. Mehn, & A. Westermann (Eds.), *Konzepte und Strategien für Omnichannel-Exzellenz: Innovatives retail-marketing mit mehrdimensionalen Vertriebs- und Kommunikationskanälen* (pp. 3–35). Wiesbaden: Springer Gabler.

Merz, M. A., He, Y., & Vargo, S. L. (2009). The evolving brand logic: A service-dominant logic perspective. *Journal of the Academy of Marketing Science, 37*(3), 328–344. https://doi.org/10.1007/s11747-009-0143-3.

Michaeli, R. (2006). *Competitive intelligence: Strategische Wettbewerbsvorteile erzielen durch systematische Konkurrenz-, Markt- und Technologieanalysen.* Berlin: Springer.

Mower, S. (2017). How Christopher Bailey transformed burberry and redefined brand revivals in the 21st century. *Vogue.* Retrieved from https://www.vogue.com/article/burberry-christopher-bailey-legacy

Naisbitt, J. (2015). Der Horizont reicht meist nur bis zum nächsten Wahltag. In Bundeszentrale für politische Bildung (Ed.), Megatrends?. *Aus Politik und Zeitgeschichte, 65*(31–32), 3–6. Retrieved from https://www.bpb.de/apuz/209953/der-horizont-reicht-meist-nur-bis-zum-naechsten-wahltag

Nemko, M. (2017). *Marketing is evil: Marketers use many psychological ploys to make you buy what you shouldn't* [Blog post]. Retrieved from https://www.psychologytoday.com/us/blog/how-do-life/201701/marketing-is-evil

Nielsen. (2018). *Sustainable Shoppers buy the change they wish to see in the world* [Report]. Retrieved from https://www.nielsen.com/wp-content/uploads/sites/3/2019/04/global-sustainable-shoppers-report-2018.pdf

Noll, B. (2002). *Wirtschafts- und Unternehmensethik in der Marktwirtschaft.* Stuttgart: Kohlhammer.

Nolte, H. (1998). Aspekte ressourcenorientierter Unternehmensführung. In H. Nolte (Ed.), *Aspekte ressourcenorientierter Unternehmensführung* (pp. III–VIII). München: Rainer Hampp. Retrieved from http://hdl.handle.net/10419/116857

North, D. C. (1990). *Institutions, institutional change, and economic performance: Political economy of institutions and decisions.* Cambridge: Cambridge University Press.

Of, J. (2014). *Brand formative design: Development and assessment of product design from a future, brand and consumer perspective.* Doctoral thesis. Retrieved from http://d-nb.info/1053319665

Ohmae, K. (1982). The strategic triangle: A new perspective on business unit strategy. *European Management Journal, 1*(1), 38–48. https://doi.org/10.1016/S0263-2373(82)80016-9.

Oliva, R., Srivastava, R., Pfoertsch, W., & Chandler, J. (2009). *Insights on ingredient branding, ISBM Report 08–2009.* Pennsylvania State University, University Park, PA.

Orton, K. (2017, March 28). *Desirability, feasibility, viability: The sweet spot for innovation* [Blog post]. Retrieved from https://medium.com/innovation-sweet-spot/desirability-feasibility-viability-the-sweet-spot-for-innovation-d7946de2183c

Osterwalder, A., Pigneur, Y., Smith, A., Bernarda, G., & Papadakos, P. (2014). *Value proposition design.* Hoboken, NJ: Wiley.

Otte, M. (2019). *Weltsystemcrash: Krisen, Unruhen und die Geburt einer neuen Weltordnung.* München: FinanzBuch.

Özbölük, T., & Dursun, Y. (2017). Online brand communities as heterogeneous gatherings: A netnographic exploration of Apple users. *Journal of Product & Brand Management, 26*(4), 375–385. https://doi.org/10.1108/JPBM-10-2015-1018.

Payne, A. F., Storbacka, K., & Frow, P. (2008). Managing the co-creation of value. *Journal of the Academy of Marketing Science, 36*(1), 83–96. https://doi.org/10.1007/s11747-007-0070-0.

Pfeiffer, S. (2015). Industrie 4.0 und die Digitalisierung der Produktion – Hype oder Megatrend? In Bundeszentrale für politische Bildung (Ed.), *Megatrends?. Aus Politik und Zeitgeschichte, 65*(31–32), pp. 6–12. Retrieved from https://www.bpb.de/apuz/209955/industrie-4-0-und-die-digitalisierung-der-produktion

Pfoertsch, W., Beuk, F., & Luczak, Ch. (2007). Classification of brands: The case for B2B, B2C and B2B2C. *Proceedings of the Academy of Marketing Studies, 12*(1). Jacksonville, USA.

Pfoertsch, W. A., & Sponholz, U. (2019). *Das neue marketing-mindset: Management, Methoden und Prozesse für ein Marketing von Mensch zu Mensch.* Wiesbaden: Springer Gabler.

Pierre Audoin Consultants. (2015). *Holistic customer experience in the digital age: A trend study for Germany, France and the UK* [Whitepaper]. Retrieved from https://www.pac-online.com/holistic-customer-experience-digital-age

Pine, II, B. J., & Gilmore, J. H. (1998). Welcome to the experience economy. *Harvard Business Review, 76*(4), 97–105. Retrieved from https://hbr.org/1998/07/welcome-to-the-experience-economy

Plattner, H., Meinel, C., & Leifer, L. (Eds.). (2011). *Design thinking: Understand-improve-apply.* Berlin: Springer.

Porter, M. E. (2011, January 5). *Rethinking capitalism* [Video file]. Retrieved from https://hbr.org/2011/01/rethinking-capitalism

Porter, M. E., & Kramer, M. R. (2011). Creating Shared Value – How to reinvent capitalism – and unleash a wave of innovation and growth. *Harvard Business Review, 89*(1/2), 62–77. Retrieved from https://hbr.org/2011/01/the-big-idea-creating-shared-value.

Prahalad, C. K., & Ramaswamy, V. (2000). Co-opting customer competence. *Harvard Business Review, 78*(1), 79–87. Retrieved from https://hbr.org/2000/01/co-opting-customer-competence

Prahalad, C. K., & Ramaswamy, V. (2003). The new frontier of experience innovation. *MIT Sloan Management Review, 44*(4), 12–18. Retrieved from https://sloanreview.mit.edu/article/the-new-frontier-of-experience-innovation/

Precht, R. D. (2018). *Jäger, Hirten, Kritiker: Eine Utopie für die digitale Gesellschaft* (6th ed.). München: Goldmann.

Reich, R. (2017). *Saving capitalism: For the many, not the few*. London: Icon Books.

Reinartz, W. (2018). Kundenansprache in Zeiten digitaler transformation. In M. Bruhn & M. Kirchgeorg (Eds.), *Marketing Weiterdenken: Zukunftspfade für eine marktorientierte Unternehmensführung* (pp. 123–138). Wiesbaden: Springer Gabler.

Reiss, R. (2011, October 4). How CEOs view the digital transformation. *Forbes*. Retrieved from https://www.forbes.com/sites/robertreiss/2011/10/04/how-ceos-view-the-digital-transformation/#26072ce72631

Reputation Institute. (2019). *Winning strategies in reputation: 2019 German RepTrak® 100* [Report]. Retrieved from https://insights.reputationinstitute.com/website-assets/2019-germany-reptrak

Reutemann, B. (2017). *Service design: Der Turbo für Ihr Business* [Presentation]. Retrieved from https://bernd-reutemann.de/wp-content/uploads/2017/02/Servicedesign.pdf

Richert, M. (2019, July 3). *Tschüss Bargeld, Hallo Libra! Facebooks schwingt sich zum weltgrößten Finanzdienstleister auf*. FOCUS Online. Retrieved from https://www.focus.de/finanzen/boerse/gastkolumne-tschues-bargeld-willkommen-libra_id_10892195.html

Ries, E. (2011). *The lean startup: How today's entrepreneurs use continuous innovation to create radically successful businesses* (1st ed.). New York, NY: Crown Business.

Rittel, H. W. J., & Webber, M. M. (1973). Dilemmas in a general theory of planning. *Policy Sciences, 4*(2), 155–165. https://doi.org/10.1007/BF01405730.

Robier, J. (2016). *UX redefined: Winning and keeping customers with enhanced usability and user experience*. Cham: Springer.

Robinson, P. K., & Hsieh, L. (2016). Reshoring: A strategic renewal of luxury clothing supply chains. *Operations Management Research, 9*, 89–101. https://doi.org/10.1007/s12063-016-0116-x.

Robra-Bissantz, S. (2018). Entwicklung von innovativen Services in der Digitalen Transformation. In M. Bruhn & K. Hadwich (Eds.), *Service business development:*

Strategien – Innovationen – Geschäftsmodelle: Band 1 (pp. 261–288). Wiesbaden: Springer Gabler.

Rohrbeck, R. (2014). Trend scanning, scouting and foresight techniques. In O. Gassmann & F. Schweitzer (Eds.), *Management of the fuzzy front end of innovation* (pp. 59–73). Cham: Springer.

Rosling, H, Rönnlund, A, & Rosling, O. (2018). *Factfulness: Ten reasons we're wrong about the world – and why things are better than you think.* Flatiron Books.

Ross, J. W., Beath, C. M., & Mocker, M. (2019). *Designed for digital: How to architect your business for sustained success (Management on the Cutting Edge).* MIT Press.

Rossi, C. (2015, May 27–29). *Collaborative branding* [Conference paper]. Paper presented at the MakeLearn & TIIM Joint International Conference, Bari, Italy. Retrieved from https://www.researchgate.net/publication/282763907_COLLABORATIVE_BRANDING

Rühl, W.-D. (2017). *Measuring fake news – Die Methode* [Report]. Retrieved from Stiftung Neue Verantwortung website: https://www.stiftung-nv.de/sites/default/files/fake_news_methodenpapier_deutsch.pdf

Rumler, A., & Ullrich, S. (2016). Social-Media-Monitoring und -Kontrolle. *PraxisWISSEN Marketing, 1*, 94–112. https://doi.org/10.15459/95451.7.

Rusnjak, A., & Schallmo, D. R. A. (2018). Gestaltung und Digitalisierung von Kundenerlebnissen im Zeitalter des Kunden Vorgehensmodell zur Digitalen Transformation von Business Models im Kontext der Customer Experience. In A. Rusnjak & D. R. A. Schallmo (Eds.), *Customer Experience im Zeitalter des Kunden: Best Practices, Lessons Learned und Forschungsergebnisse* (pp. 1–40). Wiesbaden: Springer Gabler.

Saam, M., Viete, S., & Schiel, S. (2016). *Digitalisierung im Mittelstand: Status Quo, aktuelle Entwicklungen und Herausforderungen* [Research project]. Retrieved from https://www.kfw.de/PDF/Download-Center/Konzernthemen/Research/PDF-Dokumente-Studien-und-Materialien/Digitalisierung-im-Mittelstand.pdf

Sängerlaub, A. (2017a). *Deutschland vor der Bundestagswahl: Überall Fake News?!* [Report]. Retrieved from Stiftung Neue Verantwortung website https://www.stiftung-nv.de/sites/default/files/fakenews.pdf

Sängerlaub, A. (2017b). *Verzerrte Realitäten: Die Wahrnehmung von "Fake News" im Schatten der USA und der Bundestagswahl* [Report]. Retrieved from Stiftung Neue Verantwortung website https://www.stiftung-nv.de/sites/default/files/fake_news_im_schatten_der_usa_und_der_bundestagswahl_0.pdf

Sarkar, C., & Kotler, P. (2018). *Brand activism: From purpose to action* (Kindle edition). n.p.: IDEA Bite Press. Retrieved from www.amazon.com

Schäfer, A., & Klammer, J. (2016). Service dominant logic in practice: Applying online customer communities and personas for the creation of service innovations. *Management, 11*(3), 255–264. Retrieved from https://econpapers.repec.org/article/mgtyoumng/v_3a11_3ay_3a2016_3ai_3a3_3ap_3a255-264.htm

Schlick, J., Stephan, P., & Zühlke, D. (2012). Produktion 2020: Auf dem Weg zur 4. industriellen revolution. *IM: Die Fachzeitschrift für information management und consulting, 27*(3), 26–34. Retrieved from https://www.econbiz.de/Record/im-schwerpunkt-industrie-4-0-produktion-2020-auf-dem-weg-zur-4-industriellen-revolution-schlick-jochen/10010019258

Schlotmann, R. (2018). *Digitalisierung auf mittelständisch: Die Methode "Digitales Wirkungsmanagement"*. Berlin: Springer.

Schuett, P. (2013). *Der Einstieg in die Resonanzgesellschaft* [Presentation]. Retrieved from https://de.slideshare.net/pschu/knowtech2013-peter-schuettibmresonanzgesellschaft?from_action=save

Schultz, D. E., Tannenbaum, S. I., & Lauterborn, R. F. (1994). *The New marketing paradigm: Integrated marketing communications*. Lincolnwood, IL: NTC Publishing.

Schulz, M. (2011). *New mindsets for service-orientated marketing: Understanding the role of emotions in interpersonal relationships*. Doctoral thesis. Retrieved from https://ourarchive.otago.ac.nz/handle/10523/1928

Schulze, G. (1992). *Die Erlebnisgesellschaft: Kultursoziologie der Gegenwart*. Frankfurt: Campus.

Schwab, K. (2019). Davos Manifesto 2020: The Universal purpose of a company in the fourth industrial revolution. *World Economic Forum*. https://www.weforum.org/agenda/2019/12/davos-manifesto-2020-the-universal-purpose-of-a-company-in-the-fourth-industrial-revolution/

Scott, W. R. (2008). *Institutions and organizations: Ideas and interests*. Los Angeles, CA: Sage.

See Edman, K. W. (2009). *Exploring overlaps and differences in service dominant logic and design thinking*. In her contribution to the First Nordic Conference on Service Design and Service Innovation she compared DT and S-DL and demonstrated the overlap. Available under http://www.ep.liu.se/ecp/059/016/ecp09059016.pdf

Sherry, J. F. (2005). Brand meaning. In A. M. Tybout & T. Calkins (Eds.), *Kellogg on branding: The marketing faculty of the Kellogg school of management* (pp. 40–69). Hoboken, NJ: Wiley.

Sheth, J. N., & Parvatiyar, A. (2000). The evolution of relationship marketing. In J. N. Sheth & A. Parvatiyar (Eds.), *Handbook of relationship marketing* (pp. 119–148). Thousand Oaks, CA: Sage.

Sheth, J. N., & Sisodia, R. S. (2002). Marketing productivity: Issues and analysis. *Journal of Business Research, 55*(5), 349–362. https://doi.org/10.1016/S0148-2963(00)00164-8.

Sheth, J. N., & Sisodia, R. S. (2005). Does marketing need reform? In marketing renaissance: Opportunities and imperatives for improving marketing thought, practice, and infrastructure. *Journal of Marketing, 69*(4), 1–25. https://doi.org/10.1509/jmkg.2005.69.4.1.

Sheth, J. N., & Sisodia, R. S. (2007). Raising marketing's aspirations. *Journal of Public Policy & Marketing, 26*(1), 141–143. https://doi.org/10.1509/jppm.26.1.141.

Simon, H. (2015). *Confessions of the pricing Man: How price affects everything*. Cham: Springer.

Sinek, S. (2009). *Start with why: How great leaders inspire everyone to take action.* New York: Penguin.

Sisodia, R. S., Sheth, J. N., & Wolfe, D. (2014). *Firms of endearment: How world-class companies profit from passion and purpose* (2nd ed.). Upper Saddle River, NJ: Pearson Education.

Smith, P. G., & Reinertsen, D. G. (1991). *Developing products in half the time.* New York, NY: Van Nostrand Reinhold.

Spanier, G. (2017). The now economy: 'Uber's children'. *Business Transformation,* 12–13. Retrieved from https://www.raconteur.net/business-transformation-2017

Speaker's Corner. (2019, March 3). *"Es ist eine verdammte Lüge" – Dr. Markus Krall (Roland Baader-Treffen 2019)* [Video file]. Retrieved from https://www.youtube.com/watch?v=AWCyL3gcOzw

Sprout Social. (2017). *Championing change in the age of social media: How brands are using social to connect with people on the issues that matter* [Report]. Retrieved from https://media.sproutsocial.com/pdf/Sprout-Data-Report-Championing-Change-in-the-Age-of-Social-Media.pdf

Stone, M. L. (2014). *Big data for media* [Report]. Retrieved from Reuters Institute for the Study of Journalism website https://reutersinstitute.politics.ox.ac.uk/sites/default/files/2017-04/Big%20Data%20For%20Media_0.pdf

Tarnovskaya, V., & Biedenbach, G. (2018). Corporate rebranding failure and brand meanings in the digital environment. *Marketing Intelligence and Planning, 36*(4), 455–469. https://doi.org/10.1108/MIP-09-2017-0192.

Teknowlogy. (2020). *IoT C&SI Survey 2020* [Study report]. Retrieved from https://75572d19-371f-4ade-aeb6-61dbca89834b.filesusr.com/ugd/f21868_2f8ab8213a00460f8777de2057430fb0.pdf

Ternès, A., Towers, I., & Jerusel, M. (2015). *Konsumentenverhalten im Zeitalter der Digitalisierung: Trends: E-Commerce, M-Commerce und Connected Retail.* Wiesbaden: Springer Gabler.

Trommsdorff, V., & Steinhoff, F. (2013). *Innovationsmarketing* (2nd ed.). München: Franz Vahlen.

Vargo, S. L., & Lusch, R. F. (2004). Evolving to a new dominant logic for marketing. *Journal of Marketing, 68*(1), 1–17. https://doi.org/10.1509/jmkg.68.1.1.24036.

Vargo, S. L., & Lusch, R. F. (2008). Service-dominant logic: Continuing the evolution. *Journal of the Academy of Marketing Science, 36*(1), 1–10. https://doi.org/10.1007/s11747-007-0069-6.

Vargo, S. L., & Lusch, R. F. (2016). Institutions and axioms: An extension and update of service-dominant logic. *Journal of the Academy of Marketing Science, 44*(1), 5–23. https://doi.org/10.1007/s11747-015-0456-3.

Vargo, S. L., & Lusch, R. F. (2017). Service-dominant logic 2025. *International Journal of Research in Marketing, 34*(1), 46–67. https://doi.org/10.1016/j.ijresmar.2016.11.001.

Verganti, R. (2009). *Design-driven innovation: Changing the rules of competition by radically innovating what things mean.* Boston, MA: Harvard Business Press.

Vitsœ. (n.d.). *The power of good design: Dieter Rams's ideology, engrained within Vitsœ.* Retrieved from https://www.vitsoe.com/gb/about/good-design

Voeth, M. (2018). Marketing und/oder marktorientierte Unternehmensführung? In M. Bruhn & M. Kirchgeorg (Eds.), *Marketing Weiterdenken: Zukunftspfade für eine marktorientierte Unternehmensführung* (pp. 67–78). Wiesbaden: Springer Gabler.

Volvo Trucks. (2013). *Volvo trucks – The Epic Split feat. Van Damme (Live Test)* [Youtube video]. Retrieved from https://www.youtube.com/watch?v=M7FIvfx5J10

von Hirschfeld, S. T., & Josche, T. (2018). *Lean content marketing: Groß denken, schlank starten. Praxisleitfaden für das B2B-Marketing* (2nd ed.). Heidelberg: O'Reilly.

Wackernagel, M., & Rees, W. E. (1996). Our ecological footprint. *The New Catalyst Bioregional Series, 9.*

Wallaschkowski, S., & Niehuis, E. (2017). Digitaler Konsum. In O. Stengel, A. van Looy, & S. Wallaschkowski (Eds.), *Digitalzeitalter – Digitalgesellschaft: Das Ende des Industriezeitalters und der Beginn einer neuen Epoche* (pp. 109–141). Wiesbaden: Springer.

Wang, W. L., Malthouse, E. C., Calder, B., & Uzunoglu, E. (2019). B2B content marketing for professional services: In-person versus digital contacts. *Industrial Marketing Management., 81,* 160–168. https://doi.org/10.1016/j.indmarman.2017.11.006.

Wani, T. (2013). From 4Ps to SAVE: A theoretical analysis of various marketing mix models. *Business Sciences International Research Journal, 1*(1), 1–9. https://doi.org/10.2139/ssrn.2288578.

Weiss, A. M., Anderson, E., & MacInnis, D. J. (1999). Reputation management as a motivation for sales structure decisions. *Journal of Marketing, 63*(4), 74–89. https://doi.org/10.1177/002224299906300407.

Wilken, R., & Jacob, F. (2015). Vom Produkt- zum Lösungsanbieter. In K. Backhaus & M. Voeth (Eds.), *Handbuch Business-to-Business-Marketing: Grundlagen, Geschäftsmodelle, Instrumente des Industriegütermarketing* (2nd ed., pp. 147–164). Wiesbaden: Springer Gabler.

Wolf, T., & Strohschen, J.-H. (2018). Digitalisierung: Definition und Reife – Quantitative Bewertung der digitalen Reife. *Informatik Spektrum, 41*(1), 56–64. https://doi.org/10.1007/s00287-017-1084-8.

Wüst, C. (2012). Corporate reputation management – die kraftvolle Währung für Unternehmenserfolg. In C. Wüst & R. T. Kreutzer (Eds.), *Corporate reputation management: Wirksame Strategien für den Unternehmenserfolg* (pp. 3–56). Wiesbaden: Springer Gabler.

Zhu, F., & Furr, N. (2016). Products to platforms: Making the leap. *Harvard Business Review, 94*(4), 72–78. Retrieved from https://hbr.org/2016/04/products-to-platforms-making-the-leap

Company Index

© The Author(s), under exclusive license to Springer Nature Switzerland AG 2021
P. Kotler et al., *H2H Marketing*, https://doi.org/10.1007/978-3-030-59531-9

Subject Index

© The Author(s), under exclusive license to Springer Nature Switzerland AG 2021
P. Kotler et al., *H2H Marketing*, https://doi.org/10.1007/978-3-030-59531-9

CPSIA information can be obtained
at www.ICGtesting.com
Printed in the USA
BVHW012134310122
627717BV00002B/3